AF898470

The Cultural Exchange History of Ancient Currency between China and Other Countries

The Cultural Exchange History of Ancient Currency between China and Other Countries

By

Dai Jianbing, Luqian Peng and Xiaorong Chen

Translated by Luqian Peng

Cambridge Scholars Publishing

The Cultural Exchange History of Ancient Currency between China and Other Countries

By Dai Jianbing, Luqian Peng and Xiaorong Chen

This book first published 2022

Cambridge Scholars Publishing

Lady Stephenson Library, Newcastle upon Tyne, NE6 2PA, UK

British Library Cataloguing in Publication Data
A catalogue record for this book is available from the British Library

Copyright © 2022 by Dai Jianbing, Luqian Peng and Xiaorong Chen

All rights for this book reserved. No part of this book may be reproduced, stored in a retrieval system, or transmitted, in any form or by any means, electronic, mechanical, photocopying, recording or otherwise, without the prior permission of the copyright owner.

ISBN (10): 1-5275-8058-X
ISBN (13): 978-1-5275-8058-9

TABLE OF CONTENTS

ACKNOWLEDGEMENTS

Throughout the process of writing this book, many colleagues and friends have really helped to facilitate its completion. I sincerely thank all of those who have given me constructive suggestions and provided necessary materials to help the book come into being. I especially show my gratitude to Professor Sumin Zhang of Zhejiang Gongshang University for her consistent support in writing, particularly for her contribution to the final publication of the book.

PREFACE

In the currency culture of human history, there are two wonderful works that are immortal. One is the currency culture of China, an ancient Oriental civilization, which has influenced the currency culture of many Asian countries for more than a thousand years. The other is the monetary culture of ancient Greece, the birthplace of the Western monetary culture, which later gave rise to the Arab and the Indian coin systems.

From the perspective of configuration, ancient Chinese coins pay attention to the characters, and the beauty of calligraphy lies underneath the square and circle world of the coins. Greek money, on the other hand, features the patterns, which are mainly made up of the images of gods, heroes, animals and plants.

Since the Half-Liang money of the Qin dynasty (*Liang* is a measure unit), Chinese coins have generally been circular-shaped with a square hole in the middle, which are called, jokingly, "Brother Kong Fang." (*Kong* means a hole and *Fang* means a square shape.) In the beginning, the coins were weighed, such as Half-Liang in the Qin dynasty and Five Zhu in the Han dynasty (*Zhu* is a unit of weight). However, since the Tang dynasty, money with the title of an emperor's reign began to prevail, which continued until the early years of the Republic of China.

The influence of the ancient Chinese currency culture on the currencies of Asian countries is mainly reflected in the following aspects.

First, the shape, weight and even name of the coins in many Asian countries are basically the same as those of the Chinese coins. They are generally round-shaped with a square hole, using Chinese characters with the name of Tong Bao or Yuan Bao. As early as the first year of He Tong (708) in the Nara Age, Japan minted the coins with Chinese characters 'He Tong Kai Zhen.' In the fifteenth year of Chong Zong's reign (996), North Korea began to imitate China's Qian Yuan Zhong Bao money. The King of the Ryukyu dynasty minted the Da Shi Tong Bao coins in 1453. In 970, Vietnam cast the coins with Chinese characters 'Tai Ping Tong Bao' on them. Until modern times, these countries still minted the Chinese character coins for circulation, which are similar to the coins of China. The round shape with a square hole became the symbol of the currency circle of Chinese culture, and many countries in ancient Central Asia and Southeast Asia adopted this type of system. The coins basically use Kai Yuan Tong Bao money of the Tang dynasty as the standard, with a diameter of about 2.5 cm and a weight of 4 g or so.

The second aspect is the complete imitation of Chinese currency in some countries. In the exchanges between ancient China and other Asian countries, Chinese coins were once widely spread in Asia as a messenger of friendship. Many countries imitated Chinese currency. For example, Japan forged thirty-six kinds of Nian Hao Qian (money with the title of an emperor's reign). Vietnam forged fourteen kinds. Korea also copied the Tang dynasty coins. Indonesia imitated the ancient Chinese money of Tang and Song dynasties.

Third, the money of many Asian countries uses Chinese characters, and, as with the Chinese ancient coins, the calligraphy art beauty is painstakingly pursued to achieve an aesthetic effect. For example, the Chinese character 'dragon' on the bronze coin of Ryukyu could not have been written vividly without a solid foundation of Chinese calligraphy. The gold and silver coins with Chinese characters have also been found in Thailand. Overseas, China also issued Chinese currency in Southeast Asian countries.

Fourth, Asian coins inherited some of the traditions of ancient Chinese coins. In ancient China, coins often had characters on the back of them, indicating the place and time of casting. And the coins of Japan, Korea, Vietnam and other countries also have characters added to them, such as Korean coins, in 1678, cast with Chang Ping Tong Bao, Japanese coins, in 1625, cast with Kuan Yong Tong Bao and so on.

Fifth, ancient Chinese paper money had a great influence on Asian countries. Korea, Japan and Vietnam all issued paper money in ancient times, so did the Persian Ili Khanate in the Yuan dynasty. Iranians still call paper money *Chao*. (*Chao* is the pronunciation of 钞, which means paper money in Chinese).

Sixth, both the coins in China and Southeast Asian countries are made by pouring molten metal into the mold, which, after cooling down, is taken out and reprocessed.

Money is the blood of trade, while trade is the base of currency cultural exchange. China's ancient Silk Road has played a very important role in the economic and cultural exchange between China and foreign countries. Broadly speaking, there were four ancient Silk Roads. The traditional one started from Luoyang and Chang'an, going westward to Hexi Corridor, Yangguan, along the south of Tianshan Mountain, across the Green Ridge (today's Pamir) into Central Asia, to the Mediterranean. The second was the maritime Silk Road from the Southeast coast of China to Europe, which can be dated back to the Tang dynasty. It was also known as the silk and silver road, after the discovery of the new world, because it was by this route that Europeans transported American silver to China in exchange for Chinese silk. The third was the southwest Silk Road, which runs from Chengdu through Yunnan and Myanmar to India and through Central

Asia to Europe. The fourth was the grassland Silk Road, through the Mongolian steppe in the north.

Chinese coins used to be the world currency in international trade and the medium of the Silk Road trade, especially, in Asia. In ancient times, China had very close economic and trade relations with Asian countries. Many of them traded with China just because they wanted Chinese copper coins. As early as the Song dynasty, "the tall ships of the sea, mostly covered with cargo, were inside full of copper coins waiting to be shipped to foreign countries. Although the imperial court set an official ban, how could it be checked out!"[1] Japan sent people to China many times during the Ming dynasty to trade for copper coins. Ma Huan, who travelled to the west with Zheng He, said in his book, *A Journey to Japan*: "Java, Jiugang (today's Palembang on Sumatra Island) and Ceylon all used Chinese money." The large numbers of the Ming dynasty coins unearthed in the Xisha islands are the remains of Zheng He's Voyages to the western seas.

Ancient Chinese coins were also unearthed far away in Africa, and about 330 are known to date, including one of the Tang dynasty, 142 of the Northern Song, sixty-four of the Southern Song, ten of the Ming dynasty, and four of the Qing dynasty. Still, there are 105 coins for which the years are unknown, and the characters are unclear.

In the middle of the ninth century, the Chinese Square Hole money was circulated in Siraf in the Persian Gulf. According to the article "Chinese Cultural Relics Found in East Africa," "a surprising amount of Chinese porcelain and coins have been found on the East African coast, which is very helpful for the determination of the dates of the history of the East African coast in the middle ages." Most

[1] Jingde Li, ed., *Zhuzi Yu Lei Vol. VIII*. (Beijing: Zhong Hua Book Company, 1986), 48.

Chinese coins were found in Mogadishu, Bulava and Merka (in Somalia), and Zanzibar, Mafia, Kilwa islands (of Tanzania), on the coast of East Africa.

As early as 1888, Zanzibar already had the Song coins unearthed. In 1944, a Chinese coin hoard was discovered in Kajengwa, southeast of Zanzibar island. About 167 coins were found, including four Kai Yuan Tong Bao coins from the Tang dynasty, 108 from the Northern Song dynasty and fifty-five from the Southern Song dynasty. The hoard was found close to Vongguja, a place that Chinese galleons had frequented.[2] The Song dynasty coins, mostly from the eleventh to twelfth centuries, were found in three locations in Mogadishu, Somalia, in 1898. Later, Yong Le Tong Bao was also discovered. In 1959, the Song dynasty and Shun Zhi Tong Bao coins were unearthed in Bulawa. Ancient Chinese coins have also been unearthed in Mekal.[3] One coin from the Emperor Shenzong period was unearthed on the island of Mafia in Tanzania in 1916, and another two coins, Qing Yuan Tong Bao and Shao Ding Tong Bao from the Southern Song dynasty were found in 1954.[4] One Chun Hua ingot, four Xi Ning ingots and four Zheng He Tong Bao coins were also found in Kilwa, Tanzania.[5] Another two Southern Song coins were found in the ancient city of Gedi, near Malindi, Kenya. Five coins from the Song dynasty and one

---

[2] Guanxi Sheng, "The Overseas Circulation and Significance of Ancient Chinese Coins," *Asian Coins*, no. 1 (1999).

[3] Yizhong Yu, "Research on the Influence of Chinese Currency Culture on Neighboring Countries from the Perspective of Their Coins," in *Proceedings of the Sixth Symposium on Southeast Asian Historical Currencies and Maritime Silk Road Currencies*, ed. Zhejiang Coin Society (Ningbo: Ningbo Numismatic Society, June 1995).

[4] Ping Wu, "Exploration of Maritime Silk Road Currencies," *Fujian Currency*, no.3-4 (1994).

[5] Sheng, "The Overseas Circulation."

from the Ming dynasty were also found in Angowana.[6]

More than 90 percent of the Chinese coins unearthed in Africa are of the Song dynasty. Of these large quantities of Chinese copper coins, most were carried to African countries by the Chinese merchant fleet at that time and left there as a result of commercial trade. The discovery of Chinese coins in Africa further confirms that the ancient sea passage extended to the African continent as early as the Song dynasty.[7]

The exchange of currency cultures is a two-way process. In China Persian silver, East Roman gold coins and Arabic coins were found, as well as the ancient coins of Japan, Korea or Vietnam, some even in large stock. Since the mid-Ming dynasty, silver coins from Western countries have flowed into China. Foreign copper money also flooded into the Chinese market, after the opium war. The commonly used coins in the Chinese currency market at that time were Japan's Kuan Yong Tong Bao, North Korea's Chang Ping Tong Bao, Annam's Guang Zhong Tong Bao, Jing Sheng Tong Bao, Jing Xing Tong Bao, Jing Xing Ju Bao, Jing Xing Quan Bao, Jing Xing Da Bao, Jia Long Tong Bao, etc. Among these, Annam's Guang Zhong, Jing Sheng, Jing Xing, and Jia Long were called "Yi Qian," "Foreign Light Money," "Piggy Money," or "Water Floating," because they were thin and light. In the ninth year of Dao Guang, Li Hongbin, Governor of Guangdong and Guangxi, banned foreign light money from flowing into China.

> *...In Guangdong Province, Guang Zhong Tong Bao and Jing Sheng Tong Bao are the most circulated, with Jing Xing Tong Bao, Jing Xing Shi Bao, Jing Xing Da Bao, Jia Long Tong Bao being occasionally used. The so-called "Yi Qian" occupies 7 out of 10 of the money in circulation, even a higher percentage in Chaozhou and is exclusively used in a few places. Finding it thin and light, some evil people counterfeit the casting, making the number increase day by day. We are also afraid that some might make*

[6] Yu, "Research on the Influence of Chinese Currency Culture."
[7] Sheng, "The Overseas Circulation."

their own money in the name of Yi Qian. ...Anyone who has Yi Qian in store may be given 60 Wen (unit of Chinese money) for each Jin in hope that all be surrendered within 6 months... Adulterated with lead and sand, Yi Qian can't be tempered for long. What's more, sporadic collection consumes too much. Therefore the counties are ordered to collect them by the deadline and turn in the coins to the province to be destroyed... [8]

We may notice that coins were circulated in certain areas, serving as a standard currency. Meanwhile, fake foreign coins were used in some coastal areas in China.

There are huge differences between the Chinese and Western currency cultures, ranging from their evolution, their economic forms, their roles in the transition from one economic form to another, to their currency theories, the government control over currency, and the standard systems of currency. It is these differences that have led to the development of different social economy and finance, on which different socio-economic structures have been constructed. The exchange of currency culture is an important issue in economic history, and, also, is closely related to the path of modernization in China. Either the establishment of the modern currency system or the transformation of the financial systems contains the trail of currency cultural exchange.

In addition to being imported from Guangdong, foreign coins also flowed in from Fujian and Shandong. In the ninth year of Daoguang, Sun Erzhun, governor of Fujian and Zhejiang, and Han Kejun, grand coordinator of Fujian, sent a memorial to the throne, which said, "Foreign coins have been collected within a time limit and exchanged into forged Chinese coins in Quanzhou and Zhangzhou." Naerjinger, grand coordinator of Shandong, reported, at the end of the same year, "Money with such words as Guang Zhong or Jing Sheng has been

[8] Han Li, "Foreign Copper Coins in Chinese Market in Late Qing Dynasty," *Chinese Currency*, no.1 (1985).

found occasionally in Yanzhou. We plan to buy it twice its value…" In the twentieth year, Huang Juezi reported, in his memorial, "Yi Qian not only came from the foreigners, but it was also forged domestically in secret. Among those circulating in Zhangzhou and Quanzhou, Guang Zhong have been the most, Jing Sheng being the second. Still some were made in Chaozhou or Jiaying in the name of Yi Qian…" The same year, Wu Yiji, Official Decadence, also wrote, in his memorial to the Emperor, "Yi Qian in Tingzhou, known as Pi Qian, was mixed into sand so much in the making that it could be broken by pinching."[9]

Before the U.S. dollar, such currencies have also functioned as world currencies in the history of human civilization, i.e., the currencies of ancient Greece and Rome, especially the Byzantine coins in the later period; the Arab currency; the ancient Chinese currency, especially the copper coins after the Tang dynasty; the Persian silver coins; and the Spanish silver dollars, in sequence. These currencies have played an important role in the world trade and people's economic life.

Due to trade, foreign coins have long since been recorded in ancient Chinese historical documents. According to *The Historical Records* and *History of the Han Dynasty*, currencies from Parthia "took silver as money on which the king's face was carved." "They would cast more money in memorial of a king if he died." *History of Quan*, a book of the Southern Song, is a complete collection of foreign coins at that time. (*Quan* is the name of ancient coins.) Textual research has developed since the mid-Qing dynasty. Weng Shupei's *Summary of Ancient Quan*, written in the years of Qianlong, paid more attention to foreign currencies. During the Republic of China, especially in the

[9] Han Li, "Foreign Copper Coins in Chinese Market in Late Qing Dynasty," *Chinese Currency*, no.1 (1985).

1930s, the famous scholar Ding Fubao devoted himself to the study of ancient money and established the Association of Quan. His *Ancient Money Dictionary* contains hundreds of foreign coins. Contemporary, well-known scholar Zhang Xinglang compiled *The Historical Materials of Chinese and Western Transportation*, which has kept many documents about foreign currencies. The historian Xiang Da translated Stein's archaeological achievements in Central Asia and published *Stein's Archaeological Book of Central Asia*, which included an overview of the ancient coins excavated by Stein in Central Asia. Professor Peng Xinwei's book *History of Chinese Currency* can be called the pioneering work of Chinese history of currency and numismatics, in which special attention was paid to the foreign coins passed into China over the Silk Road, and the discovery and circulation of East Roman gold coins and Persian Sassan silver coins in China were also highlighted.

The Chinese archaeological community attached great importance to the foreign coins unearthed in China, with the famous archaeologists Xia Nai and Huang Wenbi as the main representatives. In the 1930s, Huang Wenbi discovered many foreign coins on the Silk Road during his Archaeological Survey in Xinjiang. In the 1940s, Mr. Xia Nai made investigations along the Silk Road from Shaanxi and Gansu to Xinjiang, which contributed to the publishing of dozens of research papers on Parthia coins, East Roman gold coins, Persian Sassan silver coins, Arabic gold and silver coins, and other Central Asian coins.

Since the 1980s, with the impetus of the Chinese Numismatic Society, the Silk Road Currency Research Group has been established, consisting of eleven provinces and autonomous regions — Gansu, Inner Mongolia, Xinjiang, Tibet, Qinghai, Ningxia, Shaanxi, Henan, Shanxi, Sichuan and Yunnan. It has promoted the development of China's Silk Road currency research, and a number of high-level research findings have emerged, which help with the Chinese Numismatic Society's foreign academic exchanges. Until now, ten monographs have been published by Lanzhou University Press, including *Silk Road Currency*.

In recent years, the research on Chinese and foreign currency exchanges has been very hot in China, with the appearance of a series of papers and monographs. Xinjiang is the most authoritative place in China to study the Silk Road currency and the related national currencies, to which Mr. Jiang Qixiang has made outstanding contributions. In addition, some coin researchers from northwestern provinces have also conducted in-depth studies on this, such as Kang Liushuo and Liu Dayou in Gansu Province. Mr. Lin Meicun's research on ancient Silk Road currency has always remained in a leading position in China. Mr. Du Weishan of Canada had an abundant collection of Silk Road currency, which he donated to the Shanghai Numismatic Museum. He also wrote monographs on it. Mr. Wang Guizhu of Guangdong conducted in-depth research on Persian silver coins unearthed there, while Taiwan's Dai Xuewen produced many masterpieces of Spanish silver coins study.

Numismatics have occupied a very prominent position in the Western academic circle, for example, well-established scholars and experts on numismatics can be found in many countries from the United Kingdom, France, the United States, Japan, Germany, to Sweden, the Netherlands, Russia, and India. British Stein, French Pelliot, German Lecoq, Russian Kozlov, Japanese Tachibana Zuicho, and Swedish Sven Hedin, all excavated precious cultural relics and coins from Xinjiang, Inner Mongolia, or Gansu during their archaeological investigations in Central Asia and Western China from the late nineteenth century to the early twentieth century. The relics were kept in the British Museum, the French National Museum, the

Russian Petersburg Museum, the German National Museum, and the Otani Longzang Temple in Japan. The amount of these numismatic materials is quite huge.

The numismatic research on ancient Greek, Roman, and Indian coins have prevailed in the Western countries for a long time, so we'll not dwell on it here.

Some numismatists in the West also involved themselves in the study of certain countries' currencies that were related to Chinese coins. In Western countries, a bunch of monographs on Persian Sassanid coins were published, such as *Handbook of Ancient Oriental Coins,* by Morgan; *Arabian-Sassanian Ancient Coins Directory,* by Walk; and *Persian Art Review,* by Pubo, in the 1950s. Valentine's *Sassanian Coins* is the first monograph about the coins of this dynasty. His other masterpieces include *Indian Coins* and *Modern Copper Coins of Muhammad State*s, a book about Arab coins. In 1968, Yi Bell published *Sassanian Numismatics*, then Baruch published *Sassanian Currency,* in 1976, and Sellwood published *Introduction to Sassanian Currency,* in 1985; Sellwood had also earlier published *Parthian Coins.*[10] The former Soviet Union had some outputs on the ancient coins of Central Asia. Since the 1970s, there have been more foreign papers and books on Silk Road currencies, and the scope of research has been more extensive, among which are India's research on the coins of Kushan Empire, Kleb's research on the coins with both Chinese and Kharosthi inscriptions, the Dutch scholar Yi Zhongting's research on the Harahan dynasty coins, the Russian Petersburg Museum's research on the Central Asian coins, French scholar Thierry's research on Byzantine gold coins, Polish scholar Popelawicz's research on Bactrian coins, Japanese scholar Hirayama

[10] Tiesheng Li, "Four English Monographs about Sassanian Coins," *Special Issue of Inner Mongolia Financial Currency,* no.3 (1994).

Ikuo's collection of coins throughout Central Asia, etc. It is worth mentioning that foreign numismatic scholars tend to be interested in Chinese coins discovered in Central Asia, India, Japan, and Southeast Asia, when studying the Silk Road coins. They have published many research papers. For example, Professor Smirnova of the former Soviet Union made research on China's Kai Yuan Tong Bao money unearthed in Tajikistan in Central Asia. Indian scholars researched the Chinese Song dynasty coins unearthed in Tamil Dupont, India, and Russian scholars researched the Chinese Five Zhu coins unearthed in Fergana in Uzbekistan. Japanese scholars researched Chinese coins found in Japan, too. [11]

As to the study of Islamic coins, Hennequin of France edited *The Catalogue of Islamic Coins—The Seljuk Dynasty and Subsequent Dynasties until the Mongolians' Invasion into Asia* (the 1985 edition of the National Library of Paris, consisting of 932 pages, among which fifty pages were illustrations). A total of more than two thousand coins have been collected, with sixty-two photos of the original size in the fifty pages of illustrations. Since the coins collected in this catalog were issued during the dynasty of Seljuk, up until the Mongolian invasion, there were no Turkish coins. Geographically the region corresponds to present-day Syria, Iraq, Iran and the Asian part of Turkey. In terms of the age, it is about 433 to 869 of the Islamic era (between AD 1041 and 1464). The British Museum has compiled a relatively complete catalogue for its collection of Islamic coins, the last volume of which was published nearly a century ago. This ten-volume catalogue has great value for reference. John Walker started to revise it in 1941 but hadn't completed Volume 2 until now. Still, the British Museum is an important base for the world study of the oriental coins,

[11] Liushuo Kang, "Silk Road Currencies Study: Present and Forecast," *Lanzhou Finance*, no.2 (1995).

with the achievements of Cleb, Wang Hailan and others in studying Chinese coins and the exchange of Chinese and foreign coins. What's more, its Oriental Numismatic Society (ONS) is extremely influential in the world.

As early as 1881, Britain published *Mongolian Coin*, a book edited based on the collection of the British Museum, which was later translated by Hong Wenqing, when he was in Britain, in the sixteenth year of Guangxu, and renamed *The Money Book of the Mongolian Western Regions*. There were 687 pictures in the original book, but only some of them were selected in the translated version.

Japanese scholars' research on ancient Chinese currencies was done to a depth and breadth that was worth studying by Chinese numismatic scholars. In recent years, some scholars in South Korea have also begun to pay attention to the issue of currency cultural exchanges between China and Korea, and have published some papers.

Singapore numismatic experts, such as Huang Hansen, have organized the Asian Numismatic Society, making the exchange of currency culture between China and Southeast Asia their major subject of research and *Asian Coins*, their journal, in which they have had a series of publications.

Thierry, of France, and Dr. T. D. Yih, of the Netherlands, because of their special interest in the currency culture exchanges between China and foreign countries, have published a series of related articles in various media.

Chapter One

History of Chinese Currency through the Ages

I. Ancient Money

In legends, Dayu was said to be the first person to coin money in ancient China. The book *Guanzi* said, "Yu coined with Lishan's copper." According to *On Salt and Iron*, black shells were used as money as early as the Xia dynasty. It is generally believed that, in the Shang dynasty, our ancestors used shells as currency.

Shang was the most developed dynasty in Chinese slavery society. Due to the great development of the social economy, plus the three major divisions of labor at that time, currency began to appear in social and economic life, as shown in the large numbers of inscriptions on the unearthed bones or tortoise shells of the time. Of course, the Chinese characters currently in use also suggest the relationship between shells and currency. For instance, Chinese characters related to money often have a 贝 as a component, such as 货 (goods in Chinese), 财 (wealth in Chinese), 赋 (taxes in Chinese), etc.

There were, naturally, some favorable conditions for seashells to be a currency. They were valuable in themselves, easy to count, strong and durable, portable, and not in large numbers. In our country, the reason why seashells could become a currency was very closely related to their scarcity in the Central Plains region. There were only two kinds of seashells that could be used as money in ancient China, one was Huo Bei (money cowrie), and the other was A-patterned Shou Bei

(Arabian cowrie). At first, shellfish were used as ornaments. Seashells were unearthed from Erlitou ruins of Yanshi, Henan Province, which represents the culture of Xia dynasty. More seashells were found in the tombs of the Shang dynasty, basically buried as funerary objects. In Pudu Village, Shaanxi, thousands were found in the 1970s. Among the fifty-one civilian tombs of the Shang dynasty excavated in Dasikong Village of Anyang, Henan in 1958, eleven were buried with shells, generally with one shell in a tomb, and thirteen pieces at most. The unit of measure for shells is Peng, and there are now three definitions of how many shells a Peng is: two, five, and ten pieces.

Seashells at the time had a high value, eighty Peng could be exchanged for ten pieces of land. An awarding higher than fifty Peng was rarely recorded in Oracle scripts. Archaeological discoveries prove that Chinese ancients not only obtained seashells from the far south, but also manufactured various types of seashell substitutes. For example, pottery shells made of pottery clay were unearthed in Yin Ruins. Bone shells polished from animal bones were unearthed in large quantities in Henan, Shanxi, Hebei, Shandong, and even Qinghai. There were also mussel shells, which were from ground clam shells. It is still debatable as to whether these imitations were currency or not, and some think they were only ornaments.

The unearthed shell coins made of metal are relatively few, but they are thought to have been popular currencies then. Some copper shells were coated with gold, and lead shells also were found in some places. What's most peculiar is the discovery of the shell coins made of gold or silver in the tombs of the Zhongshan Kingdom from the Warring States period. By the time of the Zhou dynasty, metal coinage began to appear in large numbers, bringing about the withdrawal of seashells in circulation. However, seashells called Haibeiba remained popular as a currency in Yunnan until the end of the Ming dynasty and the beginning of the Qing dynasty.

Currency came into being as a consequence of the production of commodities in human society. The formation of currency has gone through several stages, from the direct exchange of commodities, to the exchange of goods based upon a general equivalent, i.e., a special commodity with which all others must be compared before an exchange for the determination of their value. Therefore, the general equivalent can reflect the value of other commodities. Gradually, it developed into a standard measure of the value of social commodities in circulation, from which the primary function of currency was generated.

Agriculture developed early in China, so the agricultural tool *bo* (a tool used to hoe up weeds) became the earliest form of general equivalent in the history of ancient Chinese currency. As an ancient shoveling tool, bo had a handle, and the upper end of bo was designed as a hollow square cone for the handle to be inserted. Later, in the shape of this tool, people cast a currency that was easy to carry and store, durable and light-weight. That was the future, so-called, "Empty-Headed Bu" (*bu* means cloth in Chinese). Since the word bu, in ancient times, was interchangeable with that of the agricultural tool, bo, people later called the currency, deriving from the agricultural tool, bu.

The Empty-Headed Bu was the earliest metal coin in China. In the past hundred years, a large number of oracle bone inscriptions were excavated in the Yin Ruins. The text on the Empty-Headed Bu was found to be inherited from the oracle inscriptions, with similar brushwork and writing techniques. Most of these currencies were unearthed in some areas of Henan, with Luoyang as the center. It was recorded that King Wu, after overthrowing King Zhou of the Shang dynasty, enfeoffed Wu Geng, the son of Zhou, the land of Yin, who, however, rebelled, under the help of Guan Shu and Cai Shu, after King Wu's death. The rebellion was suppressed by Zhou Gong, who then migrated the people of Yin to Luoyi. Since then, the cultural center of Yin was moved to Luoyang. As is shown above, the text on the Empty-Headed Bu was consistent with the original oracle bone inscriptions. Therefore, the earliest metal coins in China had an extremely close relationship with the people of the Shang dynasty. In addition, the Empty-Headed Bu remained basically the same shape as the original farm tool. The upper end of the currency, or the head part, was empty and could have a wooden handle inserted.

The development of currency itself required it to be more convenient to carry and count, which resulted in the appearance of "Flat-Headed Bu," in the later Spring and Autumn Period. As the name indicated, the head of the currency was no longer empty, and it was smaller too.

Both Wei and Zhao, in the Spring and Autumn Period, have coined this kind of currency. The earliest form of currency in the region of Zhao, Wei and Han was the Empty-Headed Bu, with pointed shoulders and feet part. Different from the currency unearthed in the region of Henan, it had a longer head, pointed shoulders and feet, and three parallels at the back. It had no or few inscriptions.

In recent years, Chinese scholars have discovered, in the land of ancient Wu, a batch of bronze blocks from the kilns of the Western Zhou dynasty and the Spring and Autumn Period. Since these bronze blocks were broken when discovered, and the blocks, even in the same kiln, were found not to be of the same bronze cake when tested, it is justified to say that these bronze blocks were, indeed, the circulated weighing currency of ancient China, specifically, of the ancient state of Wu in China.

Now, Chinese archaeologists have discovered large numbers of "Ge coins" of the State of Yue during the Spring and Autumn, and the Warring States periods, which are basically the same as the weapon, *Ge*, used in ancient battles, only smaller in size. They're generally assumed as the currency of the state. People divide these coins into four types, in terms of size and weight: extra-large, 120 mm long, weighing more than 10 g; large size, about 110 mm and 5.8 g; medium size, 90 mm and 3.8 g; small size, 80 mm and 3.3 g.

In the Warring States period, the states of Qi, Chu, Yan, Zhao, Han, Wei and Qin were the ones possessing ten thousand carriages. There were also states with one thousand carriages. Currencies were generally cast in the states due to the need for the development of social production and economic exchanges. China's bronze culture reached its climax in this period, and it was also in this era that Chinese currency culture approached maturity. Let's see the metal currencies in the various states at that time.

The state of Qi, a major coastal country in the East, was well-developed in fishing and hunting since ancient times. The role of knives was so important in this area that they became the general equivalent from which the currency of Qi was transformed. The knife coins of Qi were made thick and delicate, with characters, such as "Qi Fa Huo," on them. Seven kinds of Qi's large knife coins have been found so far. It is now believed that Qi Zhi Fa Huo, cast in the early Spring and Autumn Period, is the earliest coinage of Qi, while Qi Fa Huo was made in the middle of Warring States period. Some round coins were also cast in Qi, the late Warring States period, of which there were 3 kinds: Yi Hua; Yi Four Hua; and Yi Six Hua, respectively. *Hua* was the unit of measure; some scholars think one Hua was one knife coin.

The state of Yan is a northern fishing and hunting country close to the sea. In ancient Yan, the earliest currency was the sharp-pointed knife coins. With a character of "Ming" on it, the knife coin, popular here, was called "Knife of Ming." Recently, people have discovered some more knife coins of Yan State during the Warring States period, through archaeology or other means. Yan once cast a kind of knife coin that only circulated in Shandong—which was unearthed for the first time in Xiangyu Village of Boshan, Shandong Province—in the Jiaqing years of the Qing dynasty, thus named as Boshan Knife or Qi Ming Knife. This was the knife coin that was minted in Qi after the army of Yan captured the place. Yan also had its own Bu coins cast, characterized by shrugged shoulders, tightened waist and long feet. This Bu currency has been found with seven inscriptions, most of which are the names of places that are on the border of the states of Yan and Zhao. The early currency of Yan had no place names on it. Scholars believe that some coins were marked with place names later due to the influence of Zhao State.

Like Qi, Yan State, in the later Warring States period, made a lot of round coins. There were three kinds of round coins in Yan, i.e., Ming Four, Ming Hua and One Hua. Ming Four coins were relatively rare, while One Hua were the most numerous. The production of this kind of coins was coarse, with only "One" or "Hua" on the face sometimes. This currency was derived from the "Ming Knife" coins of the state of Yan. One Hua coins may have been the last currency of Yan, circulating for quite a short time. Most of the One Hua currency was found in the north of the state, the final base of Yan in the late Warring States period. Judging from the areas where it was unearthed, it should have been the latest currency cast in the history of Yan. It didn't circulate long because Yan had soon been defeated by Qin. Another feature of the currency of Yan was the discovery of lead in all the forms of currencies, whether Ming Knife, One Hua or Small Bu.

The state of Zhao, the land of San Jin, still used Bu coins, which were much lighter than the Empty-Headed Bu in the past. Bu currency usually had the parts of head, shoulders, crotch, and feet. The currency in Zhao was flat in head, shoulder, and crotch, with square feet and a thin body, called "Square-Feet Bu," in brief. Place names of Zhao were cast on it, "Anyang" was the most frequently used one. In the later

Warring States period, the Bu currency of Zhao State slowly changed in the direction of roundness in head, shoulders, and feet, in accordance with the developing law of currency itself—to be more endurable and suitable for circulation. The kingdom also had its own knife currency, "Gan Dan" and "Bai Ren" were the two most used inscriptions. It was always called "Straight Knife" because of its straight blade. Besides, round coins were also made in Zhao, inscribed with the words "Lin," "Li Shi," etc.

The Bu currency that was popular in the kingdom of Han was very peculiar. Having two acute angles in the head, it was called "Acute-Angle Bu," or "Abnormity Bu." Five kinds of words have been found on such currency so far: "Bai Nie;" "Zhou Bai Nie;" "Lu Shi Bai Nie;" "Rong;" and "Chui," respectively. Used originally as auspicious words, Bai Nie later became the name of currency storehouses, then the mark of currency. The words before Bai Nie were names of the places proved to be within the territory of Han. The excavation sites of the currency were also within ancient Han.

The Bu currency in the state of Wei was bridge-shaped with flat head, round shoulders, flat feet, and curved crotch. It was also called "Bridge-Shaped Bu" because the crotch seemed like the arc of a bridge. It had three ranks: Two-Jin of An Yi; One-Jin of An Yi and Half-Jin of An Yi. There were also coins with other words inscribed, such as "Gao An" and "Liang." Wei state was the earliest to make round currency in the Warring States period. The newly found round coins of One-Jin of Qi Yuan and Half-Jin enabled people to know more about the currency system of the state. Other inscriptions on the round coins included "Yuan," "Gong Tun Chi Jin," "Gong," "Xiang Yin," "Gu," etc., most of which were place names.

Qin had three kinds of currency during the Warring States period, all were round shaped. One was One-Liang money, one was Two-Zi money and the other was Half-Liang money (both Liang and Zi were units of weight). Half-Liang had been circulated in Qin before the state united China. Qin's currency derived from the spinning wheel, having One-Liang and Half-Liang types, according to weight. Both were circular with a round hole in the middle, so some thought the Chinese character 珠 (pronounced as *zhu*, meaning pearls in English) resembled their shape. It was said in *Historical Records* that the money was used for the first time in the second year of King Qin Hui. Qin also had some round currency cast on the newly conquered land of Zhao, such as Lin, Li Shi and Wu An. The same was done after it conquered the state of Wei.

With the small-sized bronze shells spread most widely in Chu, the state had the most peculiar currency at that time. It was called "mosquito-nosed" money or "grimace money" because of the clumsily written words on it. There was also some special Bu currency in the state. Chu was extremely famous for its golden coins, called "Yin Zi Jin," in ancient times. In 1980, the Museum of Henan, in collaboration with the Museum of Fugou County, announced the discovery of a batch of golden and silver coins of Chu, among which were the eighteen pieces of silver Bu coins—the most precious coins, as the earliest silver coinage in the history of China.

Gold had been in circulation as currency since the Warring States period. Judging from the gold coins unearthed so far, most were round-cake shaped, known as "Persimmon Gold" by the ancients.

The economic development of the Warring States period has a unified trend, which can be seen from the forms of currencies and the currency exchanges among the states. First, each state forged various kinds of currencies so that it could trade with others by using a certain form. For instance, Zhao had currencies of knife and Bu; Yan had knife, Bu and round coins; Qi had knife and round coins; and Chu had gold, silver and Bu currency—linking up the originally clearly divided districts of knife, Bu or round coins. Second, round coins appeared in almost all the states as a result of the law of currency development. Third, some states imitated others' currencies on such a large scale that they enhanced economic association with them. The state of Zhong Shan, besides making its own knife currency, was found to imitate the money of its neighbors, Zhao and Yan. In the Xinzheng ruins of the state of Han, round-foot coins were unearthed together with some non-Han-styled moulds of money. The Bu currency of Wei was also found in Linzi, the capital of the state of Qi. Fourth, most of the currencies were counted by weight, but the unit of weight was different from state to state. Fifth, currency production technology peculiar to China came into being—casting, especially mold casting. The evolution of currency during the Warring States period has foreshadowed the unification of China.

II. Circular Coin with a Square Hole

Emperor Qin Shihuang began to use Qin Half-Liang, the currency of Qin, to replace those of other states after he unified the whole country. The casting of Half-Liang money began at the age of Emperor Xiao Wen of Qin. Those made in the Warring States were heavy and thick with clumsy words on the surface. For example, one kind of the Pre-Qin Half-Liang was made by putting two molds together. The evolution of Qin Half-Liang itself reflects the development of China's casting technology.

Qin Shihuang only unified the unit of currency; he did not unify the casting and issuing rights of currency. Qin Half-Liang was still cast by the states, respectively. That's why the money that we have discovered so far varies in weight, size and inscriptions—some weighing 20 g or more, some only 5 g-6 g. Qin Half-Liang unified the various forms of the Warring States currencies into circular money with square holes, from which the saying "Brother Kong Fang" derived. The Square Hole round money symbolized the ancient people's view of the universe as a place of round sky covering square land. Most importantly, it was determined by the intrinsic requirements of currency itself, which needed resistance against wear and tear, as well as convenience in circulation and counting.

During the Warring States period, gold coins, in Qin state, were listed as superior, while copper coins were inferior. The system was continued after Qin's unification of China. The gold coins of the Qin dynasty were usually cake-shaped, as seen in the twenty pieces discovered in Shanxi Province from 1929 to 1963. About 50 mm-60 mm in diameter and 250 g in weight, the gold coins generally had a word in *Zhuan* style that was related to Liang in meaning (Zhuan is a style of Chinese calligraphy).

It is recorded that the currency system was changed nine times in the West Han dynasty. At the beginning of the Han dynasty, Emperor Han Gao Zu had a small coin minted that weighed only three Zhu, for the Qin Half-Liang was too heavy to be circulated. It was called elm pod money by later generations because it looked like an elm pod growing on the tree. The circulation of the small money almost resulted in inflation.

In the second year of Empress Lv, the elm pod money was replaced by Eight Zhu money, which weighed eight Zhu, though the words inscribed on the surface were unchanged. In the sixth year, Five Fen money was issued, which had a diameter of 5 Fen and a weight of 2.4 Zhu. In the fifth year of Emperor Wen, the central authorities began to cast Four Zhu money, for which the right of coinage was also permitted at local government level.

In the first year of Emperor Wu (140 BC), Three Zhu money was used, which was replaced by Half-Liang again in the fifth year. 118 BC saw the coinage of Five Zhu money, a significant event in the history of ancient Chinese currency because the age of Five Zhu started from then on, in which Zhu, instead of Liang, became the basic unit of Chinese currency, which then did not change until the Tang dynasty. Having an appropriate weight, Five Zhu money exerted a far-reaching influence on Chinese currency. In the second year of Yuan Ding (115 BC), Emperor Wu ordered the use of money cast by the central government because that made by locals varied in weight. Two years later, only the three central authoritie, Jun Shu, Zhong Guan and Ban Tong, were allowed the official right to cast money, and the currency issued before could not be used anymore. Five Zhu money remained in circulation until the early years of the Tang dynasty.

In the fourth year of Yuan Shou (119 BC), Emperor Wu ordered the casting of gold coins in three ranks: the most superior were the circular coins of the dragon, worth three thousand; of medium superiority were the square coins of the horse, worth five hundred; and the inferior elliptical coins of the turtle were worth three hundred. Additionally, money of white deer fur was made, which was worth four hundred thousand. People used to say that this was the earliest paper currency in China, but from the perspective of its scope of use, it would be more accurate to say that it was the earliest public debt in China. There was also an extremely small kind of Five Zhu money in West Han, known as "the eyes of a chicken" or "eyes of goose," at the time.

Five Zhu money was still used in East Han. It was a local warlord named Gongsun Shu who cast the first iron money recorded in Chinese history, a kind of iron-made Five Zhu. Five Zhu of East Han was made in large amounts from the sixteenth year of Emperor Guang Wu in imitation of that of West Han.

After Wang Mang took power, the new Emperor even carried out four large-scale currency reforms in the period of eight years. The first reform occurred in the second year after Wang Mang's usurp. It applied the legendary law of "daughter phase weight" —a currency law that used two monetary systems of different weight at the same time—to real life to replace the popular Five Zhu. Wang Mang had three kinds of currency cast: Big Quan; Qi Knife; and Gold Cuo Knife, respectively. Big Quan was worth fifty pieces of Five Zhu. Qi Knife, in the shape of keys, was worth five hundred pieces. Gold Cuo Knife, similar to Qi Knife in form, was quite precious because it had five gold-made Chinese characters on it. In the second reform, Wang Mang issued two kinds of currency—Big Quan and Small Quan. On Small Quan, the characters "Xiao Quan Zhi Yi" were cast (*Xiao* means small).

One year later, Wang Mang began his third reform. This time, Xiao Quan Zhi Yi was used as the standard money unit, based on which gold, silver, turtle, shell, and copper money was circulated for trade. The system was so complicated, with twenty-eight ranks, that people could hardly identify them. In the year of Tian Feng (AD 14), Wang Mang had his fourth reform in which the previous currency was abolished and only Huo Bu and Huo Quan were circulated. Huo Quan had a larger amount of coinage. The frequent reforms caused disorder in the social economy.

The currency in the Three Kingdoms period was complicated too. Cao Cao believed that Qin united the countries because they had given priority to agriculture and Emperor Wu of Han settled the West Regions by way of *Tun Tian* (a system in which the government organized farming for fear of the outbreak of a war). With this idea as the guideline, Wei state encouraged Tun Tian and a thrifty policy, which entitled Wei to a better economic condition than the other two kingdoms—Shu and Wu, thus, paving way for its unification of the other two kingdoms in the future.

In 214, Liu Bei captured Ba Shu. He had big money cast in Shu because of a shortage of military expenditure. He also ordered money to be cast with lighter weight. In later years, as the economy deteriorated, Shu cast “small money” and “iron money” in great quantities.

Wu circulated the currency of Han dynasty at the early times, mostly the Five Zhu and the money of Wang Mang. In 236, Sun Quan cast Da Quan 500, and later cast Da Quan 1,000, Da Quan 2,000 and Da Quan 5,000. The weight of the money didn’t increase, but the nominal worth increased again and again, making the prices rise higher and higher until the economy collapsed finally.

Wei established West Jin after the unification of the three kingdoms. The central government of West Jin didn’t cast money, but Zhang Gui, the governor of Liang Zhou, cast copper money, named “New Quan Made in Liang.” Generally, in East Jin, they continued to use the money of old times, and cast their own money at the same time, but most of it was private because of a lack of administrative interference from the government. Song, Qi, Liang and Chen, of the Southern dynasties, had all cast money. In 523, Emperor Xiao Liang Wu forbade the use of copper coins. As a result, iron money circulated on a large scale, which was inconvenient for trade. Having been used to build Buddha statues, copper was rarely used for money, which contributed to the huge amount of iron money in the market. But iron money was ceased in the early years of the Chen dynasty. In 579, Emperor Yi issued Tai Huo Six Zhu, which, at first, was equal to ten pieces of Five Zhu, then of equal value to one piece of Five Zhu later.

Northern Wei was set up by Xian Bei, whose emperor, Xiao Wen, admired the culture of the Han ethnicity; he reformed and cast Tai He Five Zhu, in the nineteenth year of Tai He. In the third year of Yong Ping, Emperor Xuan Wu cast Yong Ping Five Zhu. The size of Northern Wei money continued to dwindle to such a degree that it could float on water in the wind. In the second year of Yong’an, the money was changed into Yong’an Five Zhu. Later, Northern Wei broke into Eastern and Western parts. East Wei was soon replaced by

North Qi, whose emperor cast Chang Ping Five Zhu as a substitute of Yong'an Five Zhu. It was neatly made with a relatively high value. But the corruption of North Qi brought about a great disorder in the currency market, which was flooded with the private casting from members of the public. The authorities of West Wei cast Zhi Yang Five Zhu, an imitation of Yong'an Five Zhu—except for a vertical written character, "Wu," on the money. West Wei was soon overthrown by Yu Wen Tai of North Zhou. Yu Wen Yong, Emperor of Wu, in 561, had Bu Quan money cast, with the calligraphy of "Yu Jin Zhuan." In 574, Wu Xing Da Bu was cast, which equaled ten pieces of Bu Quan but weighed similarly to it. Yong Tong Wan Guo money was made in 579, and was worth ten pieces of Wu Xing Da Bu, or five hundred pieces of Five Zhu money.

In the first year of Kai Huang, Yang Jian, the Emperor Sui Wen, had Kai Huang Five Zhu cast. He attached importance to the law of money circulation and demanded that one hundred pieces of such money be placed at each check post as the model money. Any money that failed to meet the standard was forbidden to pass and would be melted for recasting. In this way, he controlled the currency market effectively and the economy developed rapidly in early Sui. However, the extravagant Emperor Yang Di dragged the finances into trouble and private casting prevailed again in the late years of Sui.

With the establishment of the Tang dynasty, Kai Yuan Tong Bao was cast, which would have a significant influence on Chinese currency. From then on, currency was no longer named after its weight unit and Chinese currency accomplished its transition from weight to count. This Tong Bao system lasted over one thousand three hundred years until the late Qing and early Republic of China.

Kai Yuan money replaced all previous currency and was welcomed by the merchants. Folk-forged money appeared again in the market in large quantities during the years of Tang Gao Zong. Hence,

Gao Zong ordered the casting of Qian Feng Quan Bao, which was not much heavier than Kai Yuan money but valued at ten times its worth. It was abolished in less than a year, therefore, this kind of money is quite rare now.

In the An-Shi Rebellion, Shi Siming cast two kinds of money—De Yi Yuan Bao and Shun Tian Yuan Bao. After the rebellion, Da Li Tong Bao was cast in northwest areas. Jian Zhong Tong Bao was also cast in the Northwest but was not delicate and was seldom seen. According to scholars' research in recent years, Da Li Tong Bao, Jian Zhong Tong Bao and their varieties, "Money of Character Zhong" or "Money of Character Yuan," were all made in 766-783 by the Anxi Frontier Command of Tang for the defense of the West Regions. They were cast in Kuche, and all were official money for the use of the armies at that time.

The years of Tang Su Zong saw the financial difficulties after the rebellion. Qian Yuan Zhong Bao was cast in 758, a big money with the worth of ten pieces of Kai Yuan Tong Bao. In the next year, double-circled Qian Yuan Zhong Bao was cast, with only the addition of a copper line along the outer circle of the money at the back, but it was worth fifty pieces of Kai Yuan money in value. The law of currency was disturbed. Later, one Qian Yuan was announced to be worth one Kai Yuan. The last kind of money in Tang was Hui Chang Kai Yuan, made in the years of Hui Chang by Tang Wu Zong, with the name of the casting place on its back. There were as many as twenty-two places of casting, including Chang, Jing, Luo, Yi, Lan, etc. Most of the coins were made of copper from Buddha statues, or bells, after Wu Zong ordered the destruction of the Buddhas.

In the history of more than one hundred years of the Five Dynasties and Ten Kingdoms, the currency was in disorder with changing values. The five dynasties in the North (Liang, Tang, Jin, Han, and Zhou) all cast their own currency. Kai Ping Tong Bao, cast during the years of Kai Ping of the Emperor Tai Zu of latter Liang, is especially precious, for few of them have been discovered up to now. So is the Tian Cheng Yuan Bao money, of latter Tang. Tian Fu Yuan Bao, of latter Jin, has been found in great numbers, including both the official ones and the privately cast ones. Of course, the official ones are of higher quality. It was Zhou Yuan Tong Bao, of latter Zhou, that was best cast and circulated in the largest amounts among the Five Dynasties' currencies.

In 911, a segregated government appeared in the North—Liu Rengong and Liu Shouguang's government in Youzhou. Multifarious money were cast. Some were of copper, some of iron. Some were big, some small. Some used the mould of Wang Mang's Bu currency, some the mould of Shi Siming's Shun Tian money. Finally, they even had all these currencies hidden in Mount Da'an, leaving the subordinate army with only money of mud.

In Chu, one of the Ten Kingdoms, they cast Tian Ce Fu Bao and Qian Feng Quan Bao, each in two kinds: big copper money and big iron money. In Chu, they also cast money of lead. Fujian was known as the kingdom of Min. In the eighth year after Wang Shenzhi became the King of Min, he began to have money cast: big copper, big iron and big lead money. Min made money of lead because there was a lead ore in Ninghua. Liu Long of Southern Han had a great amount of lead money cast in the year of Qian Heng. For the first time, lead money was made and circulated in large quantities in China. Having been developed in culture and economy, South Tang cast the first Dui Qian in China—Kai Yuan Tong Bao. Dui Qian is the money with words written in two calligraphic styles. The words on Kai Yuan Tong Bao were in the styles of Zhuan and Zheng. Later, private castings rampaged, causing soaring prices and the end of the kingdom.

Zhao Kuangyin unified China into the Song dynasty and the social economy developed substantially. Silver occupied a more important position in circulation. Also, in Song, the earliest paper money in the world appeared. In the first year of Jian Long (AD 960), Song Tai Zu had Song Yuan Tong Bao cast, the first kind of currency of North Song. Since then, a new currency was cast almost every time a new reign title was used. The number of currencies in North Song was especially great. For one thing, new money was cast for each new reign title; for another thing, most of the money of North Song was Dui Qian, so the words on the money were written in various styles, as Zhuan, Li, Xing, Cao, and, Kai. An average currency had words in at least two calligraphic styles, written, usually, by the famous calligraphists of the time. Thirdly, the currencies were divided into many grades. What's more, there were both iron money and copper money at the same time. Song Ren Zong (from 1023 to 1063), used ten reign titles, each with the casting of a lot of new currencies. In the years of Song Shen Zong, there were Xi Ning Yuan Bao, Zhong Bao Zhe Er and Xi Ning Tong Bao, in addition to the Tong Bao and Zhe Er money with the reign title of Yuan Feng.

Yuan You Tong Bao was cast in the years of Yuan You of Song Zhe Zong, the words on which were said to be written by Su Shi and SiMa Guang. Money was also cast during the years of Shao Sheng and Yuan Fu. Song Hui Zong had the money of Chong Ning, Da Guan, Zheng He, Chong He, Yi He and Jing Kang cast. Among the currencies discovered so far, Ying Yun Tong Bao, coined by Li Shun, in the Song dynasty, is the earliest in our country that was definitely coined by a peasant uprising. It was made either of copper or iron.

Jian Yan Tong Bao was cast first by Gao Zong, after the establishment of the Southern Song dynasty, followed by Jian Yan Yuan Bao and Jian Yan Zhong Bao. These currencies inherited the traditions of the Northern Song dynasty—they all had three kinds of face value, and they were all "Dui Qian." This was also the case with Shao Xing Yuan Bao and Shao Xing Tong Bao, the money cast during

Gao Zong's Shao Xing years. Long Xing Yuan Bao, Qian Dao Yuan Bao, Chun Xi Yuan Bao and Chun Xi Tong Bao were the money with Xiao Zong's different reign titles. Marked with *Qi* (a character that means number seven), the coins cast in the seventh year of Chun Xi became the first ones in the world that carried the year number. Characters signifying the supervising authorities were sometimes found on the back of coins; this was first established on the Chun Xi money. Shao Xi Yuan Bao, the money cast in Guang Zong's reign of Shao Xi, was all numbered with the years. The iron money that he had cast was marked with the supervising authority.

There was a new fashion of casting during the Jia Ding years of Ning Zong, i.e., money with the same reign title was given different names, making the currency names more complicated. For instance, the iron money of the reign title of Jia Ding had four names—Yuan Bao, Tong Bao, Zhi Bao and Quan Bao—while Zhe Three and Zhe Five iron money had even more names. Li Zong had many currencies cast in his reign, among which, Da Song Tong Bao Big Money Worthy of Ten counted as a treasure.

The excessive issuance and depreciation that was too fast led to the inflation of currency during the Southern Song dynasty, which, in turn, caused people to deposit copper coins. Hence, a great quantity of copper coins vanished from the market. As a result, the government ordered each region to cast a batch of regional currencies for local use, which were called "Money Cards."

Song Gao Zong had cast a peculiar money card in Hangzhou with three shapes. One was square in the upper and circular in the lower, the second, a reversal of the first—circular in the upper and square in the lower—and the third was a rectangle. Words like "Lin An Fu Xing Yong" were cast on the front, with the face value on the back. Money cards with smaller value were also found in recent years. They were cast by local governments as well, mostly in the years between Jia Xi and Chun You. The relics unearthed in Jiujiang, Jiangxi, in 1993, included money cards of South Song.

Liao Tai Zu and Liao Tai Zong began to cast their own money. Tong Xing Quan Huo, Kai Dan Sheng Bao, Dan Xun Tie Bao, and Qian Qiu Wan Sui were generally taken as money of the early years of Liao. Among the unearthed currencies of all the dynasties, those of Liao have been the most abundant. More and more money of Liao was found, such as Tian Zan Tong Bao, Tian Xian Tong Bao, Hui Tong Tong Bao and Tian Lu Tong Bao, unveiling many mysteries that have puzzled people in the past. The first currency of Liao Tai Zong was Tian Zan Tong Bao. Since then, a new currency would be issued by each emperor with a new reign title. Commemorative coins were also placed in the tombs for dead people in the Liao dynasty; these were big money coins, with the numbered year. The authority in charge of coin-casting in Liao was called the "Court of Mint."

The social economy and culture of West Xia are relatively developed. A dynasty established by the Dangxiang ethnic group, it has its own writing system and has coined its own currency. Chinese characters were also found on some West Xia money. The newly unearthed data can, basically, confirm the existence of West Xia currency, with a number of new varieties that have been unearthed. Since the late 1970s, a variety of West Xia currencies have been evacuated in Helanshan, Baotou, Yinchuan and other places. Due to West Xia's developed social economy and culture, its currency was made extremely exquisite. *Kingdom Xia* in *the History of Song* recorded that, in the tenth year of Tian Sheng, Emperor Ren Zong established Tongji Supervision Department to mint Tian Sheng Yuan Bao. Before that, West Xia's minting organization was Wen Si Yuan. Iron money was cast as well, as discovered recently in the present Hetao area, which was to the west of the kingdom of ancient times.

Jin dynasty money wasn't cast until the second year of Zheng Long, during King Hai Ling's reign. It was called Zheng Long Yuan Bao. Only two casting organizations were recorded in the Jin dynasty. One was Fu Tong Jian, in Daizhou, which mainly cast Da Ding Tong Bao. The other was Li Tong Jian in Quyang, which cast some year-numbered money, with the characters of "Shen" or "You" on the back. As with the Yu Jin Zhuan writing of Dang Huaiying, the Tai He money of Jin Zhang Zong was more delicate than the products of machines. Some iron money of Jin dynasty was discovered in recent years.

The currency of the Yuan dynasty is in relatively small numbers, mainly because of the use of the bank notes and silver ingots, which turned the casting of copper coins into a subordinate position. At the beginning of the Yuan dynasty, reforms of some currencies were carried out, based on the mould of the previous dynasties, as an imitation of the past system, shortly after the conquest of the Central Plains. Da Chao Tong Bao money of Yuan was made of copper or silver, with Mongolian marking on the back, the meaning of which was indecipherable to people, until now. In Kublai's Zhong Tong years, Zhong Tong Yuan Bao was cast as the first formally circulated currency of Yuan. It's a kind of Dui Qian with the calligraphic styles of Kai and Zhuan, only few of which have been discovered. In the twenty-second year of Zhi Zheng, Zhi Zheng Tong Bao was cast, both in Chinese and Phagspa script. It was produced in large amounts at the end of Yuan, subdivided into various kinds.

Since *History of Yuan* was compiled within a year, by more than thirty people under the command of Zhu Yuanzhang, it was not comprehensive in the matter of economic historical materials. Therefore, many unearthed or handed-down currencies were not recorded in the book, such as Da Chao Tong Bao, in the years of Shi Zu; Yuan Zhen Tong Bao, in the years of Cheng Zong, both in Chinese and Mongolian; Huang Qing Yuan Bao and Huang Qing Tong Bao of the Ren Zong years; etc. Another feature, peculiar to the currency of Yuan, is the casting of money that was used for the worship of temples. Such money was generally small and was of two kinds: one had words and reign titles, similar to the normally circulating currencies; the other used the name of the temple, or of the Buddha, as the money's name. The uprisings broke out successively at the end of Yuan dynasty. The separating powers cast their own currencies too, such as the Long Feng money of Liu Futong, Tian Qi Tong Bao of Xu Shouhui and Da Yi Tong Bao of Chen Youliang. Most of them include three kinds—Xiaoping, Zhe'er and Zhe Three money.

The money in the Ming dynasty was complicated by the frequent changes of the money system and the casting institutions. Zhu Yuanzhang established the Bao Yuan Bureau to cast Da Zhong Tong Bao as early as 1361. After he took the throne, he commanded Hu Bu and the local provinces to cast Hong Wu Tong Bao, which was divided into five ranks—Dang ten, Dang five, Dang three, Dang two and Dang one. In the eighth year of Hong Wu, Da Ming Bao Chao (a kind of paper money) was issued, while the Bao Yuan Bureau was abolished. Two years later, the Bao Quan Bureau was set up in each province to cast small coins to circulate with the paper money at the same time. In the twenty-second year of Hong Wu, the form of money was changed again by adding weight to the back of it. *Regulations on Money Casting outside Beijing* was worked out in the twenty-fifth year of Hong Wu, which stipulated that Nei Fu was in charge of money casting within the capital, while outside Beijing it was up to the Bu Zheng Si (a department responsible for civil affairs) to cast money under the supervision of the officials sent by Gong Bu. The names of money casting bureaus varied many times just in the early years of the Ming dynasty, from Huo Quan Bureau to Bao Yuan Bureau, quickly to Bao Quan Bureau, then to Bao Yuan Bureau again.

In the sixth year of Yong Le, Ming Cheng Zu began to cast Yong Le Tong Bao. The Hong Xi money was cast during Ren Zong's year of Hong Xi, which, though mentioned many times in historical documents, was rare in number because of Ren Zong's death just one year after his succession. In the eighth year of Xuan De, Ming Xuan Zong ordered Gong Bu, in Nanjing, and the four Bu Zheng Si, in Zhejiang, Jiangxi, Fujian and Guangdong, to cast Xuan De Tong Bao. No money was cast during the years of Jian Yuan, Tian Shun and Cheng Hua until the sixteenth year of Hong Zhi, when Ming Xiao Zong ordered Beijing, Nanjing and the provinces to resume the casting.

None of the money—Yong Le Tong Bao, Hong Xi Tong Bao, Xuan De Tong Bao or Hong Zhi Tong Bao—had words on the back. Most were Xiaoping coins. Ming Shi Zong started to cast Jia Jing Tong Bao in the sixth year of Jia Jing, each with the weight of 12 *fen* or 1.2 *qian* (both qian and fen are units of weight). Eunuchs began interfering with finance, from the Jia Jing years, even meddling money casting directly. Long Qing Tong Bao was cast in the fourth year of Long Qing, weighing 1.3 qian each. The Jia Jing money was Xiaoping coins, except Dang two, Dang three, Dang five and Dang ten versions. Long Qing Tong Bao was all Xiaoping coins. Since the resumption of casting in Hong Zhi, casting bureaus sprang up in the years of Jia Jing, and prevailed more in the Wan Li years. Wan Li Tong Bao, cast in the years of Wan Li, was mostly Xiaoping coins, some with such words as Gong, Hu, Tian, Zheng, Jiang, or He on the back.

In February of the first year of Tian Qi, new forms of money were established. The next year, government regulated the organizations responsible for money casting. The factories of Hu Bu were reorganized into the Bao Quan Bureau to make money for military needs. There were three casting centers all over the country—Jingshi (present Beijing), Nanjing and Sichuan. Three kinds of the Dang ten coins of Tian Qi money, all with the casting bureau names, were found—with the word Fu on the back for Xuanfu, Mi for Miyun and Zhen for Jizhen. However, the back words were more complicated for Tian Qi Xiaoping coins, including the words like Hu, Gong, Yun, Zhe, Yuan, Jing, or Fengzhi, etc. The word Yuan was supposed to indicate the Du Cha Yuan because, having been given the power to inspect money casting, it was highly likely that the Du Cha Yuan cast coins itself, especially during an age when casting was so popular.

In late Chong Zhen years, money was cast in Bing Bu, of Nanjing, Caojiang, Yingtian Fu and Guangdong, but only for their own use, and the sizes were not unified. After the soldiers of Qing entered the Shanhaiguan under the guide of Wu Sangui, the Ming dynasty collapsed, and some royal families in the South established the Southern Ming dynasty. In 1644, the first year of Hong Guang, King Fu Wang had Hong Guang Tong Bao cast. The same year, King Lu Wang had Da Ming Tong Bao cast. King Tang Wang also had Long Wu Tong Bao cast in the first year of Long Wu. Emperor Yong Li had money cast in abundance after he escaped to Myanmar. The words on the back of the coins were Hu, Gong, Yu, Chi, Du, Dao, Fu, etc., in the calligraphy of Kai, Xing, Cao or Zhuan.

The peasant uprising led by Li Zicheng and Zhang Xianzhong swept the country in the late Ming dynasty. In 1644, Zhang Xianzhong made Chengdu the capital, Da Xi the title of his reign, and had Da Shun Tong Bao cast. The money was made from the Buddha in temples or the official seals. Li Zicheng set his capital in Xi'an and called his country Da Shun. He had Yong Chang Tong Bao cast, including Xiaoping, Dang five and Dang ten coins. According to some documents, Li Zicheng had cast money in Xiangcheng, of Hubei, and Xi'an, of Shaanxi. After the death of Zhang Xianzhong, his adopted son, Sun Kewang, supported Emperor Yongli of the Southern Ming dynasty against Qing and had Xing Chao Tong Bao cast.

Qing had cast their own money before they entered Shanhaiguan. In the Tian Ming years of Nurhachi, he had Tian Ming Khan money cast in Manchu script and Tian Ming Tong Bao in Chinese. Later, Huang Taiji cast the big money of Tian Cong Khan in Manchu script.

Emperor Shun Zhi had five kinds of money cast during his time. One kind was cast in the first year of Shun Zhi, with the words "Shun Zhi Tong Bao" on the front. The second kind added the names of money casting bureaus in Chinese, like Gong, Hu, Dong and, Fu. The third kind was made in the tenth year of Shun Zhi, a One Li coin with the script "One Li" (*Li* is a money unit) and the casting bureau name on the back. The fourth and fifth were made in the same year (1660). The fourth had the word "Bao" and the bureau name on the back, both in the Manchu script, while the fifth had only the bureau name on the back, but in both Manchu and Chinese.

Kang Xi, Yong Zheng, Qian Long, Jia Qing and Dao Guang all had Tong Bao money cast in their regimes. In Xian Feng's years, the Taiping Tianguo uprising broke out, which led to a tightened finance. The government began to cast big money. The currency at that time could be divided into three kinds. One was Tong Bao, a Xiaoping coin of copper, iron or lead. The second was Zhong Bao, a big money from Dang four to Dang fifty. The third was Yuan Bao (or ingots), with a greater value, varying from Dang one hundred to Dang one thousand.

In Tong Zhi and the early Guang Xu years, only Tong Bao of small money and Zhong Bao of Dang ten were cast. Later, Empress Cixi ordered machines from abroad to cast money. Xuan Tong Tong Bao was the money for Xuan Tong years, of which there were two kinds; both kinds were small money, but one was larger in size than the other.

The money of the Qing dynasty fell into two categories: one made by the central casting factories, and the other by the local factories. Like the Ming dynasty, the Central Government of Qing also established two central mints to be responsible for money casting—Baoyuan and

Baoquan in Gong Bu and Hu Bu, respectively. In local provinces, the Qing government also set up many new mints, among which were the Xuan Fu, Mi Zhen, Ji Zhen, Bao Zhi and Bao De bureaus, in Zhili Province; Da Tong, Bao Jin and Yang He bureaus, in Shanxi Province; Sheng Jing and Bao Sheng bureaus, in Fengtian Province; etc. All provinces had money-casting factories of their own, including Henan, Hubei, Hunan, Jiangsu, Yunnan, Sichuan, Guizhou, Guangdong, Guangxi, Tibet, Xinjiang, Taiwan, etc. In addition, there was also some money in the Qing dynasty that was cast by uprising armies or local separatist forces.

III. Silver Taels

Silver coins were cast early in ancient China in the form of the silver Bu coins in the Kingdom of Chu, of the Warring States, and the silver-caked coins in the Han dynasty. In the Tang dynasty, silver was used for tax collection, as well as in fiscal expenditures. According to archeological discoveries, there existed Yongdiao silver (Yongdiao is a measure taken by government to balance the market prices), tax commodity silver, mine silver and tax silver in the Tang dynasty. Four pieces of Yongdiao silver were found in Xi'an, in 1970, in the shape of round cakes with many words on the surface. They were the Yongdiao silver handed in by Huaiji, Lingnan. In 1977, two tax commodity silver ingots were found in Shaanxi, which were also collected from Lingnan. The mine silver was discovered in Xi'an in the 1950s, weighing fifty Liang. Besides silver cakes, gold cakes of the Tang dynasty were also unearthed, such as the four found in Pinglu of Shanxi in 1979.

Silver had been an important tax of the government in the Song dynasty. Silver taels of Song can be divided into two kinds—the official casting and the folk casting. They were usually in the form of Silver Ting. The folk cast ones should have had the names of the shop and the artisan carved on them, together with the purity condition of the silver.

There were three categories of official Silver Ting. The first was cast by the local governments. The second was used for tax collection; the batch of silver ingots unearthed in Fangcheng of Henan, in 1975, turned out to be the silver collected by the Song government in the name of various kinds of harsh taxes. The third was the silver for civil use. According to the statistics of some scholars in the late of 1980s, around three hundred pieces of silver ingots had been discovered by then, among which, some were for tax, some for military use, and some were for business, on which can be seen the names of the shops. Still some were for circulation; on this kind, only the silver quality of the ingot was marked. There were specific prescriptions as to the grades of silver ingots in the Song dynasty.

The first kind of officially cast silver coins in China was born in the second year of Cheng'an of Emperor Jin Zhang Zong, that is, the Cheng'an Bao Huo coins, which were divided into five grades ranging from one Liang to ten Liang. It was the first silver coin in Chinese history to deviate from the simple weight to the indication of the currency value. Four coins of Cheng'an Bao Huo were found, for the first time, in Heilongjiang, in 1981. Another piece was found in 1985.

There were two kinds of silver ingots in the Jin dynasty. One was tax silver, for example, the Silver Ting of the second year of Zheng Long. The other was Jie Salt silver ingots, which were cast with the silver collected by the government as salt tax. There were the characters "Ti Ju Jie Yan Si" on the ingots; they account for a large proportion in Jin's silver ingots discovered so far.

The silver taels of the Yuan dynasty included Yangzhou, Pingzhun, Mengshan and Taiyuan silver, among which, Yangzhou silver is more famous. Casting place, time, weight and an inscription were carved on the unearthed silver. On the back, there were two characters—Yuan Bao—engraved in the way of Yin Ke (a method of engraving the lines under the flat surface to make it a concave pattern).

The years from the middle and late Ming to the middle Qing dynasty were the era when the Spaniards traded with China, exchanging silver coins for Chinese silk and porcelain. For this reason, China, which originally did not produce much silver, began to use a large amount of silver in circulation—a kind of money made by melting the Mexican silver coins to recast them into boat-shaped Yuanbao.

Fig. 1-1 Silver Yuanbao

First of all, fundamental changes took place in China's traditional single currency system of the combination of copper and paper currency. In the past, silver, though a member of the currency family from an early time, was mostly limited to saving purposes. The wealthy Chinese buried silver as the treasure to bless their house, so the circulation attributed to silver did not exemplify itself in Chinese traditional social and economic life. After the flow into China of American silver in large amounts since the middle and late Ming dynasty, the status of silver in the Chinese monetary system was greatly strengthened. The government's policy of levying silver in taxation further enhanced the importance of silver in China's social economy. Silver played a role in large transactions and government finances that was irreplaceable by paper money or copper coins.

Secondly, the shape of the Chinese silver also underwent great changes. Silver in the Song and Yuan dynasties was usually cast into a narrow-waist lump. However, it took the shape of a boat from the Ming dynasty, the so-called Yuanbao that people see often in movies now. The reason for this change in form has not been studied in depth, but it is definitely related to the influx of silver into China.

The Silver Ingots Inscription Regulation of the eighth year of Jiajing demanded that the names of the officials and the silversmith be chiseled onto every piece of silver ingot. At first, every ten Liang amounted to one Ding. In the fourteenth year of Jiajing, it was prescribed that twenty Liang be one Ding. In the forty-first year, fifty Liang was one Ding. Thus, the three levels of silver ingots in the Ming dynasty were defined—big Ding of fifty Liang, medium Ding of twenty Liang and small Ding of ten Liang. This was also the case for the gold Ding system in the Ming dynasty.

The inscriptions of silver tael in the Ming dynasty experienced a process of simplification. Those in the periods of Zheng De, Jia Jing, Long Qing and Wan Li had been quite comprehensive, while, after Wan Li, they turned more and more simplified. There was a kind of Yuan Bao in the Ming dynasty, on which the three words "Jin Hua Yin" (gold flower silver) were inscribed, as well as the casting place, time, the names of the supervising official and the artisan. Therefore, it was called Jin Hua Yin silver. In the Zheng Tong years, Jin Hua Yin was sent to the capital as taxes, which, since then, was regulated as a practice of Ming. There have been many archaeological discoveries of this kind of silver.

From the middle and late Ming dynasty to modern China, silver taels became the most important branch of the Chinese currency system, circulating in the market in parallel with copper coins. Silver has achieved an unprecedented status.

In the Qing dynasty, there was no unification of silver taels, and the form of silver was different from place to place. That's because silver taels in the Qing dynasty were cast both by official and private mints. There were no official mints for silver taels like the casting factories of copper coins. It was not until 1932, when the government of the Republic of China announced the reform of Yuan in replacing Liang, that China's silver taels withdrew from circulation.

IV. Paper Money

The earliest paper money in the world originated in Sichuan, in the Song dynasty of China. At that time, Sichuan used iron money, which was inconvenient to trade. The large iron money weighed twenty-five Jin per thousand *Wen*, and even the small one weighed more than ten Jin. A piece of cloth cost twenty thousand *Qian*, which had to be pulled by cart (both Wen and Qian are units of money). In this case, some merchants began to issue Chu Quan (a receipt type of paper vouchers), whose amount could be filled in temporarily for circulation in the market. The merchants joined forces later to issue Chu Quan, which could be cashed at any time. The merchant who issued the money was called Jiaozi shop/household, and the paper money issued was called Jiaozi. Soon, the government nationalized the power of Jiaozi issuing. In the first year of Tian Sheng of Emperor Song Ren Zong (1023), Yizhou Jiaozi Wu was set up to issue official Jiaozi in three grades—one Guan, five Guan and ten Guan ("Guan" was the cord used to connect the coins in ancient times. One thousand coins was one Guan). In the first year of Xi Ning of Shen Zong (1068), it was changed to just two kinds—one Guan and five Guan—issued every three years and iron money was used as the reserve for paper money. During the years of Chong Ning, Emperor Song Hui Zong changed the name of Jiaozi to Qian Yin. This was printed in the fourth year of Chong Ning (1105) and distributed outside Sichuan. In the third year of Da Guan (1109), Jiaozi Wu was officially changed to Qian Yin Wu.

In the South Song dynasty, Jiaozi Wu was at first set up in Lin'an to issue Jiaozi, which was later called Guanzi, which was similar to bill of exchange. Because Bianqian Huizi, a common paper currency among the people, was circulated, the Southern Song dynasty made this Huizi government-operated in the thirtieth year of Shao Xing (1160). It was initially issued in the Liang Zhe region, then in Liang Huai, and circulated both in Zhejiang and Guangdong. The denomination was divided into two hundred, three hundred and five hundred Wen, and one Guan. One Guan was equal to one Hui. The edges of the note were uncut.

There were many kinds of paper money in the Southern Song dynasty. Jian Qian Guan Zi was issued in Wuzhou by Zhang Jun when he garrisoned his troops there in the first year of Shao Xing. During the years of Jing Ding, when Jia Sidao was the Xiang Guo (equivalent to the present prime minister), he issued gold and silver Jian Qian Guan Zi; there were also Qian Yin, in Sichuan, Huai Jiao, in Huainan, and Hu Hui, in Huguang. In the late Song dynasty, paper money began to depreciate. In the Chun You years of the Southern Song dynasty, two hundred Guan of Hui Zi couldn't even buy a pair of straw shoes. The Jin dynasty issued a variety of paper money. In 1154, Jin set up Jiao Chao Ku to issue Jiao Chao (paper money), which was divided into large and small Chao. The former included five kinds: one Guan, two Guan, three Guan, five Guan and ten Guan. The latter had also five kinds: one hundred Wen, two hundred Wen, three hundred Wen, five hundred Wen and seven hundred Wen. During the reign of Emperor Xuan Zong, in the years of Zhen You, large Chao was issued that ranged from twenty to one hundred Guan, and then from two hundred to one thousand Guan, which caused the soaring of prices. Ten thousand Guan was only enough to buy a cake. The names of paper money changed many times in the Late Jin dynasty, such as Zhen You Bao Quan, Zhen You Tong Bao, Xing Ding Bao Quan, Yun Guang Zhen Huo, etc.

At the beginning of the Yuan dynasty, all the paper money was local. In the eighth year of Emperor Yuan Tai Zong's reign (1236), Jiao Chao were issued in various places, but they were not mutually exchangeable. The paper money that was commonly used in China in the Yuan dynasty was Zhongtong Yuanbao Jiao Chao, also known as Silk Chao, which was issued by Shi Zu Kublai Khan in the first year of Zhong Tong. Two Liang of Silk Chao was worth one Liang of silver money. In October of the same year, Bao Chao was issued, which was divided into ten Wen, twenty Wen, thirty Wen, fifty Wen, two hundred Wen, three hundred Wen, five hundred Wen, and one Guan, two Guan, and so on. One Guan equated to one Liang of Silk Chao. Li Chao, issued in the twelfth year of Zhi Yuan, was a small note, which could be divided into 3 types: one Wen, three Wen and five Wen. Zhi Yuan Chao of the twenty-fourth year of Zhi Yuan was divided into eleven grades. One Guan of Zhiyuan Chao was equal to five Guan of Zhong Tong Chao. Both kinds of money were circulated in the market.

The paper money used in the Ming dynasty was Da Ming Bao Chao. In 1374, the Ming government established Bao Chao Ti Ju Si. The next year they began to issue Da Ming Bao Chao, which would be used for more than two hundred seventy years. It had six kinds of denomination: one hundred Wen, two hundred Wen, three hundred Wen, four hundred Wen, five hundred Wen, and one Guan.

There were three periods that issued paper money in the Qing dynasty. The first was the Shun Zhi years, in the beginning of the Qing dynasty, during which time Shun Zhi Chao Guan was issued. The second was the Xian Feng period. The banknotes issued at that time included Da Qing Bao Chao by the government, the official banknotes, by Hu Bu, and the banknotes issued by local financial institutions. The third period was during the reign of Guang Xu, when the Qing government ordered local financial institutions, which were set up in different places, namely, the official banks, Qian Hao, to issue paper money.

In the eighth year of Shun Zhi (1651), due to the urgent need of the government's military forces, Shun Zhi Chao Guan were issued. Ten years later, they were withdrawn and abolished. The Taiping rebellion, during the years of Xian Feng, led to the issue of paper money financially. The issue of paper money by local financial institutions in modern China also originated in the Xian Feng period of the Qing dynasty.

天津宫南庆隆银号伍圆（尺寸：15.2X10.3）

Fig. 1-2 Paper money, Five Yuan, of Qing Long Yin Hao, in Tianjin

From this acquaintance with the history of Chinese currency, we can sum up several characteristics of Chinese currency culture. First, there were many kinds of coin materials, copper being the main one, while other metals such as iron and lead were sometimes used too. Second, in the early stage of coinage, mould casting was often adopted, and then the sand-turning method, rather than hammering, was used to increase output. Third, the copper coins of counting currency and the silver Taels of weighing currency were mixed in circulation, and the system of silver and copper as duplicate standards was formed in the

Ming and Qing dynasties. Fourth, paper money appeared prematurely, and it was national paper money, not credit currency.

CHAPTER TWO

CURRENCY CULTURE EXCHANGE BETWEEN CHINA AND ANCIENT GREECE AND ROME

I. Currency Legacy of Alexander the Great

Ancient Greece is the birthplace of Western monetary culture. The origin of Greek monetary culture is in some areas of Western Asia, but soon Greek civilization became dominant in this culture. Greek coins are well-known for their designs, with gods, heroes, animals and plants forming the main motifs.

Alexander the Great had a great influence on the history of the Western world. He was an unconquerable military genius in the Western world. In the West, he created an ideal society that conforms to all people's dreams and a dictatorship without any restrictions. All these ideas have been deeply integrated into Western legends, and they still affect the West, twenty-four centuries later. The exchange of currency culture between the East and the West is inseparable from the Eastern expedition of the great emperor. The valiant young man began to control the whole of Greece in 337 BC. Three years later, he started the Eastern expedition with his Greek army, successively conquered Syria, Egypt and Persia, crossed the Hindu Kush Mountains, and reached the Indus River region in 327 BC. Here, Alexander, who defeated the West invincibly, met with strong resistance and had to withdraw to Babylon. However, a new empire spanning Europe, Asia and Africa was formed. The great empire, which was only maintained by military forces, disappeared immediately after the death of Alexander.

Nevertheless, the currency culture of Greece came from the West to the East. Before Alexander the Great, gods, animals and plants were designs that Greek coin makers used to show their talents. The coins of Alexander the Great had exerted an immeasurable influence on the world's currency culture. The inscriptions and patterns on the coins ushered the world into the Hellenistic period and influenced the history of the world's currency.

Unlike Chinese coins, the ancient coins in the West were made by striking. Each coin had its own characteristics. When making coins, the engraver first reversed a bronze or iron die left and right, then placed it on the anvil. This fixed die was called the surface die. Then he prepared the second print, which was a beater with a handle that would be blown directly by a hammer. This print was called the back die. Place the heated unprocessed blank coin on the surface die, then the back die on the blank coin, and then hammer. In this way, coins were made. The back die and the surface die were driven into the blank coin at the same time. Usually, after producing about five thousand to ten thousand coins, the surface die would be damaged.

Since the back dies of ancient Western coins were generally engraved the symbol of the city, the name of the chief executive, the symbol monogram, etc., we can find the connection between different back dies and a same surface die. In addition, the fact that some surface dies have been used continuously for a long time is helpful to reveal the relationship between coins, and to explore the status of the issuer and the history at that time.

When Alexander the Great died in 323 BC, his empire, from Epirus to the Indus, had twenty-four mints, all of which produced different types of gold, silver and copper coins. For example, the main casting in Amphipolis, in Macedonia, and Babylon, in Mesopotamia, was silver coins, Drachmas, while Abydus and Lampsacus, of Hellespont, mainly cast gold coins, Starters. Through the study of coins, we can see that these coins underwent dramatic changes in the decades after Alexander's death. Greek city-states used coins with their own marks, rather than an Alexander-type mark.

The first obvious change took place around 320 BC. When Ptolemy became the ruler of Egypt, he began to replace the standard pattern of Hagras on the coins with Alexander in elephant's scalp, thus, dramatically breaking through the Greek tradition. The pattern of coins was originally occupied by gods and heroes in myths and legends, but, at this point, it became a ruler—a human being. However, Ptolemy still compared Alexander the Great to Dionysius, the conqueror of India in Greek legend. Also, Alexander had a little curly ram horn on his head, which meant that his father was the King of Gods, Zeus. This was actually a declaration that Alexander was also a god, and the Ptolemaic dynasty was blessed by this god, because it was Ptolemy who snatched the body of Alexander the Great from its way to Macedonia and buried it in Alexandria.

Fig. 2-1 Greek rulers' coin under the influence of Alexander the Great

Before long, Lysimachus, following Ptolemy's example, ruled what is now the Europe's rich coastal regions of Turkey and Bulgaria. Like Ptolemy, Lysimachus attached great importance to his connection with Alexander the Great and decided to use his coins to convey this message. In this way, a beautiful pattern appeared on the coin. The irresistible energy, strong and decisive quality, violent personality and even the maintenance of the gods were all reflected in the horns of Zeus. The essence of Alexander's legend is all condensed in the portrait on ancient coins.

While the portraits on Ptolemaic coins were changed every few years, the portraits of Alexander the great on Lysimachus coins had never been changed since he served as a magistrate and later established the Kingdom (which ended in 281 BC). On the contrary, with the victories of Lysimachus in politics and military affairs, his coins were widely recognized. By 281 BC, their abundance had earned Lysimachus coins a position of international currency, and they were was recast many times throughout the ancient Greek era (until the first century AD).

In about 305 BC, after the Cyprus naval battle, the victors, Antigonus and Demetrius, were proclaimed kings, and soon Demetrius gave up all types of Alexander's coins and substituted a brand-new design to commemorate the victory of the naval battle, as well as the new inscriptions—"the coins belong to Demetrius." The original change was inspired by the competition with Ptolemy who established his reign at about the same time. Demetrius used a kind of imitation of Alexander's portrait coins, on which he had his own portrait and bull horns engraved. Bull horns declare Demetrius to be a relative of Dionysius and Poseidon. Demetrius, thus, set a precedent by casting the portrait of a living ruler on coins, an influence that felt itself fast and lasting in the world of coins. Later, in Greek history, nobody who won an independent kingdom could ever resist the temptation. Even the generals of the Republic of Rome could not be exempted from it.

In the ten years after Alexander's death, the ever-changing alliances and wars of various competitors made the single city-states in a very difficult situation, and some of them succumbed to the rule of Alexander's successors. In 281 BC, due to the barbarian invasion, the Greek city-states had to rely on the protection of the heirs of the great emperor to survive, and when the turmoil occurred, the currency was in urgent need, so that many Greek city-states turned their coins to the pattern of Alexander the Great, and the Alexander coins were generally accepted in the city-states to be used internally or in international trade.

In the Hellenized city-states in Europe and Asia, the coins of Alexander the Great or the coins with the design of Lysimachus were always accepted, especially the latter, having become the generally accepted medium in the Black Sea and Balkans region. The city-state emblems can be found on these coins, which were usually engraved on the back. In addition, composite scripts and even symbols are often found too. The coins of these city-states were important products under the influence of the coins of Alexander the Great.

Before the middle of the second century BC, most of the Greek city-states gave up the Alexander the Great coins, this was closely related to the strengthening of Roman rule in the East. More than twenty Greek city-states began to use their own city-state coins again, most of which were engraved with wreaths on the back. However, the neighboring countries to Greece still preferred the Lysimachus coins. In the regions along the Black Sea coast and the Balkan Peninsula, the demand lasted until the first century BC. As the supply of standard city-state coins decreased, imitations multiplied. Thus, the second and early first centuries BC saw a "golden age" of unbridled counterfeit of the coins of Alexander the Great and Lysimachus.[1]

The Eastern expedition of Alexander the Great left many Hellenistic city-states in Asia, which later formed Bactria and Kushan. These two countries kept the monetary culture of ancient Greece in Asia, which, in turn, exerted a great influence on that of India.

---

[1] Robert A. Bauslaugh, "The Numismatic Legacy of Alexander the Great," *Archaeology*, no.7-8 (1984).

Fig. 2-2 Greek ruler's coin in Asia, influenced by Alexander the Great

The earliest Indian coins were produced around 700 BC by melting and casting, with square or round holes on the coins. However, the technique of using two sides to strike Indian coins was influenced by the coins of Alexander the Great. When Bactria broke away from Syria and became independent, it often invaded India in the second century BC. As a result, it controlled Afghanistan, Baluchistan and Wuhe Province, and Hellenized these areas. From AD 1 to 150, the coins in this area were all Hellenized types deeply influenced by Alexander the Great. Due to the complexity of the ethnicity, there were generally two kinds of inscriptions on the coins.[2]

In the first century AD, the Kusanas conquered Afghanistan and Wuhe Province, and established the Kusanas Empire. They also accepted the Alexander types of coins. In this period, as the Roman Empire began to develop eastward, the coins in Central Asia began to be Hellenized and Romanized. The coins of Kadiphises (145-85), after he occupied the Kabul River, have the obverse motif of the portrait of Augustus. His son, Kadiphises II, conquered Northern India, thus making the coins more Hellenistic, and the weight of his gold coins was equal to that of Aurei, the Roman gold coins. At the same time, the coins had the characteristics of Indian culture, such as the god Shiva on the back.

[2] Arthur Anthong MacDonnell, *History of Culture in India*, trans. Long Zhang (Beijing: Zhong Hua Book Company, 1948).

Greek coins have been found in Mulei County, Xinjiang, China.[3]

Who would have thought that the two great monetary cultures, China and Greece, had been perfectly integrated as early as the beginning of the first century? Two kinds of currency culture, one from the East to the West, and the other from the West to the East, finally, after countless tribulations, met in Xinjiang, China.

II. Hotan Horse Money

Fig. 2-3 Hotan horse money

The result of the meeting was the appearance of a coin with the distinct characteristics of the two currency cultures in the years of 100-220, in Khotan—Hotan horse money, also called the Chinese-Kharosthi coin because both the Chinese and Kharosthi characters were found on it. According to Lin Meicun, a Chinese scholar, this kind of coin was produced in between the years of 175-220.

One legacy of Alexander's Eastern expedition on currency culture was that, after Alexander's withdrawal from the East, his subordinate generals who were left in the East made themselves kings and, for the first time, cast Alexander on coins instead of gods or the representatives of

[3] Elken Rozi, "On the Ancient Coins Found in Mulei County," *Xinjiang Finance*, Supplement II (1988).

gods, such as an olive branch and an owl. Since then, it has become a major feature of Greek monetary culture to cast the portrait of one's own king, or the name of the king, on coins. At this time, or later, this kind of coin, and the culture it represented, crossed the Karakoram Pass and came to Khotan, the main road of the Silk Road.

The Han Five Zhu money, from the Central Plains, had an early and large circulation in Xinjiang. Having been in use for 739 years in more than ten dynasties, such as Han, Wei, Shu, Jin and Sui, Five Zhu money was one of the currencies that had been used longest and most successfully in Chinese history.[4] Before the Han dynasty, although market transactions existed in the Western Regions, there was no fixed currency as a general equivalent.[5] Since Zhang Qian got through the Western Regions, the Han dynasty attacked the Huns three times. In the second year of Shenjue (60 BC), Emperor Xuandi of the Han dynasty set up Protectorate of the Western Regions, with field officer as the commander, and soldiers were sent to garrison the fields. The Silk Road began to enter the era of prosperity. China's silk, tea, handicrafts, spices and medicinal materials were traded with Western gems and glaze. Goods were gathered from all sides. The Silk Road trade produced thick profits and a bright future. In addition to the two important trading media of gold and silk, Five Zhu money, having flourished in international trade, was active in Western Regions and Central Asian countries, and became the earliest and most crucial international currency in this trade channel. A country's currency cannot circulate across the borders of different regions without the support of a strong economy.

[4] Xinwei Peng, *History of Chinese Currencies* (Shanghai: Shanghai People's Publishing House, 2007), 84.

[5] Jianyi Du and Doudou Du, "The Management and Influence of the Central Dynasty on the Western Regions from the Perspective of the Coinage History of Xinjiang," *Xinjiang Coins*, no. 4 (2010).

At the beginning of the last century, Stein found more than one hundred seventy pieces of Five Zhu coins at the Yotecan site of Khotan. Mr. Huang Wenbi found more than six hundred pieces in the Lopnur area. In 1999, while digging an irrigation canal, a farmer in Yingyar Township, Moyu County, Hotan District, discovered a depot of coins of twenty-seven Jin in weight, most of which were Five Zhu money. Along the ancient Silk Road, Uzbekistan, Kazakhstan, Afghanistan, India, Sri Lanka, Cambodia, Thailand, Vietnam and other countries have also found ancient Chinese Five Zhu coins.

Fig. 2-4 Hotan horse money

"Hotan horse money," influenced by the West, adopted a round shape without a hole. In the center of the front was the image of a horse or a camel, around which was a circle of Kharosthi letters. On the back, there were Chinese seal characters, "copper coin weighing twenty-four Zhu" and "six Zhu coin." The use of Zhu as the weight unit of currency was obviously influenced by the Five Zhu money of the Han dynasty.

The second half of the nineteenth century was a time when China fell behind in the world and was vulnerable to attacks. Cultural bandits from various powers came to Xinjiang in the name of "archaeology" or "scientific investigation." In 1876, the British published the results of their investigation, among which there were two obscure coins, each with the pattern of a horse or a camel in the center of one side surrounded by a circle of Kharosthi, and Chinese characters on the other side. By the late 1980s, 352 coins had been published in the world that bore distinctive characteristics of both Chinese and Western cultures, including 259 in Britain, twenty-one in the Soviet Union, fifty-six in India, four in private collections of foreign countries, and only thirteen in China. Of the thirteen Hotan horse coins in China, one was discovered in Xinjiang by Huang Wenbi, a Chinese scholar. Eleven were collected by a Japanese researcher, Otani Mitsui, in Xinjiang, at the beginning of the twentieth century, and were, later, sold to Lvshun Museum. Fortunately, they were not transported to Japan by the Japanese Army during the Chinese Anti-Japan War. In recent years, Chinese archaeologists have made new achievements in Xinjiang. In November 1989, Liu Wensuo, a Chinese scholar, found another Hotan horse coin at Xiayangtag site of Andir River in Xinjiang, i.e., the thirteenth piece of Hotan horse money in China.

The Western characteristic of Hotan horse money was embodied in the horse and camel patterns of coins and the Kharosthi name of the king, while the Chinese feature was reflected by the Chinese characters and use of the balance system of Zhu. There was a very close relationship between cultural and economic exchanges, and we can see the origin of the economic exchanges between China and the West from the coins.

III. Lead Cake-Shaped Currency with Foreign Words

The Han dynasty also left a mystery related to the coins of Western countries—the lead cake of the Han dynasty. Many people associate this kind of lead cake with the three platinum products issued by Emperor Hanwu.

According to *Pingzhun Book* of *Historical Records*, "platinum was made of silver and tin. It was divided into 3 ranks used respectively by the heaven, the earth and the human beings. Dragon was used for the first rank, weighing eight Liang and in circular shape with the word dragon on it. It was worth two thousand. The second was horse, square shaped with the word horse on it, valuing 500. The third was turtle, small and elliptical, with the word turtle on it, worth 300." Since it was convenient to cast, and profitable, private casting became a common practice in the West Han dynasty. The historian Sima Qian said, "Those who stealthily cast money were sentenced to death, but the countless people committing casting were more than officials could punish."

Oddly enough, such platinum products cast in large numbers have never been found so far, but a kind of lead cake money is often obtained in archaeology. In 1949, Huo Mingzhi, an antique businessman, bought a copper cake coin in Linxia. The inscription and stamp were the same as the later, commonly found lead cakes, with a diameter of 5.4 cm and a weight of 104 g. The original object is now in the Chinese History Museum. In March 1963, a batch of thirteen lead cake coins, weighing between 142.4 g and 119.6 g, were found at the site of Hancheng, northwest of Xi'an. In 1971, two lead cakes were found in Yechi village, Li County. One of them is 5.5 cm in diameter and weighs 126 g, with clear inscriptions and marks. In 1972, two lead cakes, 5.3 cm in diameter, 1 cm at the thickest part and 120.1 g in weight, were found in the Jiangyuan group of Rougu commune, Fufeng County, Shaanxi Province.[6]

In October 1976, a pile of rare lead cake coins in foreign languages was unearthed in Zaoshutai, outside Lingtai city. At a time of climax in farmland infrastructure construction, the hillside around Zaoshutai was turned into a large construction site. The workers found a man-made pit, at the bottom of which was a layer of fist-sized white pebbles, about 33 cm thick. In the middle of the stones were two pieces

[6] Huo Zhu, *New Classic of Ancient Money* (Xi'an: Sanqin Publishing House, 1994), 175.

of Han dynasty cylinder tiles. People put the lead cake coins into a cupola and covered it with the two tiles, and then placed a bluestone tablet on each end of the tiles. Two hundred seventy-four lead cakes were neatly stacked on top. The diameter of the lead cakes was generally about 5.5 cm, with an average weight of 116 g and a total weight of 31,806 g. According to the laboratory test of the Institute of Archaeology, Chinese Academy of Social Sciences, lead was the main composition of the lead cake money.[7]

In 1986, farmers in Liu'an County, Anhui Province, discovered, in one site, two foreign language lead cakes, one horse-pattern lead cake, two turtle-back pattern lead cakes and some Five Zhu coins. In October 1990, several lead cakes in foreign languages were found among a batch of Four Zhu and Half-Liang money unearthed in Baoji, Shaanxi Province. One was of dragon pattern, three of horse pattern and one of turtle pattern. According to the research of Dang Shunmi, now there are about 315 round foreign lead cakes, eight square horse coins and four oval turtle coins collected in the Chinese History Museum, the Xi'an Research Office of the Institute of Archaeology of the Chinese Academy of Social Sciences, the Shaanxi Fufeng Cultural Center, the Shaanxi History Museum, the Xi'an Cultural Administration, the Shaanxi Changwu Cultural Center, the Gansu Lixian Cultural Center, the Gansu Lingtai Museum, the Xihe County Museum, and the Xi'an antique market, etc.[8]

---

[7] Dezhen Liu, "Discovery of Lead Cakes with Foreign Inscriptions in Lingtai, Gansu Province," *Archeology*, no. 6 (1977).

[8] Liushuo Kang, "An Overview of the Silk Road Foreign and Western Regions Currency Unearthed in Gansu Province", *Inner Mongolia Finance Research Special Issue of Coins*, no. 4 (1993).

Fig. 2-5 Lead cake currency with foreign words

There has been a long history of research and debate over the copper and lead cakes with Greek inscriptions. In 1913, Zheng Wenhan put forward the theory of "Rutin gold plate." Cai Jixiang claimed "Horseshoe gold of Da Qin" in 1943. During the period of the Republic of China, Cai Jixiang published an article in *Quan Coin*, maintaining that this kind of lead cake was made in Da Qin. After studying this kind of copper and lead cake for several decades, in 1952, the German scholar Maenchen-Helfen first proposed the theory of "Parthian Coins," and then diagnosed that the dragon shape of this kind of coin was Chinese style, and that the inscription was the Chinese copy of the distorted Greek. In the 1960s, they were believed to be the coins of Parthia, most similar to the drachma of the late Parathia. Due to the influence of Hellenization, the rulers of Parthia used Greek, while the common people used various kinds of languages, bringing about a misspelling of Greek. In 1961, Xia Nai wrote an article to introduce Helfen's point of view. At the same time, he thought that these things might be from the Han or Wei dynasties, but that they were not made by Chinese people because there was no precedent for copying foreign languages onto Chinese coins. Xia Nai thought that the content of lead writing should be Greek "king," "king of kings" and "great." In the 1970s, Mr. An Zhimin believed that these copper and lead cakes were copies of the inscriptions on the Parthian coins in the first and second centuries.

In the 1980s, there was a heated discussion on copper and lead cakes in China's numismatic circle, and several opinions appeared successively. In 1988, Lin Haicun considered the lead cakes as the relics of Kusana. In 1990, Wang Yudung and Xu Weiyi put forward the idea that the lead cakes were "Tianzhu coins." According to Kang Liushuo, a Chinese scholar, they were not made in China in the Han dynasty, judging from the Greek inscriptions on the copper and lead cakes. The view that they were the dragon coins of the three platinum products of the Han dynasty, though novel, was obviously far-fetched. He thought this kind of copper and lead cake should be made by the Hellenistic countries in Central Asia. In these countries, the first to trade with China was Bactria. When Zhang Qian went to the Western Regions for the second time, he brought with him not only herds of cattle and sheep, but also thousands of millions of pieces of gold and silk. According to the objects unearthed in Xi'an, this kind of gold coin may have been persimmon gold cake. After being given to Bactria as a gift, it might have been imitated. The shape of the copper and lead cakes was similar to that of the persimmon gold cakes in Han dynasty. Therefore, he speculated that, after Zhang Qian's second visit to the Western Regions, Bactria, in the Western Regions, would have liked to pay a visit back to China. In addition to the local special products, they imitated China's gold cakes by using lower materials, such as copper or lead, to cast currency, and brought them to China to exchange for Chinese local products and silk. Of course, on the imitated currency, they had to print the characters and emblem of their own country—the circle of Greek inscriptions and the two stamps on the back of the copper and lead cakes. The bulged patterns on the front of the money seemed to be animals, something like dragons or snakes. On some lead cake rubbings, the eyes, heads and tails of animals seemed identifiable. However, this kind of design was exaggerated by art. It might be that, after the spread of Chinese silk and bronze wares in the West during the Warring States period, Qin dynasty and the early Western Han dynasty, countries, like Bactria or Parthia, were influenced by the patterns on Chinese silk and bronzes, and cast, seemingly, dragon or snake decorative patterns on the copper or lead cakes for circulation in China. These kinds of copper or lead cakes were recognized by the Han dynasty, after they entered China. They had a high value of use, and, thus, appeared in large numbers around Chang'an, the capital of Han. Other scholars, like Yu Liuliang, Liu Chaojin, Ren Shuanying, Yuan Lin, Li Yong, Yao Jianqiang, etc., insisted that the lead cakes were the dragon coins of the three Platinum products of the Han dynasty. People are still debating the issue.

In 1955, some Ming Bi coins (coins for the dead) were unearthed in Yanjialing, Hengyang, Changsha. The Ming Bi were similar to the three kinds of platinum coins. Of the two unearthed West Han platinum coins, one was rectangle, with its four corners slightly rounded, a flat back, with the character of "five" on it, 13.5 cm in length, 7.7 cm in width, 2 cm in thickness, and painted white on the surface. The fact that the horse-pattern platinum coin was worth five hundred explains why "five" was on the coin. The other was an oval coin, 10.5 cm long, 6.7 cm wide, 1.5 cm thick, with a flat back and a hole in the slightly humped face. In addition, many dragon-shaped copper cakes have been unearthed in the area, some of which were gilded, with a diameter of 6.4 cm, a thickness of 1 cm and a weight of 108 g.[9]All of them reveal the secrets of the three platinum products to the world. Liu Sen, a Chinese scholar, thinks that the Ming Bi are basically the same in weight as the regular ones at that time, though the weight and size of them might be slightly different from those of the

[9] Shirong Zhou, "A Study on the Coins of the Western Han Dynasty Unearthed in Hengyang, Changsha," in *Anthology of Chinese Coins*, ed. Chinese Numismatic Society (Beijing: China Financial Publishing House, 1985).

current articles.[10]

The diameter of lead cakes was about 5.5 cm, the same as the gold cakes of the Han dynasty. In addition, they were cast coins, rather than being stricken into coins as the traditional Greek ones, and they were similar to the golden cakes of the Qin and Han dynasties. No matter which country turns out to have made them, they were deeply influenced by Chinese traditional currency culture, which is, indeed, a mystery in the world's numismatics circle.

IV. Currency from Ancient Rome

Ancient Rome, located in the Apennine Peninsula, once had splendid culture and highly developed commerce. When the Roman Empire prospered, it inherited the currency culture of Greece and forged a large number of coins. The people of the Roman Empire loved Chinese silk very much, so the Silk Road was an important commercial route to the Roman Empire. In the period of Olivier (270-275), a pound of silk weighed the same as a pound of gold, so a large amount of Roman gold flowed to the East. Pliny, a Roman in the first century, estimated that as many as fifty million Roman gold coins flowed into India for the payment of trade, while the amount that flowed to China was about thirty-five million to one hundred million.[11] In recent years, people have become very interested in the ancient Roman cultural relics in Northwest China, but few ever know that copper coins of ancient Rome, from as early as the Qing dynasty, were unearthed in Shanxi, China.

A piece of news was recorded in the Tianjin "Zhi Bao" Newspaper on June 5, 1896, that read, "As for foreign money, it is rare

---

[10] Sen Liu, "On the Three Platinum Products of Emperor Wu of the Han Dynasty," *Anhui Coins*, no. 1 (1995).

[11] Mingwei Li, *History of Trade on the Silk Road* (Lanzhou: Gansu People's Publishing House, 1997), 360.

in the Central Plains, not to mention the money of thousands of years ago. Wang Yunshan recently returned to Beijing from Shanxi Province. In his suitcase were stored 14 pieces of Roman copper coins, all weirdly colorful, being ancient artifacts at first sight. On the coins were cast the Roman Emperors' years, basically corresponding to the West and East Han Dynasties in the Chinese era."[12]

The Eastern Roman Empire spanned Asia, Europe and Africa, with Balkan Peninsula as its center. Its capital, Constantinople, was the former Byzantine capital, therefore, it was also called the Byzantine Empire. Generally speaking, AD 395, the year of partition between East and West Rome, was taken as the beginning of the Byzantine Empire. In 1453, when Turkey captured Constantinople, the Byzantine Empire was destroyed. Lasting for 1123 years, it has coexisted with China's Eastern Jin, Southern and Northern dynasties, Sui, Tang, Yuan and Ming dynasties.

In the heyday of the Byzantine Empire, it reached the Italian Peninsula in the West, Asia Minor and Syria in the East, bordered on the Sassanian Persian Empire, and had contacts with China in the Northern and Southern dynasties. In the historical books of Sui and Tang, it was called "Fulin." Pei Ju of the Sui dynasty recorded the business route from Dunhuang to Byzantium in his *Records of the Western Regions*.[13]

At that time, the Eastern Roman Empire was the richest country in Europe. The East Roman gold coin was an international currency, widely circulating in Western and Central Asia. In the middle of the sixth century AD, Eastern Rome (Byzantium) and Persia signed a peace agreement to jointly control the silk trade. The Eastern Roman

[12] Elken Rozi, "On the Ancient Coins Found in Mulei County," *Xinjiang Finance* (1988).

[13] Nai Xia, "Byzantine Gold Coins Unearthed in the Tomb of Li Zongxi in Zanhuang," *Archeology*, no. 6 (1977).

Empire paid eleven thousand pounds of Roman gold coins a year to the Persian Empire to buy Chinese silk. The Sassanian Empire of Persia had made great profits from the silk trade. In order to fight for the Silk Road, two silk wars broke out between Persia and Eastern Rome, in 528 and 540, respectively. Rome had been fighting with other countries for the commercial road for five centuries.

In the early Byzantine period (498), the coins of the Empire inherited the system of the Roman Empire. Constantine the Great changed the gold coins from Oreas to the lighter Solidus and established a monetary system with Solidus as the core. The standard Solidus contained seventy-two pounds of pure gold, weighing 4.4 g-4.54 g. The face of the coin was the emperor in armor, and the reverse was often the goddess of victory.

From 498 onwards, the obverse of the Byzantine gold coins was usually an emperor in a suit, the reverse was an angel or a cross, and, later, Jesus or the Virgin. The inscriptions changed from Greek to a mixture of Greek and Latin. This kind of currency system lasted until 1092, when Alexius I (1081-1118) carried out a new reform of the currency system.[14]

As for the East Roman gold coins found in China, Mr. Peng Xinwei said, in his book *The History of Chinese Currency*, in the 1950s, that, since the end of the Qing dynasty, twenty-two East Roman gold coins and one Persian Sassanian silver coin had been unearthed in China.[15] Yuan Kewen recorded one East Roman gold coin in *the Diary of Bingyin*. In 1935, Huang Jun also included three gold coins of Eastern Rome in his *Records of Gold and Stone in Hengzhai.*[16] Before

---

[14] Xia, "Byzantine Gold Coins."

[15] Xinwei Peng, *The Currency History of China* (Shanghai: Shanghai People's Publishing House, 1965).

[16] Jun Huang, *A Brief Record of Gold and Stone in Hengzhai* (Beiping: Zunguzhai, 1935).

the Liberation, one gold coin of Justinian I (527-565) was found in Astana, Turpan.

Since the founding of the People's Republic of China, there have been many reports of the discovery of Persian and Eastern Roman coins. In October 1970, more than one thousand hoarded Tang dynasty cultural relics were found in Hejia village, in the southern suburb of Xi'an. Among these cultural relics, there was a collection of ancient Chinese coins, from the knife money of the Spring and Autumn, in the Warring States periods, to the other hundreds of coins in circulation at the same time. More importantly, there were some foreign coins circulated then, such as the Japanese He Tong Kai Zhen silver coins, Persian silver coins and East Roman gold coins. According to research, the collector of these coins was Prince Zhang Huai of Tang dynasty.

Some of the Eastern Roman gold coins unearthed in China may be Chinese imitations. They are, roughly, as follows: the three imitations of the Eastern Roman gold coins discovered by Stein in Astana cemetery, Turpan, Xinjiang, in 1915; one imitation unearthed in Tumen village, in the suburb of Xi'an, in 1956; a batch of imitations unearthed in Astana cemetery, Turpan, Xinjiang, in 1966-1969; one imitation found in a Tang tomb in the eastern suburb of Xi'an, in the summer of 1989.

What is worth mentioning, in particular, is the cemetery of the family of Shi in Guyuan, Ningxia. In November 1981, an Eastern Roman gold coin was unearthed from Shi Daode's tomb of the Tang dynasty in the southern suburb of Guyuan. He was buried in the third year of Yifeng (678), during Tang Gaozong's reign, and the coin is a Solidus of Theodosius II (408-450). In 1982, another Eastern Roman gold coin was unearthed from the tomb of Shi Suoyan in the southern suburb of Guyuan. In 1986, people found a gold coin of Eastern Rome in each of Shi Tiebang's and Shi Kedan's tombs. In April 1996, another message came from Guyuan, Ningxia. Chinese and Japanese archaeologists had jointly found some fragments of Eastern Roman coins and Roman glass from an ancient tomb of the Tang dynasty, in the southwest suburb of Guyuan County, Ningxia. This was the latest disclosure of the discovery of Eastern Roman gold coins in China. It turned out to be the tomb of Shi Daoluo, buried in the third year of Xianqing (658). According to historical records, the family Shi was one of the famous "nine families of Zhaowu" of the Tang dynasty, moving from Central Asia to the East. The analysis of their skulls proves that these people were Aryans. The excavation of the tomb, once again, uncovered materials for cultural exchanges between China and the West, especially for the study of the northern route at the eastern end of the Silk Road.

In recent decades, there have been more than twenty Eastern Roman gold coins unearthed in the scientific research of archaeology. These gold coins came from Xinjiang, Shaanxi, Inner Mongolia, and other regions; apparently brought to China by the merchant envoys of the Eastern Roman Empire, through the land Silk Road.

In 1959, an Eastern Roman gold coin was found in the northeast of Bikeqi Town, Tumetzuo Qi, Inner Mongolia, a coin of Leo I (547-474). Having been unearthed in Shuimogou, Bikeqi Town, the edge of the gold coin was cut, with a diameter of 1.4 cm and a weight of 2 g, and cast at the time of Leo I (457-471), after the currency system reform of Constantine, the emperor. There were images and inscriptions on both sides of the gold coin. On the obverse was the bust of the emperor, wearing a helmet, with a ribbon flapping beside the ear, in a cross-necked armor, which was outlined by some small dots in the shape of beads. On the back was the winged statue of the goddess of victory, wearing a hat and a gown, with the right hand holding the object and the left hand below her stomach. The inscription around the gold coin was Latin. This was the earliest Byzantine gold coin unearthed in China, also at the northernmost site of excavation. The casting time corresponded to the years of Emperor Wencheng and

Emperor Xiaowen, in the Northern Wei dynasty. At that time, the Tuoba Xianbei ethnicity had just set its capital in Shengle, i.e., the present Tumote Plains, where Hohhot is now located. This place can connect Mobei, in the north, with Central Plains, in the south. After the development in the Northern, Sui and Tang dynasties, it grew into a central area connecting the grassland and the Central Plains. Shuimogou, where the gold coin was unearthed, was right on the road from Chang'an, the capital of the Tang dynasty, directly to the north of the Yinshan Mountain, through Chan Yu Du Hu Fu. It was an important passageway to the north and south of the Daqingshan Mountain, from where one could go to Central Asia, in the west. Therefore, it was a gold coin from the grassland Silk Road.[17]

In 2002, Qinghai archaeologists found an Eastern Roman gold coin in the tomb of the Tuguhun people, in the Northern dynasty, in Xiangride Town, Dulan County. This was the second Roman gold coin found in Qinghai, with a diameter of 14.5 mm and a weight of 2.36 g. On the obverse, was the bust of the emperor, wearing a helmet and armor, plus a war robe, a javelin in the right hand and a shield in the left. On the back of the gold coin, was the goddess of victory, marching to her right side. She held a long-handled cross in her right hand, a star between her head and the cross. There were inscriptions on both sides of the gold coin, a shear wheel on the edge, and two perforations on the upper and lower sides of the emperor statue. It belonged to the gold coins of Theodosius II of the Byzantine dynasty (AD 408-450). In the past, we used to think that the eastern end of the "Silk Road" was from Lanzhou, through the Hexi Corridor into today's Xinjiang. The important discoveries in Dulan Tubo tomb cause this view to be reconsidered.

---

[17] Zhihua Xiao, "East-West Communications and Byzantine Gold Coins," *Newspaper of China Cultural Relics*, no. 7 (February 1999).

The Byzantine gold coins of Eastern Rome played the role of an international currency in the Silk Road trade. As the capital of Byzantium, Constantinople (Istanbul), located at the intersection of Europe, Asia and Africa, was a place where merchant ships gathered from all over the world. At the same time, it was the Western end of the Silk Road. The developed international transaction has brought huge wealth to the local residents. With the territory of the Byzantine Empire approaching the East, the interest in Oriental luxury goods, especially Chinese silk, was growing day by day. Princes, nobles and Christian churches had become the important consumer groups for Oriental silk, spices and other luxury goods, and even people from the lowest level of society were interested in silk. However, the trade between Byzantium and China was not a direct one, but a transit through Persia, Turkic, or their controlled countries, such as Sogdiana. So, the price of silk was very high. The best equivalent to silk was the Byzantine gold coin. With its high purity and exquisite production, it maintained an amazing stability for quite a long time, and with its high value, purity and stability, it was widely accepted in the world, and known as the "medieval American dollar."[18]

Sogdian merchants in the fourth century brought Byzantine gold coins and glass, coral, agate and wine along the Silk Road to Xi'an, Luoyang, Jizhou and other places, to purchase batches of silk and sell them to Central Asia. Fu Lin (the name of Rome in the Tang dynasty) sent envoys to the Tang dynasty seven times. In the seventeen years of Zhenguan, the Emperor of Fu Lin sent his envoys to offer the royal court red glass, green gold essence and other things. In return, Emperor Tang Taizong gave them a large amount of silk. From this point on, Roman merchants came to China in the name of "contribution," which

[18] R.S. Lopez, "The Dollar of the Middle Ages," *The Journal of Economic History*, vol. II, no.3 (1951), 209-234.

became a significant feature of Silk Road trade. Since Stein discovered the Eastern Roman gold coin in Xinjiang, in 1915, there have been more than two hundred Eastern Roman gold coins and their imitations unearthed in China. The excavation sites were basically along the ancient Silk Road, including Xinjiang, Qinghai, Gansu, Ningxia, Henan, Hebei, Inner Mongolia, Liaoning, and other places. According to the statistics of Rebecca Dali, a British scholar, the total number of Byzantine coins found in India was more than four thousand, mainly copper, coins. Of the 189 gold coins, imitations have accounted for nearly one-third. Professor Nemak, the American Central Asian scientist, found in his research that there were about twenty Byzantine gold coins and their imitations in Central Asia. The above findings objectively reflect the status of Byzantine gold coins in the world trade at that time.

V. Venetian Silver Coins Unearthed in China

In 1964, the Guangzhou Administration of Cultural Relics cleared the tomb of a Ming dynasty eunuch, in Dongshan, Guangzhou. The tomb had been raided in the early years, but three foreign silver coins were still found in the tomb, two of which were Malaga silver coins, and the other one was made by Pasquale Malipiero, governor of Venice from 1457 to 1462.

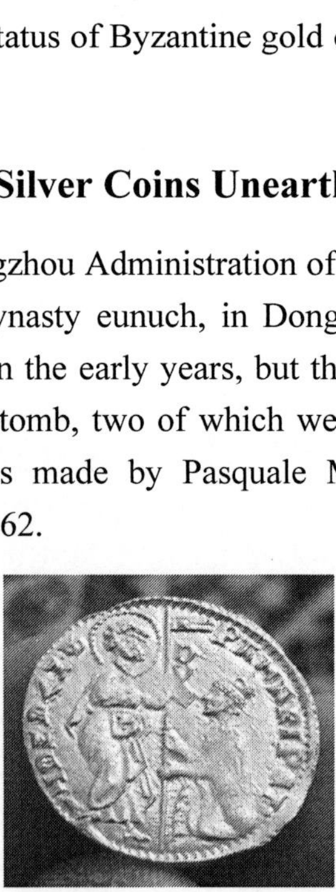

Fig. 2-6 Venetian coin unearthed in China

That silver coin was the only ancient Venetian silver coin unearthed in China, with a diameter of 1.3 cm-1.9 cm and a weight of 1.4 g. It was the "Grosso" or "Grosetto" of the Republic of Venice. The obverse of the silver coin was the statue of Saint Marco, the patron saint of Venice, and the statue of Maliero, the governor. In the picture, Saint Marco is handing a military flag to the governor. The reverse of the silver coin was the statue of Jesus.

This coin was not unearthed in Guangzhou by chance. In the third year of the Hongwu period, in the Ming dynasty, the Ming government established three Shi Bo Si in Ningbo, Quanzhou and Guangzhou, and regulated that Ningbo was the port to Japan, Quanzhou to Ryukyu, Guangzhou to Zhancheng, Siam and the Western countries. Later, the eunuchs were in charge of the Shi Bo Si. The owner of the tomb is Wei Juan, the famous eunuch of the Ming dynasty who was responsible for the Shi Bo Si in Guangzhou. His term of office was from the eleventh year of Chenghua to the first year of Hongzhi (1475-1488). Of the three ports for foreign trade, Guangzhou was the most prosperous. Moreover, the eunuch was recorded in *the History of Ming* to have embezzled the silver of Arab merchants when he was in charge of the Shi Bo Si in Guangzhou, so it was not surprising that Venetian coins were unearthed in his tomb.

The discovery of Venetian silver coins in China proved the view of some scholars in the past—that Venice played a particularly important role in the trade between the East and the West from the thirteenth to the fourteenth century. That is to say, before the discovery of the new route, by way of the Cape of Good Hope, to India, in 1498, almost all trade between Europe and the East was controlled by Italian merchants, especially Venetian merchants. According to the article "The Discovery of the 15th-Century Silver Coins of Venice in China," published by Banggeli, an Italian scholar, the silver coins of Venice were mainly used for East-West trade.[19]

[19] Ping Wu and Lanying Chen, "On the Currency of the Maritime Silk Road," in *Proceedings of the Sixth Symposium on Southeast Asia Historical and Maritime Silk Road Currency*, ed. Zhejiang Coin Society (Ningbo: Ningbo Numismatic Society, June 1995).

CHAPTER THREE

CURRENCY CULTURE EXCHANGE BETWEEN CHINA AND ANCIENT WESTERN ASIA

I. Persian Silver Coins

Persia was called Parthia state in the Qin and Han dynasties. In 226, Ardashir I of Persia overthrew the Parthian Empire and established the Sassanian Empire, which was named Persia in history. In 1935, it was renamed Iran. The Sassanian Empire, a new centralized Persian Empire, had long fought with Rome, Byzantine Empire and Hephthalite, and its territory was constantly changing. At its peak, it reached the Euphrates River in the west, the Persian Gulf in the south, the Caucasus, Armenia and the Amu Darya River in Central Asia in the north, and the Pamir Plateau in the east, occupying the core area of the Silk Road. The Sassanid Empire existed for 425 years before it was destroyed in 651, having coexisted with the Eastern Han dynasty, the Three Kingdoms, the two Jin dynasties, the Southern and Northern dynasties, the Sui and the early Tang dynasties, in Chinese history. During this period, Persian culture began to spread both to the East and the West. From the third century to the end of the seventh century, Persian silver coins were not only the common currency of the ancient Persian country, but also the world currency through the centuries because of the Sassanian Empire's important geographical position on the Silk Road.

In terms of foreign trade, Sassanid Persia had frequent contacts with China, India, Egypt and Byzantium. It enjoyed the most famous wool and brocade industry, and a high level of metal processing and weapon manufacturing. The exquisite gold and silver fine works were well known in the world. The Persian Empire took control of the Silk Road by fighting against the Kushan Kingdom in the East and the Roman Empire in the West. The Persian Sassanian silver coins also became the international currency at that time, because of their consistent weight, pure silver and convenient use, and were circulated in Central Asia, Western Asia, the Western Regions and the vast areas of the Hexi counties.

After its first king, Ardashir, the Sassanid Empire abandoned the style of Parthian coins. Instead, it adopted the king's portrait on one side and the fire worship altar on the other. Zoroastrianism was the national religion of Persia. The Sassanian silver coins reflected the revival of ancient Persian culture, with the portrait of the king on the obverse, surrounded by a circle of Pahlavi inscriptions, and the altar and priests on the reverse, also circled by the inscriptions. The contents of the inscriptions were mostly the king's name and glorification of him. The weight of Sassanian silver coins still followed that of Drachmas of ancient Greece. The standard weight of each silver coin was one Drachma, about 4 g, but the coins were relatively thinner and larger.

According to the records of *Han Shu* (History of Han dynasty), in the year of 119 BC, Zhang Qian, an envoy of the Han dynasty, sent his deputy envoy to visit Parthia for the second time. The Sassanian Empire of Persia had had frequent contacts with the outside world since the fourth century. By fighting with Kushan and Hephthalite, Sassanid Persia's power reached today's Afghanistan. In 382, China's Qianliang army attacked the Western Regions and destroyed Qiuci. It must have been then that China had contact with Persia. The communications between China and Persia were rather frequent from the second half of the fifth century to the beginning of the sixth century, and were recorded in many Chinese historical books. In the sixty-six years from 455 to 521, Persia sent envoys to China more than ten times, sometimes with the envoys of Hephthalite. Among the Persian coins found in Dingxian, Hebei, one had inscriptions of Hephthalite words.[1]

In the middle of the sixth century, the Sassanian Empire was revived. They jointly attacked and destroyed Hephthalite, with the Western Turks. Hence, the Persian forces reached the Amu Darya River, which was closer to China. With a developed economy, there were as many as eighty-two minting places in Sassanian Persia, at that time. *Biography of Foreign Lands* of *Zhou Shu* (History of Zhou) recorded that, in the second year of Emperor West Wei Fei Di (553), Persian envoys had come to China. According to the Arabian masterpiece *Golden Prairi*, Chinese envoys had also been to Persia. It was also recorded in *the Biography of the Western Regions* in *Sui Shu* (History of the Sui dynasty) that Sui Yang Di had sent envoys to Persia. In Tang Gao Zong's reign, Persian king, Piruz, was appointed Governor of Persian Dudu Fu, making Zaranj the capital. In the fourth year of Xian Heng (674), Piruz came to Chang'an and later died there. Emperor Gaozong of the Tang dynasty also sent troops to escort Piruz's son Niebsi to restore his country, but failed. He returned to China and was awarded the position of General Zuo Wei Wei. Before long he died of disease. That was an important reason why very few of the silver coins of late Persia that were cast could still be found in China.

Persian silver coins were produced by pressing technology. The obverse of the silver coins was the bust of the king. The Iranian hair style, clothes and crown of the king, together with the unique patterns, constitute the Iranian charm of the coins. The back of the coins was the altar of the Zoroastrianism, on which the fire is burning, symbolizing

---

[1] Nai Xia, "A Review of the Silver Coins of the Sassanian Dynasty of Persia Unearthed in China," *Journal of Archeology*, no. 1 (1974).

the struggle between justice and evil. What is conspicuous on the crown on Persian coins is the pattern of a new moon and the stars held by the new moon. It is believed that this is the origin of the star moon pattern on the back of ancient Chinese coins. The art of Sassanian Persia, besides Roman and Indian culture, became another important source for the culture of the Six Dynasties and the Tang dynasty.

In the 1970s, Mr. Xia Nai wrote, "In an era of prosperous international trade, one country's coinage often served as an international currency, that is, was generally used as a currency on the trade channels between countries with trade relations. In the Middle East, the Near East and Eastern Europe, the Sassanian silver coins, the same as the Byzantine gold coins, are widely used as such an international currency."[2]

In the western part of the Northern dynasty, the gold and silver money of the Western Regions were officially permitted to circulate. Persian silver coins, with their good reputation and strong purchasing power, were often cut into halves in transactions, known as "half of a silver coin." It was recorded in the Turpan books many times. The objects were also evacuated in the Turpan area.

Persian and Greek silver coins had the same name of Drachma, with an average weight of about 4 g each. Among the foreign ancient coins unearthed in China, the silver coins of the Sassanian Empire, in Persia, were the most common. Persian silver coins were discovered extensively in China—ranging from Xinjiang, Qinghai and Gansu to Shanxi and Shaanxi, from Inner Mongolia, Hebei and Henan to Guangdong. According to statistics, from 1949 to 1981, one thousand two hundred silver coins of the Sassanian Empire were successively discovered in China.[3] This shows that Persia had close economic

---

[2] Xia, "A Review of the Silver Coins."

[3] G. Konig, "Byzantine and Sassanian Coins Unearthed in China," In *Collection of Papers at the First Annual Meeting of Shanghai Numismatic Society*, ed. Shanghai

relations with China during the Sassanid Empire.

As for the situation of China's copper coins in West Asia, according to Mr. Zhu Jieqin's *History of Relations between China and Iran*, as early as the middle of the ninth century, Chinese copper coins prevailed in the port city of Siraf (now known as Tahira), in the Persian Gulf.[4] They were once used as a local currency.

Chinese circular coins with square hole (Fang Kong Yuan Qian) and the Persian silver coins belonged to different cultural systems. But there is a subtle relationship between the two. The first is the connection between weight and balance systems. In 1955, ten Sassanian silver coins were unearthed in Gaochang, Xinjiang, eight of which weighed 4.2 g, on average. Compare those with the coins of the Northern and Southern dynasties of China in the same period. The Changping Five Zhu coin of the Northern Qi dynasty also weighed 4.2 g, and the Bu Quan coin of Northern Zhou weighed 4.3 g, indicating that the weight of Persian silver coins was very similar to that of the Northern Qi's and Northern Zhou dynasties' coins. Second, after Sassanian Persian silver coins began circulating in Gaochang and Hexi regions, as an international currency, Wen was used as the monetary unit. In the unearthed documents of Turpan and Dunhuang, the valuing unit of almost all silver money was Wen, which illustrated how profound an influence the silver coins of Sassanian Persia had on the coins of the Central Plains, at that time.

Under the influence of the Sassanid Empire, Persian silver coins were taken as the prototype for the coins of Hephthalites, West Turk, Arab, Central Asia Cheeyana, and even India's Chalajian and Balamara dynasties, whose forms and styles were all Sassanian.[5]

Numismatic Society (Shanghai: Shanghai Numismatic Society, 1986).

[4] Jieqin Zhu, *History of Relations between China and Iran* (Urumqi: Xinjiang Publishing House, 1988).

[5] Liushuo Kang, "Some Problems in the Circulation of Persian Sassanian Silver

In addition to Persian silver coins, Persian silver ingots were also unearthed in China. In 1989, three Silver Ting were unearthed at the south entrance of Fengdeng Road, in the western suburb of Xi'an. One of them was a 274 mm long and 61 mm wide rectangular ingot, weighing 2,130 g, with four lines of inscription on the front that indicated the value of fifty Liang and the names of the officials who offered it to the emperor.

This Silver Ting should have been consecrated around the twelfth year of Dali (777), no later than the third year of Jianzhong (782), in Tang De Zong's reign. It was the heritage of Ishaq, a Persian businessman, who died in Guangzhou at the end of Dali and the beginning of Jianzhong. His assets were unclaimed within three months and confiscated by the Guangzhou government. The Lingnan provincial governor and the Shi Bo Shi in charge of Guangzhou's foreign trade management offered them to the emperor. The offering of dead Persian Ishaq's silver embodies the system of dealing with foreign business heritage in the middle of the Tang dynasty.[6]

II. Persian Paper Currency

China was the first country in the world to invent and use paper money, which has had a profound impact on neighboring countries. Persia (Iran), Japan, North Korea and other countries have used paper money in imitation of China. In the first year of the Yuanyou of

Coins in Northwest China," in *Anthology of Chinese Currency,* vol. 5, ed. Chinese Numismatic Society (Beijing: China Financial Publishing House, 2010), 464~474; Li Tiesheng, "Examples of Multi-currency Culture on the Silk Road," in *Collection of Papers on Ancient Coins and Silk Summit Forum and the Fourth International Symposium on Turpan Studies*, ed. Academy of Turpan Studies and Turpan Museum (Shanghai: Shanghai Classics Publishing House, 2015), 8.

[6] Jinxiu Li, "A study of Yin Ting of Persian Ishaq unearthed in Xi'an," in *Silk Road: a Study of the History of Relations between China and Foreign Countries in Ancient Times,* vol. II., ed. Yu Taishan and Li Jinxiu (Beijing: Commercial Press⊠ 2012), 250-273.

Emperor Song Li Zong (AD 1253), Hulagu, the son of Tolui, Genghis Khan's fourth son, started the third western expedition. During this expedition, he successively attacked Persia, killed the Caliph and his family of the Abbasid dynasty, and captured most of the regions in the present Transcaucasia and Asia Minor. In 1264, he established IlKhanate. Among the four Khanates, IlKhanate had the closest relationship with Kublai Khan of the Yuan dynasty, and they kept good contact for a long time.

The coins of IlKhanate kept their unique characteristics, since Hulagu, and they were the most unified and complete among the four Khanate countries. The use of Persian paper money, in imitation of the Yuan dynasty, took place during the reign of Qihedu (1291-1295) of IlKhanate. Qihedu's extravagance and excessive reward resulted in the Treasury emptiness. A minister named Yzz-ud-din Mozaffer thought of the effective paper money of the Yuan dynasty and proposed it to the Prime Minister Saduhan, in the hope of helping IlKhanate get rid of the financial difficulties. Saduhan immediately reported the suggestion to Qihedu, who, after consulting Fengluo, the Minister of the Yuan dynasty in charge of IlKhanate affairs, decided to copy the Yuan dynasty—"to print paper money quickly." On September 12, 1294 (October 19, 693 in the Islamic calendar), paper money was officially issued in the capital city of Tiberius (present-day Tabriz, Iran).[7]

The paper money issued by the IlKhanate was not handed down in kind. There are more detailed records in the *Vasaff Book,* written by the historian at that time, Ordura, and, later, in the *History of Mongolia,* by Duosang, which show that the paper money of the IlKhanate was printed on paper in a rectangle with Chinese characters, Arabic chronology and Muslim prayers. Based on gold and silver, the

[7] Rashid, *Collections of Historical Documents*, vol. III (Beijing: Commercial Press, 1997), 227.

denomination is divided into several grades from half Drachma to ten Dinars. Reward and punishment regulations were printed on the paper money, while forgery was strictly prohibited. In order to promote paper money, Chao Ku (warehouses of paper money) were set up all over the country, responsible for the exchange of gold and silver and the recovery of torn paper money from overseas merchants. The cost of production was charged at one percent of the face value of the notes. The circulation of gold and silver was strictly prohibited. Anyone who refused to use paper money would be executed.[8]

The IlKhanate notes were all designed and issued in imitation of the Yuan dynasty's paper money system. On the money, were printed the words of the Islamic prayer: 'there is no other God except Allah, and Muhammad is the messenger of Allah.' This was also the common motto on the Islamic coins in Central Asia. The Chinese characters on the face of the money may have been the Chinese seals, stamped by the Yuan dynasty government. A cost as high as one percent of the face value, compared with that of Yuan's paper money, which was only three Fen for each Guan, fully reflects that Qihedu's purpose of issuing paper money was to snatch wealth.[9]

In summary, IlKhanate almost completely copied the paper money system of the Yuan dynasty, from its shape and denomination to its issuance management. Paper money is still called *Chao* (Chao means paper money in Chinese) in Persian, which shows how deep Chinese influence is on Persian currency.

---

[8] D'ohsson, *History of Mongolia,* trans. Feng Chengjun (Beijing: Zhong Hua Book Company, 1962), 249.

[9] Yongsheng Wang, "The Imitation of the Currency System of the Yuan Dynasty by the Persian Ilikhanate," *Chinese Coins*, no. 4 (1994).

III. Arabian Coins

Around the rise of Islam, silver coins of Persia circulated in the Arabian Peninsula, which was called Dirham. At that time, Byzantine gold dinars (also known as "Caesar gold coins") and Byzantine copper coins were also used. In AD 636, Khalid Ibn Walid cast gold dinars in Tiberius, in imitation of the Byzantine Dinar. Besides images of scepter, crown and cross, the initials of the Greek name of Khalid were also on the coins. In AD 639, during the reign of Caliph Omer Ibn Hatabu, the coins of Persia were imitated and marked with such words as "praise Allah; Muhammad is the emissary of Allah" and "praise belongs to Allah," "Muhammad is the messenger of Allah," "there is no other God, only one Allah," in Arabic. The coins of the Islamic Republic, or of the period of Four Wise Caliphs (632-661), with both Sassanian Persian patterns and Arabic words on them, can be called rare treasure because of their scarcity in existence.[10]

The real Arab Islamic currency was coined at the end of the seventh century, by Abdul Malik. At that time, with the Arab Empire basically settled down, and a booming political and economic construction, it was urgent to have reforms of administrative institutions and financial affairs. Abdul Malik was determined to unify the various currencies of the Empire's provinces and issue a conformed currency throughout the Empire. It was during the period of Abdul Malik that the coins of Dinar and Dirham were minted in pure Arabia for the first time, and they were widely used. He also ordered the conversion of all old coins and the prohibition of the circulation of old coins within the Empire.[11]

---

[10] Issat al Nuss, *Outline of Syrian Geography and History* (Shanghai: Sanlian Publishing House, 1974), 93-94.

[11] Nuss, *Outline of Syrian Geography*, 93-94.

Abdul Malik carried out three monetary reforms. In the first reform, gold coins were struck according to the pattern of Byzantine coins, that is to say, on the one side of the gold coins, the words "Allah alone" were pressed in Kufic Arabic; on the other side, the portraits of the Byzantine Emperor Heraclius and his two sons were retained. The second reform of Abdul Malik eventually eliminated all traces of Byzantium on the gold coins, replacing the portraits of Heraclius and his two sons with his own; and on the other side, "the seventieth year of the Islamic era" was inscribed, surrounding the edge. The gold coin with the portrait of Abdul Malik had aroused the opposition of Muslim scholars, who thought it was against the Islamic law. In AD 696, a new coin was cast, which was the third reform. On the obverse of the gold coin, were the words, "Nothing is master," "Allah is the only master;" on the edge was "Muhammad is an emissary sent by Allah to guide the Orthodox Church." On the back, the words, "Allah is the only Lord, the Lord that all things trust," were in the middle, while in the margin were the inscriptions, "In the name of Allah, this gold coin was cast in the seventy-seventh year of the Islamic era."[12]

Akadu Malik ordered that coins made in the eastern and western parts of the Islamic world be engraved with the Koran excerpt, around which was the year and address of the coinage. This order became the model for later Arabic coins. Many cities created a large number of silver coins in 698 and 699. Gradually, the silver coins took a formula: the Islamic motto was engraved, "Nothing is Master but Allah, Muhammad is the messenger of Allah."[13] Words, but no portraits, were cast on the coins, which has become the tradition of Arabic coins

---

[12] Na Zhong, *Inheritance and blending: Arab Culture* (Hangzhou: Zhejiang People's Publishing House, 1993), 70-71.

[13] Xian Song and Suzhen Zhou, "The Circulation of Ancient Arabic Coins in China," *Research on Western Regions*, no. 3 (1993).

ever since.[14] This influence gradually found its way throughout the Arab world in West Asia, Central Asia, South Asia, and such countries as India and Indonesia.

When, in 695, the capital Damascus had its first mint, producing Dinars—gold coins with Arabic on both sides—for the first time, it adopted the legal measure system of the Roman Empire in Western Asia—4.25 g. Two years later, silver coins with pure Arabic, Dirham, were created. Their legal weight was six tenths (2.97 g) of the gold coin. In addition, there were copper coins—fils. Weighing only a few carats, a fil had a price of one forty-eighth of a silver coin. Arabic gold, silver and copper coins have become the prototypes of various kinds of coins in the Islamic world since the Middle Ages.[15]

Ancient Arabic money was introduced into China in the Tang dynasty. Its shape has had an obvious influence on the coins of China, and its weight and balance may have an even closer relationship with Chinese coins.

The weight of Kaiyuan coins of the Tang dynasty was similar to that of Arabian gold coins. A standard Kaiyuan Tongbao weighed 4.25 g, and the legal weight of an Arabian gold coin was also 4.25 g. Since the Tang dynasty, China has had a unit of weight measure called *Qian*. In the Tang dynasty, one Jin weighed 680 g, and one Qian weighed 4.25 g. As Dirham was not only the name and legal weight of silver coins, but also the Arabic unit of measurement, there was no doubt that the appearance of Qian as a measurement in China was closely related to this. It shows that China was influenced by the economy and culture of the Western Regions at that time. The weight and balance of coins in the Tang dynasty were both influenced by Byzantine and Arabic currency.

---

[14] Nai Xia, "Arab Gold Coins Unearthed from the Tombs of Tang Dynasty in Xi'an," *Archeology*, no. 8 (1965).

[15] Song and Zhou, "The Circulation."

In April 1964, three Arabic gold coins were unearthed from a Tang tomb in Xi'an, with the Islamic mottos and the making time on them. All three gold coins were dinars, each weighing 4.2 g-4.5 g. The emergence of ancient Arabic coins in China was, indeed, a historical witness to the transmission of Arab Islamic culture to China and its integration with Chinese traditional culture.

IV. Chinese Records of Seljuk Coins

In the documents before before the Northern Song dynasty, "Fulin" generally refers to the Roman Empire and Asia Minor. In the eleventh century, the Seljuk Turks rose in Central Asia. In 1055, the leader of the Seljuk Turks, Tugrilneg, led his army to Baghdad and became "Sudan" and "King of the East and the West." By the reign of Maliksha (1072-1092), the Seljuks had developed into a great power ranging from Central Asia to the eastern Mediterranean.

In order to facilitate the communication between the East and the West, Maliksha sent an emissary to the Northern Song dynasty. On October 6, in the fourth year of Yuanfeng (1081), when the emissary arrived in Bianjing, he sent horses, saddles, swords and pearls to Emperor Song Shen Zong, and introduced the status quo of the Seljuk dynasty to the Emperor. In his account, his country "is rich in gold, silver, pearl, Hu brocade, cattle, sheep, horses, single-humped camels, apricots, pears, sugar, Millennium jujube, etc. Gold and silver are used as money, with no perforation. The name of Maitreya Buddha is chiseled on the face of coins, and King's name on the back. Private coinage is prohibited." [16] Since there had been no official contacts between China and Fulin for more than nine hundred years,[17] this visit

---

[16] Song Xu, *The Important Manuscripts of Song Dynasty: Foreign Land*, book 4 (Shanghai: Shanghai Classics Publishing House, 2009), 19.

[17] Tao Li, *Continuation to Zi Zhi Tong Jian*, vol. 317 (Beijing: Zhong Hua Book Company, 2004), Item Oct. 1081.

from the Seljuk dynasty was of great significance in the history of communication between China and the West.

In 1091, the envoys of the Seljuk dynasty arrived in China again. Song Zhe Zong gave them two hundred bolts of silk, silver bottles, clothes and gold belts as presents. Since then, "the communication continued until Xuanhe years."[18]

[18] Tuo Tuo and Arutu, *History of Song Dynasty Vol. 490: Foreign Countries VI Khotan* (Beijing: Zhong Hua Book Company, 1985).

CHAPTER FOUR

CURRENCY CULTURE EXCHANGE BETWEEN CHINA AND ANCIENT EASTERN ASIA

I. Currency Culture Exchange between China and Japan

China and Japan are close to each other, having frequent economic and cultural exchanges since ancient times. *The Classic of Mountains and Seas*, written in the Warring States period, clearly indicated the navigation route to Kitakyushu via Tsushima, at that time. Along the route, bronze swords and daggers, used in the Warring States period, have been successively discovered in Gyeongsangnam-do, Tsushima, Hakata Bay, Kitakyushu and other places. At the same time, large quantities of currency of the state of Yan—"Ming Knife"—have also been unearthed in this area. If these excavation sites were marked on the map, the line that they create, from the Shandong Peninsula and the Liaoning Peninsula, of China, to Tsushima and Kitakyushu, of Japan, would show the earliest sea route to Japan, opened up in the Warring States period of China.

As far as the unearthed ancient Chinese coins in Japan are concerned, the earliest ones that flowed into Japan were those of the Warring States period. In 1923, Ming Knife money was first found in Okinawa County, and, later, in Hiroshima and Okayama counties too. Anyang Bu Bi was unearthed as well. According to the research of Japanese scholars, the excavation site of the Ming Knife money, in Okinawa, belonged to the late period of Japanese Sheng Wen culture (roughly equivalent to the Warring States period in China), which meant that Ming Knife probably entered Japan around the time of Qin Shi Huang's unification of China.[1] There were also a lot of ancient Chinese coins unearthed in Japan, after the Qin and Han dynasties. In the fifth year of Yuan Wen (740), twenty pieces of Half-Liang coins and 105 pieces of Five Zhu coins (including fragments) were unearthed, at the same time, in Xiaochuan village, Yamaguchi. According to the initial records about the communication between China and Japan in *the Book of Geography* in *Han History*, "Japanese people had an audience with the Sovereign from Lelang across the sea." Lelang Jun was set up in the northern part of the Korean Peninsula, before the middle of the Western Han dynasty, and the Japanese often crossed the sea for trade. There was a great development in the relations between China and Japan in the Eastern Han dynasty. According to *the Book of the Later Han Dynasty*, during the reign of Emperor Guang Wu (AD 57) and Emperor An Di (AD 107), the kings of Japan successively sent envoys to Luoyang for pilgrimage. In the year of AD 57, "envoys from Japan paid tribute to Emperor Guang Wu of Han, who, in return, granted them a gold seal." In 1784, the gold seal was unearthed in Shiga Island, Japan, inscribed with the words "King of the slave country of Han dynasty" on it. In 1988, Da Quan Fifty was unearthed from the remains in Fukuoka, which was first cast in the year of AD 7, when Wang Mang was reigning. In the era of the Three Kingdoms, relations between China and Japan were even closer. In the Eastern Han and Wei Jin dynasties, more Japanese engaged in folk trade through Lelang and Daifang Jun. Chinese Square Hole money was widely imported into Japan. According to the statistics of Japan up to 1985, Half-Liang, Five Zhu, Huo Quan, Huo Bu and other Square Hole coins of Han and Wei Jin dynasties have all been unearthed from the

---

[1] Aiping Zhou, "The Flow of Chinese Currency to Japan and Its Influence," *Chinese Coins*, no. 4 (1995).

twenty-five sites and tombs in Prefectures of Nagasaki, Saga, Fukuoka, Oita, Kumamoto, Miyazaki, Yamaguchi, Hiroshima, Nagano, etc.

According to Japanese historical records, 3 BC to AD 3 belonged to the Japanese Misheng era, when Japan was still in a society of article-for-article exchange, and coinage was not the main means of exchange. The input of Chinese Square Hole money showed the radiation strength of Chinese coin culture and the absorption of Chinese culture by ancient Japan. The spread of Chinese Square Hole money in Japan also depended on the relations between the two. For example, in the 260s, the Japanese had no contact with China, and the fourth century was called the blank century of Sino Japanese relations; in the one hundred twenty years from the late fifth century to the end of the sixth century, the Japanese, for a long time, had no contact with China either, so nearly no coins of the Eastern Jin and the Southern and Northern dynasties of China were found in Japan, except the Five Zhu coin of Northern Wei dynasty unearthed in Fukuoka.

At the beginning of the seventh century, Japan began to send envoys to the Sui dynasty, and then to the Tang dynasty, after the 730s. They actively carried out cultural exchanges between Japan and China, which resulted in the new deal of *Da Hua Gai Xin* (great changes for new things), in 646. Japan's politics and economy developed greatly, thereafter. Under the influence of China's currency culture, Japan began the history of self-coinage. In recent years, the first kind of official coins have been found in the site of Tengyuan Palace (194-710), the first capital city in Japan, as well as the clay model of the coins.

In 708, Japan began to use the Kai Yuan Tong Bao of the Tang dynasty as the sample to cast the He Tong Kai Zhen coin. It was also the oldest legal currency in Japan.[2] During the Tang dynasty, one of

[2] He Tu, "On Japanese Gold and Silver Coins," *Chinese Coins*, no. 3 (1985).

the important missions of Japanese envoys was to carry out tribute trade. In the tribute trade before the Tang dynasty, Chinese currency was not found on the list of the items given to Japan by China (at least there were no historical records about this), but there are many reports about the coins of the Tang and Song dynasties unearthed in Japan. The total number of coins unearthed in Japan is 554,714, from eighteen places, with eighty-seven varieties, of which fifteen have more than ten thousand pieces, accounting for 17 percent of the total.

It is recorded in historical books that “all the money used by the envoys during their stay in the Tang dynasty was placer gold.” The Mikado used to give two hundred Liang of placer gold to the envoys before they were sent to Tang. Japanese students and monks also used placer gold for their expense in Tang. These sands were all wrapped in the paper or put into bamboo tubes, so they had no definite shape and were easy to disperse. Influenced by the coinage of the Tang dynasty, twelve kinds of coins, called the Twelve Coins of Imperial Dynasty, were minted in Japan in the two hundred fifty years from 708 to 958, including He Tong Kai Zhen, Wan Nian Tong Bao, Shen Gong Kai Shi, Long Ping Yong Bao, Fu Shou Shen Bao, etc. There were also some early Japanese coins in Chinese archaeological discoveries, like the He Tong Kai Zhen coins unearthed in Heilongjiang and Shaanxi. This showed that the currency relations between China and Japan were close in the Tang dynasty. In the depot of the coins of the Five Dynasties and the Ten Kingdoms unearthed in Xuchang, Henan, one was Japanese Cheng He Chang Bao, which meant there were exchanges between Chinese and Japanese currencies, at that time.

Around the middle of the tenth century, the developed social economy of Tang and Song dynasties led to the peak of the export of Chinese Fang Kong Qian (Square Hole money). For hundreds of years, the self-made Twelve Coins of the Imperial Dynasty were completely abolished in Japan. Furthermore, the coins of the Tang and Song dynasties, imported from China—which were called “du lai money” by the Japanese—and those from North Korea and Vietnam, were used as main currencies for a long time. In the late twelfth century, Japanese officials stopped minting coins. Chinese Square Hole coins were not only popular in Japan as an international currency, but also copied in large quantities, especially from the fourteenth to the sixteenth centuries. Most of the imitators were local governments or wealthy individuals. The counterfeited coins, called “shichusen” in Japan, were mixed with real money in use, but of an inferior quality. This phenomenon continued until the Japanese Edo Shogunate issued the Kuan Yong Tong Bao Fang Kong coins, in 1636.

The main ways of ancient Chinese money flowing into Japan can be summarized as follows, tribute trade, folk trade and semi-official trade. To those who came to pay tribute, the gifts from the Chinese Emperor would far surpass the tribute, both in quality and quantity, and so showed the “grace” of the great empire of China. The folk trade between the two could date back to the pre-Qin period. Before the Tang dynasty, traditional products, art crafts and other substantial objects were the main goods, while money was not widely used as a medium, or a commodity, for trade. It was after the Tang dynasty, especially in the Song and Ming dynasties, that money became the main body of trade. Semi-official trade referred to a kind of private-owned commercial trade with a written permission from the government.

With the further development of Japan’s commodity economy, and the economic and cultural exchanges between China and Japan, Japan’s demand for Chinese copper money increased rapidly. In order to meet this demand, Japan traded with China for copper money in various ways, as a result, a large amount of Chinese copper money flowed into Japan. Since the Tang dynasty, many kinds of money were imported into Japan—at least ten kinds of coins have been found in different parts of Japan. According to Irita Masazo's investigation on the unearthed ancient Chinese coins, money from the Northern Song dynasty accounted for the the most types and largest quantities found, accounting for 81.9 percent of the total, and the rest was 8.6 percent from the Tang dynasty, 7.3 percent from the Ming dynasty, 1.4 percent from the Southern Song dynasty, and 0.8 percent from other eras.[3]

In the Song, Yuan and Ming dynasties, Chinese copper money became not only the main medium of exchange between the two sides, but also the main commodity of trade. According to historical records, during the Li Zong period of the Southern Song dynasty, Japanese merchant ships traded copper coins in Wenzhou and Taizhou to the degree that the copper coins were not seen for a month in Taizhou city.[4] At the beginning of the Yuan dynasty, the government adopted an open policy towards the export of copper coins,[5] thus, a large amount of Chinese copper money flowed into Japan through private trade. In 1982, a shipwreck of the Yuan dynasty was salvaged in the Xin'an sea area of South Korea, on which a large number of Chinese ceramics were found. Archaeologists also found more than one hundred thousand pieces of ancient Chinese money, such as Zhi Da Tong Bao. This was a large cargo ship, en route from China to the port of Bodo, Japan. In the Yuan dynasty, the export of Chinese coins into Japan not only met the needs of Japan for money, but also played the role of world currency.[6] During this period, the gold and silver mining industry developed in Japan and so gold and silver was also exchanged

---

[3] Aiping Zhou, "The Flow of Chinese Currency to Japan and Its Influence," *Chinese Coins*, no. 4 (1995).

[4] Hui Bao, "An Application for the Provincial Decree of Copper Coins Banning," *My Manuscripts*, vol. I, http://www.guoxuedashi.com/SiKuQuanShu/2265x/.

[5] Gaohua Chen and Tai Wu, *Overseas Trade in Song and Yuan Dynasties* (Tianjin: Tianjin People's Publishing House, 1981), 193.

[6] Ai Guo, "Sino Japanese Economic Trade and the Outflow of Copper Money in Yuan Dynasty," *Zhoushan Coins*, no. 2 (1994).

for Chinese copper money.

In Muromachi period, Japan imitated China's gold and silver coins and made *Da Pan* (oval shaped gold coins) and sea cucumber-shaped silver coins. Da Pan was later included in the bamboo flowing gold system, which got its name from the gold block in the shape of bamboo. The shape of Japanese gold and silver coins, at this time, was related to the gold and silver cakes of the Tang dynasty. In 1543 (the twenty-second year of Jia Jing in Ming dynasty), the ash blowing method of silver refining in China was introduced to Japan; silver ore was first burned into lime, after the lime was weathered and blown away, the silver block was left, which was the so-called "ash blowing silver." Since then, gold and silver mining developed rapidly in Japan, and the purity of silver refining was also greatly improved.

At the end of the sixteenth century, after Toyotomi Hideyoshi unified the whole country, he took the mining rights of gold and silver in various territories into his own hands. With the development of a handicraft industry and commerce in Japanese cities, money circulated in large amounts. As a result, Toyotomi Hideyoshi created the Da Pan gold coin, with a face value of ten Liang, and cast a large number of Fama gold, Tai Ge Yuan Bu gold, Yong Le Tong Bao gold, Gu Ding silver, You Zhou Ding silver, Tian Zheng Tong Bao silver, Wen Lu Tong Bao silver, Yong Le Tong Bao silver, etc., for circulation in the market. The use of Yong Le, a title of reign of the Ming Empire, indicates the international characteristic of Chinese coins.

In the Ming dynasty, with the resumption of formal diplomatic relations between China and Japan, tribute trade rose again. By then, China's copper money had become a definite gift in the tribute trade, and the main purpose of Japan's dispatch of an emissary to the Ming Empire was to obtain Chinese copper money. The generous gifts of copper money still could not satisfy the needs of Japanese society for it, and Japan repeatedly asked for more. Generally speaking, Japan's petition would get approval from the Chinese authorities. In this way, a large amount of Chinese copper money flowed into Japan through the official tribute trade.[7] Before the second group of envoys, sent from Japan to the Ming Empire, set for the capital from Mingzhou (present Ningbo), they first transported one hundred thousand Jin of sulfur to Nanjing, but China returned their goods many times, and paid them thirty million copper coins at a time. Another thirty thousand Guan of copper coins were paid on their way back from Hangzhou to Ningbo.[8]

Because Japan used Chinese coins for a long time, it later formed a special center in Nagasaki to cast various kinds of Japanese-styled Chinese coins, which were called Du Lai Qian. In short, since the twelfth century, due to the economic development in Japan, a large amount of Chinese money, of the Song dynasty, was imported. After the fourteenth century, money of the Ming dynasty, such as Hong Wu and Yong Le Tong Bao, was imported from China. Japan could not issue a unified currency because the rulers did not have the power to unify the whole country. At that time, Japan was within the monetary and economic circle of China.[9]

In 1636, Tokugawa Shogunate began to unify copper coins, and in the same year began to cast Kuan Yong Tong Bao. In 1670, he issued an order that all coins, other than Kuan Yong, must be ancient money, and be prohibited from circulation. Therefore, ancient money began to be collected by some people in Japan. In 1695, coins from neighboring countries ceased to circulate in Japan.

---

[7] Aiping Zhou, "The Flow of Chinese Currency to Japan and Its Influence," *Chinese Coins*, no. 4 (1995).

[8] Yizhong Yu, "Research on the Influence of Chinese Currency Culture on Neighboring Countries from the Perspective of Their Coins," in *Proceedings of the Sixth Symposium on Southeast Asian Historical Currencies and Maritime Silk Road Currencies*, ed. Zhejiang Coin Society (Ningbo: Ningbo Numismatic Society, June 1995).

[9] Bank Financial Research Institute of Japan, "The History of Japanese Currency: In Relation to China," *Chinese Coins*, no. 1 (2000).

In Japan, there was Fan Zha, which was similar to ancient Chinese paper money, including the notes issued by various vassals in Edo and Meiji periods. The denomination of Fan Zha was generally based on the three currencies of gold, silver and copper, issued by the shogunate. Therefore, Fan Zha was also called gold Zha, silver Zha and Qian Zha. Usually, silver Zha was the most in number.

The designs of Fan Zha could be roughly divided into three types: printed, handwritten, and both. Most of the printed ones were printed with pictures. The front of the note was generally divided into three or four parts, namely, face value, place of issue, year of issue, inscription and the names of the issuer and the redeemer. On the back were two or three parts, also marked with face value, inscription, and the names of the issuer and the redeemer. As for the handwritten notes, the amount, the names of the issuer and the redeemer were handwritten, stamped with black or scarlet seals. The third was a mixture of the two. Anyway, the general structure was similar to that of ancient China. Usually, the size of Fan Zha was about 150 mm-160 mm long and 30 mm-40 mm wide, but there were also sizes larger or smaller than that. In 1871, the Japanese government ordered that Fan Zha must be converted into newly issued paper money. It wasn't until 1880 that the work of collection and exchange of Fan Zha came to an end. The patterns on Japan's Fan Zha, like those of China's paper money, are mostly about Japanese folk customs, mainly auspicious things, such as the god of wealth, the god of seven blessings, the treasure boat, the god Buddha, the temple scenery, sunrise, the map of ten thousand treasures, crane, dragon, phoenix, kylin, etc.

As copper money of Ming flowed into Japan, Japanese silver also flooded into China. From the beginning of the Longqing to the end of the Ming dynasty, silver of foreign countries flowed into China in great amounts, chiefly from Spain, Portugal and Japan. Silver mining in Japan reached its peak in the late sixteenth century. The Japanese government welcomed Chinese merchant ships to Japan, which promoted the development of trade between the two. The number of Chinese merchant ships increased in Japan. Japanese silver was mostly exported through Nagasaki port in two channels. First, the Chinese merchants exchanged the goods for silver and shipped it back to China. Second, Portuguese merchants sent silver back to Macao after trading in Japan, with which they bought Chinese silk, porcelain, tea and other goods, and shipped them to Japan, the Philippines or Europe. In this way, Japanese silver flowed into China through Portuguese merchants.

Ancient Chinese currency had a great influence on Japanese social economy, promoting the emergence of the Japanese monetary system and the development of a commodity-monetary economy. After the Tang dynasty, Japan absorbed the Han culture in an all-round way, and the amount of Chinese currency that flowed into Japan increased rapidly. When Japan cast He Tong Kai Zhen silver and copper coins, in 708, Japanese people were still not aware of using money. In order to promote the circulation of coins, the Nara Empire issued an order about "money storage and one's position," in 711, stipulating that a person with a certain amount of coins could be promoted. It also issued laws and decrees requiring that the fees and taxes to the government must be delivered in currency. Copper money gradually circulated in the commodity trade market. Thus, Japan's domestic economy and monetization of commodity were promoted.

Chinese coins circulated in large quantities in Japan and became the main exchange medium of Japanese commodity trade. In 958, the Ping'an Empire stopped casting copper coins. From then on, Kamakura Shogunate, Ashikaga Shogunate, Hirohito ODA and Hideki Toyotomi, basically, had no copper money cast in their reigns. China's currency had become the main medium of exchange in Japan's commodity trade market and the legal standard currency of Japan in certain periods. During the reign of Ashikaga Shogunate, the Japanese government stipulated that Yong Le Tong Bao would be the standard currency—not only were all transactions based on it, but the conversion of bad money was too.

II. Currency Culture Exchange between China and Korea

China has borders with North Korea, in the Northeast, and the two have been friendly with each other through the ages. In ancient Korea, like in China, there were legends about money casting and records of the use of mother and son money. Later, in Goguryeo as well as in Dongwoju, which was formed under the influence of the former, there were also records of money. North Korea's research on the currency of this period has achieved some archaeological results. One Hua and Ming Hua coins were found in the ancient Korean relics of Liaodong Peninsula and the Northwest of the Korean Peninsula. The diameter of a One Hua coin was about 1.8 cm-2 cm, which was very small. A Ming Hua coin had the same shape as One Hua, but, with a diameter of 2.6 cm, it was slightly larger than a One Hua coin. During this period, the currency exchange between China and Dongyi was very frequent. As a result, a considerable number of Chinese coins flowed into the areas that were under the rule of ancient Korea and Goguryo.

Judging from the relics unearthed in the ancient tombs of Silla, the casting technology at that time had reached a high level. In the Gold and Silver Tomb in Silla, which was thought to be from the end of the fifth century or the beginning of the sixth century, they found precious metals, clothing articles, copper wares, and iron wares that were unearthed from the Tianma Tomb. In addition, there were many remnants of metal Buddha-worshipping appliances, such as Buddha statues and Buddhist bells.

Silla's trade and economy got developed around its unification. It was generally believed that, by then, the concept of money had been well-accepted by the people of Silla. This custom actually came from the Tang dynasty of China. Few records and relics of Baiji's coinage have been found. Therefore, the speculations about the Baiji currency mainly revolve around Baiji people's concept of currency and their sales of land.

Various currencies have flowed from China into ancient Korea, throughout history, among which, Ming Knife money has been the most widely unearthed. It accounted for 19 percent of Korean ancient coins. Many were discovered in hundreds or thousands of pieces. In *the Historical Treatise,* compiled by the Imperial University of Tokyo, Japanese scholar Liangce Fujita introduced that a large number of Ming Knife coins were unearthed in the North of Korea. Just in 1924, there were more than one hundred Ming Knife coins found in the cave of Ningbian and 1,327 in Long Yuan cave of Weiyuan County, including fifty-one intact ones.[10] From 1924 to 1937, a large number of Pre-Qin coins were unearthed in Ningbian, Weiyuan, Ningyuan, Ping'an North Road, Ping'an South Road and other places in North Korea. Even over one thousand pieces were found at one time. According to the records of *Korean Business History*, Ming Knife money was excavated in more than twenty areas in the territory of ancient Korea. There were at least hundreds, sometimes as many as thousands of excavated coins. Ming Knife has been found even in the South of Korea and in faraway Ryukyu Naha.[11] A large amount of Chinese currency flowed into Korea and was used as a means of circulation and settlement, which proved that China had economic and trade exchanges with East Asia, in the pre-Qin period.

---

[10] Guanxi Sheng, "Overseas Circulation and Significance of Ancient Chinese Coins," *Asian Coins*, no. 1 (1999).

[11] Yuquan Wang, *The Origin and Development of Chinese Ancient Currency* (Beijing: Science Press, 1957).

It has been recorded in Chinese historical books that, in the seventh century BC, a country called Korea had trade relations with China, especially with the state of Yan, one of the seven powers of the Warring States period. At the end of the Warring States period, Yan state was extremely powerful and constantly launched attacks across the border at ancient Korea. In 284 BC, Qin Kai, the general of Yan state, captured thousands miles of territory in the western part of ancient Korea. When Yan declined, ancient Korea in turn recaptured more than a thousand miles of western territory. After the unification of China in the Qin and Han dynasties, Wei Man, who migrated from Yan state, established a new dynasty in ancient Korea.

Research on coins has made great progress, in both North and South Korea, since 1945. There are three theories about the center and territory of ancient Korea: the theory of Liaohe River Center, the theory of Datongjiang River Center and the theory of Movement (from the early stage of Liaohe River to the later stage of Datongjiang River). Just as different theories describe the situation of ancient Korea differently, the explanations for money flowing from China also differ.

In the third year of Yuan Feng, during the reign of Emperor Han Wu Di (108 BC), the Emperor destroyed the Wei family of Korea and set up four Prefectures there instead: Lelang, Lintun, Xuantu and Zhenfan. China's territory extended to the northern part of the peninsula. In the fifth year of Shi Yuan (82 BC), of Emperor Han Zhao Di, the latter three were incorporated into the Lelang Prefecture. These Prefectures, centered on Lelang, have remained for about four hundred years. During that time, Chinese culture was brought to Korea through these Prefectures, which permeated not only the whole area of ancient Korea, but also the south of the Peninsula. After this period, Korean society changed from Northern metal culture to Chinese metal culture.

This change can also be seen through currency. Five Zhu coins, first cast by Emperor Han Wu Di in the fourth year of Yuan Shou, have come up all over the Korean Peninsula. The unearthed sites include the Lelang ancient tomb around Pyongyang, the Yunshili tomb in Yinli County, the No.1 tomb in Xianfengli of Huangzhou County and the Tukuang tomb in Heiqiaoli. In some places, Five Zhu coins of the late Western Han dynasty were also unearthed, such as the money of Huo Quan, Huo Bu and Da Quan Fifty, issued during Wang Mang's time.

In the archaeological excavation, large numbers of Chinese coin, such as Half-Liang, Five Zhu, Huo Quan, Da Quan Fifty, Xiao Quan Zhi Yi, Huo Bu, etc., were unearthed from the original site of Lelang Prefecture (today's region of Qi Cheng Li on the South Bank of Datong River in Pyongyang, North Korea). Based on the analysis of the tomb structures and the brick burial rooms where the Square Hole money was unearthed, the burial age of the money was from the middle and late Western Han to the middle Eastern Han dynasty. The casting mould of Half-Liang coins was also found in Lelang, which indicated that the casting method of the Square Hole coins in the Western Han dynasty had, by then, spread to the northern part of the peninsula. The southern part of the Korean Peninsula was not under the jurisdiction of China. However, Five Zhu coins were also found to be buried in the tombs of the middle of the first century BC in Changyuan County, Gyeongsangnam-do, South Korea. In addition, the excavation of such coins as Five Zhu, Huo Quan, Da Quan Wu Yi and Huo Bu in the Muntain Port, Jianruli, Jeju-do, though not many, showed that, because of China's political influence, cultural radiation, commodity trade or other factors, Square Hole coins had also been exported to the south of the peninsula.

The circulation of Five Zhu coins on the Korean Peninsula lasted until the end of the Three Kingdoms period. About ninety pieces of Five Zhu coins were dug up in the tomb of King Wuning, which were iron coins, presumed to have been cast in 533. There were also Five

Zhu coins and Kai Yuan Tong Bao of the Tang dynasty in the relics of Silla in the period of reunification, which indicated that ancient Korea had close contacts with China at that time.

In the era of Three Hans, iron once circulated as an important means of exchange in Korea. According to *the Romance of the Three Kingdoms*, Byeonhan and Jinhan were the iron supply bases for Han (south central part of the peninsula), Sui (northeast part of the peninsula) and Wo (Japan). In the domestic market, iron was used the same as Chinese Square Hole money. At that time, trade relations were established in quite a wide range of regions. All the surrounding areas needed iron from Byeonhan and Jinhan. Iron had become the benchmark and the means of exchange in various physical transactions.

If iron were to serve as a "currency," its shape and size must be unified. This fact has been confirmed by the Iron Tings found in the ancient tombs in Lingnan area of Korean Peninsula and Kinki area of Japan.[12] As the material of agricultural tools and weapons, iron had become the basis of force and economy, either for a nation or for an individual. The use of Iron Tings as currency, thus, was regarded as a symbol of wealth, which naturally became an important burial object in the tombs of emperors and royal families. Several, or even hundreds of, Iron Tings of a certain size, with an average length ranging from 45.3 cm to 15.1 cm, have been unearthed in the ancient tomb groups of Fuquan cave in Busan, the Dacheng cave in Jinhai, the Jinling tomb, the golden crown tomb and the Tianma tomb in Qingzhou. Various Iron Tings have also been unearthed in the area where Mahan was located. It can be inferred from these relics that Iron Tings have appeared in the southern part of the Korean peninsula since the fourth century.

[12] Chao Dong, "Bianchen and Gaya's Iron," *Ancient culture of East Asia*, no. 68 (1991).

In the Three Kingdoms period of ancient Korea, gold and silver were also used actively. Fen, Jin and Liang had been used successively as the unit of gold and silver. *The Romance of the Three Kingdoms* recorded that Goguryeo exported gold and silver to the Han Empire. The silver Ting found in the foundation of tower in the temple of Gyeongju was about 4.45 cm long, 3.33 cm wide, 0.36 cm thick and weighed 53 g. Based on the historical records and relics, it could be concluded that gold and silver were both used as means of exchange in the Three Kingdoms period of Korea.

In ancient Korean society, weighing money of various shapes once circulated for a time. Not only were they used in the domestic market, but they had been circulating in trade with foreign countries since the era of the three Hans. Some of the weighing currency became very popular because they had great value, which, what's more, did not change frequently. Iron was especially important at that time, both for the country and for individuals. Not only did it play the role of a currency, but also it attracted people's attention.

While China was in the time of the Eastern Jin, Southern and Northern dynasties to Sui dynasty, the northern and southern parts of the Korean peninsula belonged to Goguryeo, Baiji and Silla respectively; in the Tang dynasty, it belonged to Andong Prefecture, Bohai Sea and Silla. In the middle of the seventh century, Silla unified most of the peninsula. During this period, bartering was the main form of exchange on the Korean Peninsula. In 936, Koryo united Korea and began to cast iron coins from 983. In 1097, coins were minted in imitation of China, including Hai Dong Tong Bao, Hai Dong Yuan Bao, Hai Dong Zhong Bao, San Han Tong Bao, Dong Guo Tong Bao and Dong Guo Zhong Bao. They were first used in the capital city and then extended to other counties.

From 1408 to the 1580s, the Korean government restricted the export of silver. Since then, silver has been widely used in Korea. As physical currencies were still in circulation in Korea, such as cloth and rice, silver was mainly used for foreign trade. Since the fifteenth century, due to the lack of copper, the copper coinage in Korea was greatly reduced, but, in the 1620s, it became active again. In 1627, casting was stopped once more because of the attack from Later Jin. In 1633, Jin Qizong proposed that copper coins be recast. This time, the famous Chang Ping Tong Bao was minted. The government set up a money casting office to manage its affairs. It was stipulated that the copper coins would be used in transactions, and a large amount of Japanese copper was imported for coinage. In 1636, the Later Jin attacked and seized Korea again, and the coinage, after a brief stop, soon resumed. By then, Chang Ping Tong Bao had circulated throughout the country.

The Confucian culture on Chang Ping Tong Bao can be sensed by its use of words selected from *The Thousand Character Classic*, which is a four-character long poem with Confucianism as its main body, in combination with natural science and social common sense too. In ancient times, it was used as a primary reading book for Chinese character study in many countries. Chang Ping Tong Bao carried a strong cultural charm because of *The Thousand Character Classic* word on its back. About one-third of the money was cast with words chosen from *The Thousand Character Classic*, which ingeniously reflected the mainstream culture of Korea at that time.

The Chinese characters of the Li dynasty, in Korea, were mainly in the style of Zhao Mengfu, a great calligrapher of the Yuan dynasty, in China. The words on the coins of Chang Ping Tong Bao were smooth and vigorous, and formed its unique style. Some Chang Ping Tong Bao coins, like Chinese ancient money; had signs of the sun, moon, cloud, thunder, Eight Digrams, or the Five Elements on the back, as if a coin carried a micro universe.

CHAPTER FIVE

CURRENCY CULTURE EXCHANGE BETWEEN CHINA AND ANCIENT SOUTHEASTERN ASIA

I. Currency Cultural Exchange between China and Vietnam

As early as the Neolithic age, the ancestors along the coast of China had "cut wood for boats" and sailed on the sea. In 1973, a boat-shaped pottery was unearthed in Hemudu, Yuyao, Zhejiang Province. The hole in the head part of the pottery looked like a mooring hole. Archaeologists believed that it was the shape of a primitive canoe. At the ruins of Hemudu, a carved wooden paddle was also excavated with a residual length of 63 cm, a width of 12.2 cm and a thickness of 2.1 cm. After C14 testing, experts believed that this was a marine tool, left seven thousand years ago. In addition, around 1958, seven wooden oars from more than four thousand seven hundred years were excavated in Shuitian and Wuxing County of Zhejiang Province. The discovery of these wooden oars fully proved that boat activities had been quite extensive in the Southeast coastal areas of China in the Neolithic age.

The Geography of Han Shu recorded the navigation of the emissary dispatched by Wang Mang to Nanyang: "In the year of Yuanshi at the reign of Emperor Ping Di, Wang Mang assisted the administration. Generous gifts were given to Huangzhi to show off the power and benevolence of the emperor. It took eight months to sail from Huangzhi to Pizong, and two months to the Xianglin boundary of

Rinan." Rinan, also known as Annam, is now Vietnam; Huangzhi is the capital of Dravida in *Records of Western Regions*. The recorded Pizong is the southern end of the Malay Peninsula, now an island of Singapore.[1] As early as the Wei and Jin dynasties, in the third and fourth centuries, the Chinese people had opened the sea routes from the South China Sea to the Bay of Bengal, the Indian Ocean, the Arabian Sea, the Persian Gulf and other places.

The Tang and Song dynasties were the prosperous periods in China's history. After the "Rebellion of An Lushan and Shi Siming," the economy of the regions south of the Yangtze River developed rapidly. The economic focus of agriculture, handicraft industry and commerce gradually shifted from north to south. Guangzhou, Quanzhou, Hangzhou and Mingzhou became the four major ports of foreign trade at that time. Jiangsu and Zhejiang also became the most developed region in China's economy.

At the beginning of the Tang dynasty, China invented the watertight cabin. Craftsmen divided the ship into several small cabins. Even if the ship ran on rocks in the wind, during the voyage, and some cabins leaked, the whole ship would not sink. Neither would the normal navigation be affected. In 1960, a Tang-dynasty wreck was unearthed in Shiqiao Town, Yangzhou City, Jiangsu Province, with watertight cabins inside. At that time, navigation ships in Europe and other places were still in the stage of leather rope bandages. The development of shipbuilding and navigation promoted the unprecedented prosperity of maritime trade.

In ninth to the eleventh centuries, the Chinese navigation technology had surpassed the Arabs and become the first in the world. In the Song dynasty, the carrying capacity of seagoing ships could

[1] Guanxi Sheng, "Overseas Circulation and Significance of Ancient Chinese Coins," *Asian Coins*, no. 1 (1999).

reach more than five hundred to six hundred tons, while the Arab merchant ships could only carry just over one hundred tons. In the twelfth century, the ships used by the Normans to cross the English Channel were only one-twentieth to one-tenth of the tonnage of seagoing ships in the Song dynasty. In the thirteenth century, the carrying capacity of British ships was only one-half of that of Chinese ships. China had its own transferring base at the southern end of India, where all people from the West and West Asia had to transfer to Chinese merchant ships before they came to China. In the Southern Song dynasty, there were more than twenty thousand small-sized boats registered in Eastern Zhejiang.[2] In the Yuan dynasty, China's coastal water transport mileage alone reached more than thirteen thousand Li.

In the early Ming dynasty, in order to promote economic development, Emperor Ming Tai Zu actively engaged in international trade and set up *Shi Bo Ti Ju Si* (a municipal shipping management department) in the southeast coastal provinces. Overseas trade had a robust growth then. Zhu Di, Emperor of Ming Cheng Zu, sent Zheng He to various countries with a huge fleet of ships. He went to the Eastern Ocean (Japan) first and then to the Western Ocean seven times, which opened a new era in the history of world navigation, developed the geographical understanding of China's navigation, enriched the connotation of foreign exchange, further strengthened the friendly relations between China and other neighboring countries in the world, and promoted the bilateral development in economy, culture, science and technology.

The Yuan dynasty adopted an open foreign trade policy, allowing businessmen from all over the world to come to China for business. The overseas Chinese, in Southeast Asia, in the Qing dynasty, formed

---

[2] Zhengzhong Guo, *A Study on the Commodity Currency Economy of Urban and Rural Areas in the Song Dynasty* (Beijing: Economic Management Press, 1997), 410.

their own economic society, through their efforts, and non-governmental trade closely related China with Southeast Asian countries, in economy. Seagoing ships and sea routes opened up trade between China and Southeast Asian countries, while currency was the blood of trade.

From the Qin and Han dynasties to the middle of the tenth century, Vietnam had always been one part of the territory of China's feudal dynasty, known as Annam in the Era of *Jun* and *Xian* (Jun and Xian were different levels of political administration in ancient time). During this period, Vietnam was subordinate to China, so it had long used the Square Hole (fangkong) money issued by the Chinese government. In Vietnam, Square Hole coins of Han dynasty and Wang Mang period have often been unearthed. In the Tang dynasty, China set up a money supervision organization in Guilin, and the Kai Yuan Tong Bao coins were also circulated in Vietnam.

In the middle of the tenth century, Vietnam's Ding Buling (923-979) unified Annam. He became the emperor in 968, established the first dynasty of Vietnam, the Ding dynasty, and titled it Da Qu Yue. In 970, the reign was named Tai Ping (peace and tranquility). In 975, Emperor Song Tai Zu granted him the title Jiaozhi Prince. In the Song dynasty, Vietnam was once known as Annam, Da Qu Yue and Jiao Zhi. In the Ding dynasty, the first Tai Ping Xing Bao in Vietnam was made by referring to the shape of Chinese coins. Volume 7 and Volume 11 of *Quan Zhi* recorded four kinds of ancient Vietnamese money: Tai Ping Xing Bao with "Ding" on the back (items 132 and 139); Tian Fu Zhen Bao with "Li" on the back (items 130 and 220); Tian Gan Yuan Bao with "Qian Wang" on the back (item 134); and Tai Ping Tong Bao with "Ding" on the back (item 133). All were Square Hole money with Chinese inscription.[3]

---

[3] Yanzhi Tu, "A Brief Account of Southeast Asian Money in *Quan Zhi* of Southern Song Dynasty," *Asian Coins*, no. 1 (1999).

In 1225, Vietnam began the reign of the Chen dynasty. In the thirteenth to the fourteenth centuries, Vietnam's coinage industry developed more rapidly than before. Coins and silver ingots were cast separately, according to the law. In 1226, Chen Tai Zong unified the currency. In the new system, one Qian was equal to seventy Yuan, one Guan was ten Qian, and one Mo was sixty-nine Wen. The paper money of the Yuan dynasty also circulated in Vietnam. It was recorded that "copper money was used in circulation. In the folk, 67 Qian equals 1 Liang of paper money while officially the rate was 70."[4] The two ways of evaluation, both in the government and in the folk, show the wide circulation of paper money in Vietnam (called Jiao Zhi then).

In 1396, the twenty-ninth year of Hong Wu in the Ming dynasty, or the ninth year of Guang Tai in the reign of Chen Shun Zong in Vietnam, the Vietnamese government ordered the recovery of all the copper money and issue paper money in imitation of China. The banknotes each had different designs: there were algae on the ten-Wen note; sprays on the thirty-Wen note; clouds on the one-Mo note; turtles on the two-Mo note; a kirin on the three-Mo note; a phoenix on the five-Mo; and a dragon on the one-Guan note. At that time, the government demanded that everyone use paper money, and whoever forged or used copper money would be beheaded. Besides, it was stipulated that 1.2 Guan copper coins should exchange for one Guan paper money.

In 1428, after Li Li defeated the Ming army in Vietnam, he established the Li dynasty and became Li Tai Zu of Vietnam. In the first thirty years of the Li dynasty, the monetary economy developed, which brought a rapid growth of the coin casting industry. From the middle of the tenth century to the beginning of the fifteenth century,

[4] Dayuan Wang, *A Brief Account of Foreign Islands* (Beijing: Zhong Hua Book Company, 1981).

the Vietnamese economy slowed down, after its independence. Although the dynasties changed several times, China's Square Hole money was still dominant in the circulation field. Even the private cast coins in the folk, which were called "Floating on the Water," also largely adopted the style of Chinese coins, with a round shape and a square hole in the middle.

Then it came to the period of the Southern and Northern dynasties of Vietnam. The northern Zheng family was conferred the title of King of Annam, in 1667, by the Qing dynasty. Before the eighteenth century, every town in Vietnam had a money foundry. In 1753, Zheng ordered the abolition of the foundries in the towns, and only the two mints near the capital were kept. In 1776, during the reign of Emperor Xian Zong, in the Jing Xing years, the Zheng family, after seizing Shunhua, began to cast money in Fuchun. Thirty thousand official coins of Jing Xing Tong Bao were cast. Silver ingots were cast into blocks of one Liang. One Liang was ten Qian and one Qian was two Fen. One Qian of silver equaled the value of two hundred Qian of coins. In the South, the coins of the Nguyen family were of two kinds: copper coins and zinc coins, both of which were engraved with the words "Tai Ping."

In 1802, Nguyen Shi Zu reunited the North and the South of Vietnam and established the Nguyen dynasty, with the title of Jia Long. In the second year of Jia Long (1803), a coin foundry was opened in Beicheng to cast copper coins and zinc coins, as well as gold ingots, silver ingots, gold taels and silver taels. The zinc coins, each weighing seven Fen, were cast with the words "Jia Long Tong Bao" on them and "Qi Fen" on the other side (*Qi* means seven). At that time, one Liang gold in Beicheng was worth ten Liang silver. Later more casting offices were opened in Jiading city and the other towns.

Since the copper money of China and Vietnam was basically the same in shape and form, the currencies of the two countries had been circulating with each other for a long time. Because of its moderate weight, China's copper money had become the international currency of Asia in certain historical periods, and Vietnam's money had long been used in the South of China. Since Vietnamese money was lighter and thinner than Chinese money, it had always been banned by the Chinese government. However, the exchange of currency culture between the two countries had never been interrupted. In particular, the Vietnamese carved some quotations from ancient Chinese classics on their currency, which confirmed the far-reaching significance of Chinese culture.

From 1820 to 1840, Annam Sheng Zu Nguyen Fujiao cast large copper money—Ming Ming Tong Bao, in the year of Ming Ming. Quotations from ancient Chinese Confucius classics were cast in Chinese on the back of the coins in two kinds, namely, four-character style and eight-character style. These were named Mei Hao Qian. The successors Annam Xian Zu and Annam Yi Zong continued the tradition of casting money with lines from Chinese Confucius classics.

Fig. 5-1 A circulating coin cast in Vietnam (left) and the folk coins cast in Fujian of the Qing dynasty (right), both with quotations from Chinese Confucian classics. The words are consistent, both in the calligraphic style and the layout.

In the Ming and Qing dynasties, Vietnam also minted some coins with the titles of reign of Chinese dynasties. Most of these coins were cast by the local government of Vietnam. They were light, small and coarse, and were made of copper and lead. Privately cast coins that have, so far, been discovered with the title of reign of the Ming dynasty include: Yong Le Tong Bao, Xuan De Tong Bao, Long Qing Tong Bao, Wan Li Tong Bao, Tai Chang Tong Fu, Chong Zhen Tong Bao, etc.[5]

Vietnam's currency was basically the same as that of China, in terms of its system and its bimetallic standard of silver and copper money. In the late Ming dynasty, due to the development of American silver mines, China gained a large amount of silver in the Southeast Asian trade, controlled by Western countries, through the export of porcelain and medicinal materials. The traditional Chinese currency system changed and began to form a bimetallic standard of silver and copper money. In other words, in the commercial trade, silver was used as a means of settlement for a large sum, while copper money was used for a small sum. Vietnam began to use this standard in modern times, and its silver flowed into China in large quantities.

Vietnam's silver, commonly known as bar money, was shaped like a long brick. This kind of silver was one of the main currencies, before the French colonialists invaded Annam. Not only was it the main subject matter of Vietnam's domestic finance and taxation, but it flowed into Southeast Asia, China, Japan and other places through trade. The bar money, cast around 1833, was usually divided into two kinds: ten Liang or five Liang, and more were of the ten-Liang kind. The original words were crossed out and the new ones were added to the bar money, so that they could be circulated in China. It can be

[5] Yixiang Weng, "Coins of Ming Dynasty Cast in Annam," *Shaanxi Finance,* Special Issue of Coins (1992).

estimated that a great amount of Vietnamese bar money was melted and recast into Chinese silver ingots, due to the rigid local circulation characteristics of Chinese silver.[6]

II. Chinese Tin Coins in Malaysia

There is a long history of trade between China and Malaysia. In the twelfth century, Chinese coins began to circulate in Samboja, of the old port of Sumatra. In the Song dynasty, Chinese copper coins were mainly paid for trading with this area. Chinese coins were also circulated in Malacca and other places during the Yuan and Ming dynasties.

In the 1870s, Sultan Abu Bakar allowed overseas Chinese to develop in Johor. These overseas Chinese established their own "harbor master" system there. They exercised their power and established villages along the river or along the route. Here, harbor masters could levy taxes, set up gambling businesses and execute administrative management. Some harbor masters were allowed to issue their own coins for daily payments or for use in casinos. These coins were usually cast in tin and used only under the control of the harbor masters, with the company of the issuer, or his name, on the surface. In the nineteenth century, there were more than one hundred such Chinese areas in Johor. In 1917, the British abolished the system of Chinese harbor masters. At that time, only six Chinese areas remained. The Chinese tin coins have been found with words on, such as He Li, Tong Rui, Zheng Kai Fu Xing, Yuan Xing Company, Zheng Xing Cheng Ji, Zhen Cheng Company, etc.

In Pahang, the Sultan who ruled in 1882 was Bendahara Wan Ahmad. During his reign, Chinese people were allowed to engage in

---

[6] Xuewen Dai, "Vietnam Bar Silver Circulating in China," *Chinese Coins*, no. 4 (1996).

the traditional gambling industry, and they could cast jokor coins to circulate in casinos and nearby areas. Jokor is Malay, and means being empty in the middle. These coins could be circulated, together with the tin hat coins of the Sultan, and there was a fixed rate. Generally speaking, four jokors were equal to one big hat coin, and one hundred jokors were equal to one silver dollar. This was very strange in the Malay Peninsula. There were only Chinese, besides Javanese, on these tin coins.

In Terengganu, in addition to the gold coins issued by the Sultan, there were also tin coins of the Sultan, some of which were Square Hole coins. The third kind were the tin coins cast by Chinese people, which circulated in the areas controlled by the Chinese. In 1919, they were banned by the local government.[7] The Chinese characters on the coins cast by Chinese people in Terengganu included Yu Cheng company, Hao Yi company, Xie Xing company, Yong Long company, De Shun company, Zhen Chun company, Da Hong company, Chang Yuan company, Shun Zhen Li Ji company, He Li company, etc.

III. Bullet Silver, Porcelain Money and Chinese Character Gold Coins in Thailand

The main coin used in Thai history was silver, and appeared in a very special form. Bullet silver was the name given, by westerners, for its resemblance to bullets. In fact, it evolved from seashells. The basic unit of bullet silver was the *baht*, a unit used to weigh silver. The market value of silver was usually large. In order to facilitate small transactions, in the mid-nineteenth century, the Thai royal family of Rama IV began to imitate the Western monetary system to make minor

---

[7] Saran Singh, *The Encyclopaedia of the Coins of Malaysia, Singapore and Brunei 1400-1967* (Kuala Lumpur: A Malaysia Numismatic Society Publication, 1996), 159.

coins. The bullet silver cast in Thailand had long been in circulation in China, and some coins were even marked with Chinese characters.

Fig. 5-2 The fourth king of the Bangkok dynasty in Thailand once issued a gold coin with Chinese characters, weighing 4 Baht (1 Liang), with the Thai "Siam capital" in the middle surrounded by the Chinese "Zheng Ming Tong Bao".

Before the Bangkok dynasty, Thailand was the Tunwuli dynasty, the founder of which was Zheng Xin, a person of Chinese origin. In 1767, the Yongjiya dynasty of Myanmar captured the capital of Thailand. At the critical moment of the nation, Zheng Xin led an army, composed of Thai and overseas Chinese, to expel the invading army and restore Siam's independence. He moved the capital from Ayudna to Tunwuli and crowned himself Emperor Tunwuli. During the fifteen years of Zheng Xin's reign, he sought to establish friendly and cooperative relations with China. In 1781, Zheng Xin launched a massive mission to visit China, taking eleven large ships carrying ivory, rhinoceros horn, sappan, gamboge, etc., to restore the traditional tributary trade between China and Thailand. However, Zheng Xin was forced to abdicate and was killed in a domestic political storm. A military officer under Zheng Xin's command inherited the throne, moved the palace to Bangkok, and, thus, started the Bangkok dynasty. In order to maintain friendly relations with China, the first emperor of the Bangkok dynasty wrote to the Qing government, claiming to be the son of Zheng Xin, named Zheng Hua. He promised that he would follow his father's instruction, stick to the old system and obey the Qing dynasty. He died in 1809. The succeeding emperors each had a Chinese Name: the second emperor, Zheng Fo (1809-1824), the third emperor, Zheng Fu (1824-1854), and the fourth emperor, Zheng Ming (1854-1868). Therefore, the gold coins issued by the fourth emperor had the words "Zheng Ming Tong Bao" written on them.[8]

The fourth emperor was determined to reform. He was proficient in English and loved natural science. After his accession to the throne, he advocated learning from the West and reforming Siam's administrative system. Before the fourth emperor, Siam's prevailing metal currency was bullet silver made by hand. In 1858, the fourth emperor introduced metal coins from England, and began to make round gold coins, silver coins and tin coins with machines. There were three denominations of gold coins: Tuocha, Picha and Pantedeng. Silver coins had four kinds of denomination: one baht, two shaleng, one shaleng and one fen. Tin coins were used as change, in two denominations: one atta and one soluo.[9]

In the nineteenth century, Western merchants traded frequently in Southeast Asia and the southeast coast of China. Influenced by commodity economy, many people in China went to Southeast Asia to make a living. Considerable numbers of them went to Siam. Although some people in Nanyang had made a fortune, most of them were still wage earners. They left their wives and children to make a living far away from their hometown, so they often lived together. In order to relieve the boredom, they often spent their spare time in hotels and casinos. At first, people were gambling with cash in casinos. The first casino owner to switch to chips was Khun Phat, who used small pieces

---

[8] Lisheng Duan, "A Thai Coin with Chinese Characters," *Chinese Coins*, no. 3 (1985).

[9] Lisheng Duan, "A Thai Coin with Chinese Characters," *Chinese Coins*, no. 3 (1985).

of porcelain, called Pi, in local dialect. After entering the casino, one first exchanged cash into chips, and only chips were used to calculate the winning and losing. After gambling, he exchanged the remaining chips for cash before he left. The workers in the tropical jungle had no other entertainment. Gambling was an important part of life. Some people took the chips out of the casinos and used them to pay debts. As long as the casinos to which the chips belonged thrived and had good credit, people would be happy to accept them. However, this situation was still accidental and mainly occurred in the vicinity of casinos. Khun Phat's Pi was easy to use and beneficial for the maintenance of the order of casinos. Gradually, other casinos adopted this method too. It later became Thai porcelain money. Many of such porcelain coins have been found now, with rough characters on them.

At the end of 1873, there was a shortage of fractional currency in the Thai market. Pi originally represented cash and was, naturally, recognized by society. As a result, it began to circulate as a fractional currency. Only then did chips have the real meaning of "money." At that time, Thailand was in the period of Rama V., a king who actively learned advanced science and culture from the West. During his reign, the monetary system of Thailand generally adopted the form of Western coins and banknotes, and bullet silver withdrew from circulation. The government's management of national currency was strengthened too. The government believed that the use of chips instead of fractional coins was tantamount to giving casinos the right to currency issuing, which was not conducive to economic management and social stability. In 1874, the government

Fig. 5-3 Porcelain coins as token money

announced that it was forbidden to replace fractional coins with chips. Instead, it issued Attkradat, a paper money of small denomination. In fact, porcelain chips only served as money for less than a year.[10]

There is no record of the use of porcelain coins in Chinese history, but several porcelain coins have also been found. In July 1994, a porcelain coin with a picture of double fish was unearthed at the ancient official porcelain kiln site in Zhitian, Gongyi, Henan Province, which was the site of Yong'an City in the Song dynasty. Later, another porcelain coin was found with the words "Tian Xia Tai Ping" (meaning "peace in the world") on it. Further studies need to be done as to what the objects were for.[11] There were also porcelain tokens in Chaoshan, Guangdong, in modern times. When the Kuomintang regime faced collapse, inflation worsened to the extreme and token money revived. The picture in Fig. 5-3 shows examples of some objects: a hexagon with the word "Huan Li" on the front, painted in red color, and a Pipa shrimp under it, in green color (left above); a flower-shaped coin with the character "Bao" on the face, painted in red, at the bottom (right above); a round coin with "Yi Cheng Tong Bao" written in red color, the rest is green (left below); an octagon with the inscriptions "Di Mao" on the front, painted with green color at the bottom (right below).

IV. Lead Coins with Chinese Characters in Indonesia

Ancient Chinese coins were circulating in Indonesia, in both ancient and modern times. Except for a small amount of Kai Yuan coins, most of the copper money found in the first half of the twentieth century was from the Northern Song dynasty. Many local copper coins

---

[10] Shuomin Yao, "Thailand's 'Porcelain Money' is Used for Gambling," *Inner Mongolia Financial Research: Special Issue of Coins*, no. 3 (1995).
[11] Yanzhao Xi, "Rare Porcelain Money," in *Research on Coins*, ed. Henan Numismatic Society (Beijing: Science Press, 1996).

from the ninth to the sixteenth centuries were also found at the same time. Historical recordings and archaeological findings are consistent with each other.

In 1956, Song Qingling pointed out in the "Report on Visiting Indonesia" (the report delivered at the forty-seventh meeting of the Standing Committee of the National People's Congress on September 26, 1956) that "in Bali, we find more facts about cultural exchanges between China and Indonesia in history than in other places. Copper money, which is not easy to see in China, can be found in every household in Bali. It is not long before this kind of copper money was stopped circulating. Now people hang copper coins in strings as indispensable artifacts in religious rituals. In a silver shop, I found strings of copper coins of different title of reigns, including Kai Yuan, Wan Li and the title of reigns in the Qing dynasty, which shows the close cultural relationship between China and Indonesia in history."[12]

The earliest Chinese copper coins introduced into Southeast Asia were the Han dynasty ones. In the Tang dynasty, there were not many Chinese copper coins flowing into Indonesia. When it came to the Song dynasty, things changed a lot. With the increasingly close diplomatic and trade relations between the Song dynasty and the Indonesian kingdoms, a large amount of Chinese copper money flowed into Indonesia through envoys, trade and merchants.

In the Song dynasty, China's economy and maritime trade were more prosperous and developed, on the foundations of the Tang dynasty. According to statistics, at that time, more than fifty countries in Southeast Asia, South Asia and other regions had trade and exchanges with the Song dynasty. There were both tributary trade between governments and private trade among the people, and copper

---

[12] "Report on Visiting Indonesia," *The People's Daily*, accessed Sept. 27, 2019. http://data.people.com.cn/rmrb/s?type=2&qs=%7B%22cds%22%3A%5B%7B%22fld%22%3A%22dataTime.

coins were the most popular currency. In the trade in Java, "Chinese copper money was used in all ages."[13] The money of the Song dynasty was the currency of many small countries in Java, during this period, and the smuggling of coins were serious.

A large number of local copper and tin coins were also unearthed, in Indonesia, which were cast from the ninth to the sixteenth centuries (mainly Majapahit dynasty). There were both similarities and differences in the shape of Java and Chinese ancient coins. They were similar in that the ancient Javanese coins were deeply influenced by China in terms of minting technology, and most of them were round with square holes. However, there were no Chinese characters on the ancient money of Majapahit, but there were various patterns related to Buddhism and Shiva belief, such as the main characters from India's two great epics—*Ramayana* and *Mahabharata*, and the images of falun, Bodhi tree, lotus, lingga, divine bird, divine cow, monster, elephant, deer, horse, horseman, seashell, boat, fisherman, house, temple, bucket, star, panji, trident, etc.[14] Materials for casting, such as copper and tin, were not found in Java at that time,[15] so they were all imported from other places. For example, copper came from China and Japan. Every ancient Javanese coin was an agglomeration of Chinese, Indian and Javanese cultures.

In the book *Nawanatya*, there were tables of the daily pay of some noble ministers of the Majapahit monarchy, which ranged from six hundred Wen (cash or Kepeng) to eight thousand Wen per day. It also mentioned that the commander-in-chief got eight thousand Wen per day from the market, which meant that there was a market tax at that time. The Royal decrees in 1366 and 1391 referred to tribute and taxes,

---

[13] Huan Ma, *Wonders Overseas* (Beijing: Commercial Press, 1935).

[14] E. Netcher and J.A. Van der Ghigs, *Dutch East Indian Currency* (Batauia: DeMunten Van Nederlandsch Indie, 1863), 135.

[15] Netcher and Van der Ghigs, *Dutch East Indian Currency*, 137.

and pointed out that the number of Chinese copper coins (mostly coins of the Song dynasty) was so great around the capital Trawulan that they were melted into copper.[16] Apart from the Chinese ones, there were also copper coins from Japan and Vietnam.[17]

As shown above, the commodity currency economy was rather developed during the period of the Majapahit dynasty; the Chinese copper coins and the local coins of Java were circulating at the same time, and the Chinese copper coins were also indispensable in religious ceremonies. Up to this point, Chinese copper coins were still used in Buddhist ceremonies (cremation and sacrifice to gods), in Bali, and were even used as amulets in some places. Since traditional Chinese medicine had been introduced into Indonesia at that time, copper coins were also an indispensable traditional Chinese medicine.[18]

There was supposed to be a period of imitation of Chinese coins in Java, between their use of Chinese coins and the production of Arabic coins under the influence of the Islamic Kingdom. Most of these coins were made of the alloy of lead and tin, and were the imitations of the Five Zhu of Sui, Kai Yuan Tong Bao of Tang, and many coins with the title of reigns in the Southern Song.

After the rise of the Islamic Kingdom, Java, Sumatra, Kalimantan and other places continued to cast coins, but they were different in shape, pattern and writing from the ancient coins of the Hindu period. First of all, after the sixteenth century, the economic strength of overseas Chinese merchants increased day-by-day. They had a close relationship with the local Muslim ruling class and contracted for the coin casting. The Dutch appointed some of these Chinese people, with prestige, the posts of Kapitan (captain in English), making them

---

[16] Jingnan Zhou, "Chinese Copper Money in Indonesia," *Chinese Coins*, no. 2 (1986).
[17] Netcher and Van der Ghigs, *Dutch East Indian Currency*, 147.
[18] Zhou, "Chinese Copper Money in Indonesia."

responsible for the management of the community, including the right of coinage. For example, in 1619, Su Minggang took the post of Kapitan in Batavia (the original name of Jakarta, the capital of Indonesia before 1949), and minted lead coins for circulation.[19] At the end of the seventeenth century and the beginning of the eighteenth century, the imperial family of Cirebon contracted the minting right to Chen Xiangge, the local overseas Chinese Kapitan and harbor owner. The coins of Cirebon were engraved with Chinese characters such as "Shi Dan Yu Min" (meaning "Sultan makes people prosperous"). Even the Dutch East India Companies, in Semarang and other places, contracted the minting right to an overseas Chinese Kapitan with the surname Huang. Other Chinese companies, like Da Gang Company in Kalimantan and San Tiao Gou Company, simply cast coins by themselves.

Secondly, with the rise of the Islamic Kingdom, Buddhist and Shiva motifs disappeared from the coins and were replaced by the name of the local monarch and the date of the Muslim calendar in Arabic.[20] There had also been great changes in shape. In addition to the round coins with a square hole, or a round hole, octagonal coins with a round hole, circular coins with an octagonal hole and so on, there were also coins without holes in Jugang and Jambi. In addition to China, Turkey, Persia, Arabia and other countries exerted an increasingly obvious influence on Aceh, Jugang, Pontianak and other places, which was mainly manifested in the poreless coins, and the gold and silver coins. In 1780, the Dutch colonial authorities in Davivia (now Jakarta) banned the circulation of copper coins from China, Japan, Vietnam and Jugang in Java, but they could still be circulated in Bali.

---

[19] Guoqing Li, *The Formation and Development of Overseas Chinese Capital* (Fuzhou: Fujian People's Publishing House, 1985), 162.
[20] Netcher and Van der Ghigs, *Dutch East Indian Currency*, 173.

From the eighteenth to the nineteenth century, Hakka from Southern China came to Banka and Borneo, where they mined tin and gold, lived in villages, and established an administrative organization known as Gongsi. Here, they maintained their own tradition, with Gongsi scattered all over Borneo. In economic life, they used self-made coins with Chinese characters in imitation of Chinese style. At present, there are more than two hundred seventy coins like this in the Museum of Human Beings in Rotterdam, the Netherlands. Before the Dutch East India Company ruled these regions, the Chinese established many Gongsi and issued a large number of coins, some of which had Manchu characters, similar to those of the Qing dynasty. Most of the coins in Borneo were of tin-lead alloy, while those on Banka Island were mostly of tin. These coins disappeared in July 1854 when the Da Gang Company was forced to submit to the Dutch East India Company.[21]

The casting quality of the Gongsi coins was poor, and the metal often could not fill the mould properly. The mould for the coins was a lead one with a wooden frame. After Gongsi finally succumbed to the Dutch government, its coins were largely melted and used to make tea and wine sets.

In the 1950s, Chinese copper money could only be used to buy "tickets" for heaven and as offerings to the dead in Bali. In Denpasar, it could be used to buy ice cream, and, in Trungen, a packet of rice. Up to this day, Balinese are not worried that they would be short of Chinese copper money someday, because they superstitiously believe that the copper money is not imported from China. On the contrary, they think the goddess of copper coins, called "Mercu," scatters the copper money from sky from time to time. When she distributes the

[21] Dr. T. D. Yih, "Cash Coins of the Gongsi on Borneo and Banka," accessed April 17, 2018, http://www.charm.ru.

money, there is thunder, lightning and flying dragons in the sky.[22]

V. Currency Culture Exchange between China and Other Southeastern Asian Countries

1. Laos

The economic exchanges between China and Laos in the Ming dynasty triggered the currency exchange between the two countries. In the second year of Yong Le, the Ming dynasty officially established a Military and Civilian Xuan Wei Shi Si in Laos, and Laotian envoys began to trade with Ming, in the name of tribute. In July of the third year of Yong Le, the Laotian envoys came to Beijing. Emperor Yong Le granted them five hundred fifty Ding of paper money. In the tenth year of Yong Le, the Laotian envoys came once more and the Emperor, again, gave them money as well as other gifts. After that, every time the Laotian envoys came to China, they were given money, which became a fixed system. It can be inferred from the above that Chinese paper money circulated in Laos.[23] Shell coins were also used in some areas of Yunnan in China in the Ming dynasty. Historical records show that some shellfish coins have their source in Laos. Having obtained these shells through trade with other Southeast Asian countries, Laos, by trading with China, introduced them into China, finally.[24]

---

[22] "Report on Visiting Indonesia," *The People's Daily*, accessed Sept. 27, 2019, http://data.people.com.cn/rmrb/s?type=2&qs=%7B%22cds%22%3A%5B%7B%22fld%22%3A%22dataTime.

[23] Liqun Ji, ed., *On Chinese Culture* (Beijing: Beijing Yanshan Publishing House, 1998), 189.

[24] Ji, *On Chinese Culture*, 189.

2. Singapore

In the item of *Dragon Tooth Door* of *Dao Yi Zhi Lue,* written by Wang Dayuan of Yuan dynasty, it was recorded that "the gate is in Temasek, where the two mountains intersect like dragon teeth, between which there is a water channel." Temasek was the name for present-day Singapore. Zhang Xie also mentioned the Gate of Temasek in his *Study of the East and the West Ocean.* According to the study of Singapore scholar Qiu Xinmin, on February 3, 1821, John Crawtard excavated a batch of ancient Chinese coins in the old moat of Temasek, including Square Hole coins from different years, during the reigns of Tai Zu (960), Zhen Zong (998-1021), Ren Zong (1023-1063) and Shen Zong (1068-1085) of Song dynasty. Along with the ancient coins, there were a large number of celadon fragments, also of the Song dynasty. The coins of Song Yuan Tong Bao, Shao Zhi Tong Bao and Xi Ning Tong Bao of the Song dynasty were found in the Victoria Peak Fort in Singapore too.

In November 1989, more than three hundred pieces of underground relics were unearthed in Singapore's parliament building. In addition to porcelain, pottery and ornaments, some ancient Chinese money was also found. From 1984 to 1988, relics such as shells, charcoal and Chinese ancient coins were excavated near the ancient tomb at the eastern foot of Fort Canning. Archaeologists' research showed that these artifacts were all the goods that were traded with China in ancient times. These relics showed that Singapore was also a prosperous trading port in the past. The abundant stone shields, stone axes, geometric pottery, oars, rice, etc. excavated there showed Singapore's close relation to the Hemudu culture and Liangzhu Culture in China.[25]

[25] Guanxi Sheng, "Overseas Circulation and Significance of Ancient Chinese Coins," *Asian Coins*, no. 1 (1999).

3. The Philippines

As early as 1555, before the Spanish occupied the Philippines, Chinese businessmen had settled there. The Spaniards envied the success of Chinese businessmen and cruelly persecuted the overseas Chinese. Lin Feng, a Guangdong pirate, once went to the Philippines to fight with the Spanish but failed and had to flee to the mountains. After that, the Spanish established a colony in the Philippines.

The Spanish regarded the Philippines as a transit point for their trade between America and Europe, which led to the yacht trade between China and America, and American silver coins flowed into the Philippines. In this kind of trade, the Philippines acted as a middleman and a transit station. Since the Spaniards had nothing to exchange with China, they could only use American silver to buy goods from China. At the same time, the abundance of American silver also devalued the silver currency, which led to the pouring of American Silver into China in large amounts, through the exchange of Chinese goods. This was once a headache for the Spanish colonists in the Philippines. In July 1584, the local government sent a letter to Philip II of Spain, saying, "Your Majesty has issued laws prohibiting taking coins outside of your territory or trading with pirates, but the Chinese have taken away all the coins every year."[26] In June 1586, a letter to the King of Spain said, "we can only trade with the Chinese with gold and silver."[27] It also showed that they had nothing valuable to exchange with Chinese people. As a result, most silver coins went to China.

After occupying the silver-producing areas in the Americas, Spain once became one of the richest countries in Europe, and the Spanish in the Philippines were the first beneficiaries of gold and silver in the Americas. Therefore, the consumption capacity of the Philippines was

---

[26] Taimin Chen, *Sino Philippine Relations and Overseas Chinese in the Philippines* (Hong Kong: Hong Kong Chaoyang Press, 1985), 144.
[27] Chen, *Sino Philippine Relations*, 152.

greatly improved, and what they demanded was mainly Chinese goods. It was under the large supply of American silver coins that Chinese copper coins lost their currency status in this region.

4. Brunei

Brunei was called Bo Ni in ancient times. In the third year of Yong Le, Abdul Majid Hassan, the King of Bo Ni, sent envoys to pay tribute to the Ming dynasty, and, in return, Emperor Ming Cheng Zu sent envoys to confer Abdul the title of king. Soon, Abdul Majid Hassan personally led a large number of officials and relatives to China and received a warm reception from the Chinese side. Unfortunately, Abdul Majid Hassan died of illness in Nanjing. The Ming government gave him an elaborate funeral. His tomb is now at the south foot of Tortoise Mountain, Dongxianghua village, in Nanjing.

Xia Wang, the son of Abdul Majid Hassan, returned home to take over the throne. The Chinese sent people to protect him back to Bo Ni. Later, he came to China again and was warmly received by China. He returned after staying in Nanjing for a few months.

Song coins have been unearthed many times in Brunei, such as Xian Ping Yuan Bao, Yuan Feng Tong Bao, Kai Xi Tong Bo, etc. Chinese shipwrecks were often found in the vicinity of Brunei, with a large number of coins on them.[28]

5. Burma

In the Funan period, Myanmar had tin coins and silver coins. In the fifth century, the coins were cast with auspicious patterns and the Chinese character "Five," which was obviously influenced by Chinese

[28] Yingsheng Liu, *Silk Road Culture: Maritime* (Hangzhou: Zhejiang People's Publishing House, 1995), 71.

Five Zhu coins.[29] In the Yuan dynasty, Wudie (present-day Burma) used silver coins, each of which weighed "2 Qian and 8 Fen, equivalent to twelve Liang of Zhong Tong banknotes."[30] It could be exchanged for 5,020 seashells.

Yunnan began to use shell coins from the late Spring and Autumn Period,[31] and there were many records of the use of shell coins in the Tang and Song dynasties. Most shell coins were in circulation in Western and Southern Yunnan. Yunnan didn't produce shellfish itself. Where did these shell coins come from? Mr. Li Yan believes that Yunnan's shells originated from Myanmar.[32] The way from Dali, Baoshan and Tengchong in western Yunnan to Myanmar, India and Western Asian countries constituted part of the ancient land Silk Road. In his book *Shell and Copper Coins in the Culture of Yunnan*, French researcher Mi Pirazoli speculated that there might have been three ways to import shellfish into Yunnan: first, southeast coast of China—Nanyue—Yunnan; second, the South China Sea—Northern Vietnam—Red River—Yunnan; third, India—Myanmar—Thailand—Yunnan.[33] Seashells had once been used as a currency in Indochina South to Yunnan, and in most countries in Southern and Western Asia, such as India, Burma, Bangladesh, Thailand and Laos.

The Yuan dynasty was the heyday of the use of seashells in Yunnan. Li Jing, in Da De period of Yuan Cheng Zong, wrote in his *Customs of Various Nationalities* of *Brief Account of Yunnan*, "They trade with shellfish, which are commonly called ba." It was recorded in

---

29 Zhiqiang Dai, "The Relationship between Chinese Ancient Coins and Coins in East and Southeast Asia," *Asian Coins*, no. 1 (1999).

30 Dayuan Wang, *A Brief Account of Foreign Islands* (Beijing: Zhong Hua Book Company, 1981).

31 Shouchuan Yang, *Study on Currency of Shells* (Kunming: Yunnan University Press, 1997), 4.

32 Yang, *Study on Currency of Shells*, 2.

33 Mi Pilazoli, "Shell and Copper Coins in Culture of Yunnan," *Academic Journal of Yunnan Nationalities Institute*, no. 1 (1994).

Biographic Sketches of Shi Zu of *History of Yuan* that "in September in the 19th year of Zhi Yuan, gold was stipulated to be used for taxation in Yunnan Province, and shell coins could be converted into gold. Each Qian of gold was worth 20 Suo of shells." Yunnan was also the only place where seashells could be used in the Yuan dynasty. Shell coins were also found in great quantities in many tombs unearthed in Yunnan Province, such as Jianchuan, Heqing, Dengchuan, Dali, Xiaguan, Binchuan, Weishan and Chuxiong.[34] As a result of the influx of foreign shell coins, those in Yunnan have even been divided into genuine and fake ones. The *Biographic Sketches of Cheng Zong* of *History of Yuan* recorded that, "in November of the 9th year of Da De, 10,000 Ding of Chao (banknotes) were assigned to Yunnan Province to circulate together with the shell coins. The shells that were not native were regarded as the fake ones."

[34] Dadao Wang, "On the Coins Unearthed in Yunnan," *Yunnan Cultural Relics*, no. 5 (1988).

CHAPTER SIX

CURRENCY CULTURE EXCHANGE BETWEEN CHINA AND CENTRAL ASIAN COUNTRIES

I. Five Zhu Coins of Qiuci

Qiuci was an oasis country on the northern route of the Silk Road. Its center was located in the area of Kuqa. It existed roughly from the first century AD to the middle and late Tang dynasty (the eighth century), with a history of about seven hundred years. It broke away from China's control for some time during the Six Dynasties. The Chinese have long enjoyed watching the dance of this country.

In 1928, Chinese scholar Huang Wenbi found a coin, in Xinjiang, with the Chinese characters Five Zhu and also some unreadable writing on it. Later, this was confirmed to be Qiuci scripts. From 1957 to 1958, the archaeological team of the Chinese Academy of Sciences discovered eight more coins like this in Kuqa. In 1980, two hundred twenty pieces were found in the Luntai ancient city, Xinjiang. In 1983, Xinjiang Archaeology Department found another two coins in Bachu County, and, in 1986, a large number of such coins were found on the high platform of Kudong County, with a total of more than ten thousand pieces.[1]

---

[1] Caijing Chen, "On the Exchange of Currency Culture between China and the West from the Perspective of the Ancient Local Currency Unearthed in Xinjiang," *Miscellaneous Cultures*, no. 1 (1991).

Fig. 6-1 The shape of the Qiuci Five Zhu is similar to that of Five Zhu coins. The front inscriptions are Qiuci words, "Five Zhu," originated from Indian Brahmi language, and the Chinese "Five Zhu" is cast on the back.

The coins with both Chinese and Qiuci words were first cast in the Three Kingdoms period, and were used in the Jin, Southern and Northern dynasties. The peak time should be in the middle of the Southern and Northern Dynasties (the fourth to the fifth century), and their circulation was not ceased until the early Tang dynasty (mid-seventh century). The currency of Qiuci state experienced four periods. The first used Five Zhu coins of the Han dynasty, then the imitation coins of the Five Zhu of Han, next the coins with both Chinese and Qiuci words, and, finally, the casting of coins with only Qiuci words.

The appearance of the coins with Qiuci words shows the minimum influence of the Han culture on the area at that time, when Qiuci was already under the control of Turks. Soon, these areas entered the territory of the Tang dynasty, due to the defeat of the Turks by Tang. Qiuci had been part of the Western Regions Prefecture and Anxi Prefecture of the Tang dynasty.

Qiuci script was a reflection of the influence of Indian culture. The letters of Qiuci script were derived from the Brahmi alphabet of Sanskrit. As Buddhism spread eastward, in the process of translating Buddhist scriptures, Qiuci people began to spell their own language with Brahmi letters, and then it gradually evolved into Qiuci writing. It belonged to Tokharian language. The early Buddhist scriptures in China were translated from this language. Later, it was replaced by Uighur scripts. After Islam came to the East, Kuqa began to be Islamized, and Qiuci writing became a dead language.

II. Western Spread of Currency Culture in the Tang Dynasty

The Five Zhu of the Sui dynasty continued to be used at the beginning of the Tang dynasty, but it was light and confusing. In the fourth year of Wu De, in the reign of Emperor Tang Gao Zong (AD 621), "Five Zhu coins were discarded and Kai Yuan Tong Bao coins were put into use, each with a diameter of 8 Fen."[2] The Kai Yuan Tong Bao coins followed the shape of the Square Hole coins of the Qin dynasty. Each Wen weighed two Zhu and four Si, equivalent to about 4 g in weight. It was stipulated that ten Wen coins should weigh one Liang, and each Wen weigh one Qian, while the weight of a thousand Wen should be six Jin and four Liang. This was also the key to the decimal changes in Chinese weight and balance measure. This reform of the currency system had a profound influence on the history of Chinese currency. Currency was no longer named according to its weight, but called Tong Bao from then on.

Kai Yan Tong Bao played an important role in the Silk Road trade. The Tang Empire held an open and tolerant policy. Through the Silk Road, merchants were attracted from Persia, Byzantium, Arabia, Africa and the Indian peninsula. By sending envoys, or paying tributes, these countries traded in Chang'an, the international city at that time. The flourishing trade enabled the Tang dynasty to reach an unprecedented

---

[2] Xu Liu, *Book of Tang Vol. 48: Food Records I* (Beijing: Zhong Hua Book Company, 1975), 2094.

degree of openness. There were many kinds of commodities traded in Chang'an by various countries, and their distribution range was very wide, almost all over Asia. Persian merchants sold rare treasures and horses, lions, rhinoceroses, etc., and were almost the most common traders on the Silk Road. During the years of Wu De, Tajik envoys paid tribute to Chang'an more than forty times. Merchants from Western Regions and Central Asia set up shops, jewelry stores and hotels in Chang'an. After having a big drink in the hotels run by the *Hu* merchants (Hu was a name for the ethnicity in the Northern and Western Regions of China in ancient times), the Chinese poet Li Bai left the famous lyric, "Where are you going after you appreciate all the flowers? Joyously you enter the wine shop of the Hu girls."

The Tang dynasty ceramics became the new favorite of the Silk Road trade, and compass, papermaking, gunpowder and movable type printing also spread widely through the Silk Road. Kai Yuan Tong Bao became the general currency of the trade there. At the beginning of the twentieth century, Stein secretly took away 311 Kai Yuan Tong Bao coins and 417 Qian Yuan Zhong Bao from Xinjiang. In the exploration of Loulan in 1979, more than 970 pieces of Kai Yuan Tong Bao coins were found in the Northeast of Lop Nur. There were also Kai Yuan Tong Bao unearthed in Uzbekistan, India and other countries.

1. Sogdiana

The central and eastern regions between the Syr Darya and Amu Darya rivers in Central Asia were known as Sogdian. It was a nation in ancient Central Asia and its people were the ancestors of Tajik and Uzbek people. The old city of Sogde, built in the fourth and fifth centuries, was once the capital of Hephthalite. The city flourished at the turn of the seventh and eighth centuries, when China's Tang dynasty was in its heyday.

With Central Asia entering the territory of China in 658, the exchanges between countries in the Western Regions and the mainland of China became more extensive and profound than ever. Naturally, Chinese coin culture would have an influence on this area.

Many round copper coins with square holes have been found in the site of Sogdiana; they were imitations of Chinese coins. They were similar to the coins of ancient China in the shape. The only difference lay in the inscriptions on the coins. On the obverse side of Sogdian coins was the king's emblem, and on the back was the king's name and title in Sogdian. The large-scale imitation and circulation of Chinese-type square-hole copper coins reflected China's influence on this area. The coins in the Sogdian area were completely in accordance with the Kai Yuan Tong Bao coins of the Tang dynasty, so they could only have been cast after 627. Now, a large number of Sogdian coins have been found in China and Central Asian countries. The Kai Yuan Tong Bao and Sogdian coins were also found in the ancient city of Suiye (today's Tokamak, in Kyrgyzstan).

Sogdian coins were first studied by Russian numismatist Smorinova. In 1981, she introduced the Sogdian coins from before 1573, in the form of a catalogue. The book *Sogde Copper Coins Catalogue* recorded 131 kinds of emblems. Different regions and leaders can be distinguished by different emblems. For example, the three-tail pattern was the mark of Samarkand, the four-tail pattern was that of Bukhara, the harp mark was that of Fergana, and the trident was that of Togus. Instead of using the traditional method of hammering and pressing in making Central Asian coins, they completely adopted the mould casting of the Tang dynasty, so did the local copper coins, without inner holes, in this period.

2. Uighur

It is now generally acknowledged that the Hui Hu people are the ancestors of Uighur. However, there is still debate over it in academia. In the late eighth century, Uighurs created their own scripts, but they were not spread widely. In the middle of the ninth century, Uighurs moved westward to Gaochang, Beiting and other places to establish their own state. It was during this period that the Uighur made coins. The Japanese researcher Opyeong Changhong mentioned two Uighur coins in his *Records of East Asia Money* and believed they were cast during Muyu Khan's time.

In 1981, a Uighur coin was unearthed in Jimusar County, Xinjiang. In addition, coin lovers in Shanghai and Tianjin also collected two Uighur coins. The Uighur coins reflect the influence of Chinese culture on Central Asia because the coins were made in round shape with square holes, imitating Kai Yuan Tong Bao's pattern from the Tang dynasty.

3. Tujishi

In *Orkhon Monuments*, Khan of Tujue described the trade between the Turks and the Han people: "I have established a friendly relationship with the Han people. They give us a lot of gold, silver and silk. The words of them are always sweet, and their goods are always exquisite. Using sweet words and exquisite objects, the Han people tempt distant residents to be close to them."[3]

Tujishi was one of the ten tribes of Western Turks who lived in the Ili River Basin. It rose in Central Asia in the middle of the eighth century. Tujishi Khanate was recognized by the Tang dynasty, and its successive Khans accepted the conferment from the emperors of the

---

[3] Chuanming Rui, *Research on Ancient Turkic Inscriptions* (Shanghai: Shanghai Classics Publishing House, 1998), 218.

Tang dynasty.

Tujishi coins are now rare, but they were found in many places, since the early twentieth century. In 1906, B. C. G. Mannerhein, a Finn, was sent to Northwest China to carry out military intelligence activities. He had obtained two pieces of Sogdian Tujishi coins in Hotan. Le Coq, a German, also acquired this kind of copper coin on his second expedition to Turpan.

Influenced by Kai Yuan Tong Bao, Tujishi coins were round copper coins with a square hole in the middle, weighing about 4.88 g-6.30 g. The inscriptions on the front were Sogdian, and on the back was a bow-like pattern. At the same time, they had some distinctive, national characteristics.

In 1938, the largest amount of Tujishi coins in one site were found in the ancient city of Talas, Kyrgyzstan. All of the money discovered was Tujishi coins, with bow-shaped emblems on the back, except some Sogdian coins.[4] They were also cast in the shape of Kai Yuan Tong Bao of the Tang dynasty, with an outer diameter of 2.4 cm and a weight of 5.1 g-5.5 g. In 1929, the archaeologist Huang Wenbi collected another coin of Tujishi, in Kuqa. In the 1950s, Soviet archaeologists found fifty-seven pieces of Tujishi coins, in Suiye; later, they collected thirty-nine more pieces. In Xinjiang, Gansu, Inner Mongolia, Shanghai and other places in China, Tujishi coins were also found. Some of them are now in private collections.

Smorinova, a numismatic scholar of the former Soviet Union, summed up three types of Sogdian Tujishi coins, either discovered by her predecessors or by herself. The inscriptions mainly had three meanings.[5] The first meant copper coin. This kind of coin not only imitated the form of the coins of mainland China, but also took its name

---

[4] A. Bernstein, "On Turkic Coins," in *Collected Papers of Oriental Museum*, ed. Winter Palace Museum, (St. Petersburg: Winter Palace Museum, 1940).

[5] Ruji Niu, "A Study of Tujishi Coins," *Chinese Coins*, no. 3 (1988).

from the Central Plains. The second was the unit of weight, which was equivalent to Qian, in Chinese. The third had the meaning of copper.

There were two kinds of symbols on the back of Tujishi coins. One was an arched mark, found in Suiye and Turpan, and the other was the pattern of two bows crossed together, found in Kucha and other places.[6] Until now, there has been no explanation about the symbols on the back of the coins.

Tujishi had a close relationship with the Tang dynasty and was highly valued by them for helping to wipe out the Western Tujue. In the Tang dynasty, Hu people in the Western Regions were assigned with military power. The famous general Ge Shuhan was a Tujishi. In Lintao County, there is a Monument of Ge Shuhan, which can be dated back to the Tang dynasty. Some poems of Tang dynasty also praised Ge Shuhan. Even Li Bai wrote poems to eulogize him. These historical backgrounds pave the way for the inflow of Tujishi coins into Gansu Province.[7]

The Tang dynasty was an age when China had the greatest influence on Central Asia. Kai Yuan Tong Bao was an international currency in this period, and it also affected the currency form of some countries in Central Asia. According to the unearthed materials, Wen was widely used in Central Asia as the unit of currency, during this period. There was also the loan word "Wen," in Sogdian, on Tujishi coins.

III. Taugast Coins of Karakhanid

The Karakhanid was called the Black Khanid in *the History of Song Dynasty*. In recent years, Chinese historians and numismatists have called it the Black Khanid dynasty. It was established in southern

---

[6] Niu, "A Study of Tujishi Coins."

[7] Liushuo Kang, "A Summary of the Silk Road Foreign and Western Region Coins Unearthed in Gansu Province," *Financial research in Inner Mongolia: Special Issue on Coins*, no. 4 (1993).

Xinjiang and Central Asia from the tenth to thirteenth centuries, with Kashgar as its center. Islam had been introduced there at that time. Kara means black, which also has the meaning of being great and supreme.[8]

The Islamic Black Khanid dynasty destroyed the Buddhist Khotan regime by force and occupied the vast land from southern Xinjiang to Central Asia. From then on, the Black Khanid had a direct relationship with the Northern Song dynasty. In 1063, the Black Khanid sent envoys to offer gifts to the Song dynasty, and, in turn, Song named its king "King of Black Khanid." Later, Black Khanid offered beads and jade to the Northern Song dynasty, and was rewarded with more than 1.5 million Qian.[9]

There were rich materials about the coins of the Black Khanid dynasty unearthed in recent years. In March 1980, Black Khanid coins, in kilns, were discovered in Ashitu, Xinjiang. It was at this time that the largest number of Black Khanid coins was unearthed in Xinjiang, with a total of about 130 kg and eighteen thousand pieces, all of which were copper coins.[10] Karakhan (Black Khanid) coins were also discovered in Gansu, in 1987 and 1992. In the former Soviet Union era, more and more Karakhan coins were found in Tajikistan, southern Turkmen, Kyrgyz, Uzbekstan and North Tajikistan.

The rulers of the Karakhanid usually had the title Taugast Khan. Taugast was the Western term for China. Some scholars believe that it was the transliteration of the West for Tangjiazi, which some Central Asian countries called themselves, while others claim that it was the

---

8 Qixiang Jiang, *Karakhanid Coins of Xinjiang* (Urumqi: Volksverlag Xinjiang, 1990).

9 Tuo Tuo and Arutu, *History of Song Dynasty: Khotan biography* (Beijing: Zhong Hua Book Company, 1985).

10 Qixiang Jiang, "A Brief Report on the Cleaning Up of the Kiln of Karahan Dynasty Coins Unearthed in Artux County, Xinjiang," *Xinjiang Finance*, supplement II (1988).

Central Asian countries' pronunciation of Tuoba, the pioneering family of the Northern Wei Dynasty.[11] The coins of Karakhanid include three kinds: Yusuf Arslan Khan's coins, Sulayman Kadrhan Taugast coins and Muhammad Arslan Khan's coins. Among the unearthed Black Khanid coins, only a few were Taugast ones.

IV. Coins of West Liao

The founder of the Western Liao dynasty was Yelü Dashi, who had presided over the military affairs of Liao state and fought against the Song and Jin dynasties. In February of AD 1130, he ascended to the throne in Yemili city and became emperor himself. At the beginning of AD 1134, he made Balashagun the capital of Western Liao. After more than ten years of war, the Western Liao Empire was established, with a vast land ranging from the upper reaches of the Tula River in the east, to the Aral Sea in the west, from the Balkhash Lake in the north, to the Amu Darya River in the south. It was known as "Hara Qidan," throughout history, which meant "Black Qidan," in Chinese. The Western Liao dynasty adopted the policy of Jimi (a policy of controlling the remote areas of different ethnicities without changing the local customs and social institutions) in the states dependent on it and created a feudal empire with the characteristics of Chinese laws and regulations.

The loose policy objectively guaranteed social stability, promoted the economic development and the prosperity of domestic and foreign trade, which led to the continuous expansion of currency circulation in Western Liao.

In 1998, the Newsletter (No.158) of *the Oriental Numismatic Society* published an article entitled "Kangguo Coins of Kara Qidan

---

[11] Mingwei Li, ed., *History of Silk Road Trade* (Lanzhou: Gansu People's Publishing House, 1997), 412.

(Western Liao)" by Dr. T. D. Yih of the Netherlands, which showed several rubbings of coins sent to him a few years ago by Mr. Wei Yuewang, a numismatic scientist in Inner Mongolia. Among the rubbings, five were Kang Guo Tong Bao coins. It is true that the coins of the Western Liao dynasty have been recorded in Chinese Numismatic works. For example, Kang Guo Tong Bao was mentioned in the fifteenth volume of *Gu Quan Hui* (Collection of Ancient Quan). So far, a large number of coins of ancient Central Asian countries have been found in China, the former Soviet Union and some countries in Central Asia. Documents and archaeological materials have proved that the Western Liao dynasty allowed the coins of Karakhanid to circulate within the dynasty and in the areas directly under its control. What's more, the original mints in the territories under the direct control of the Western Liao dynasty were also allowed to continue to make Karakhan coins.

The Western Liao dynasty was located on the Silk Road, and the society was stable. Since it adopted the policy of using the original currencies in its affiliated areas, there was no unified currency in the dynasty. Gold, as a natural currency, began to circulate smoothly in West Liao. As a result, gold coins, or Dinar, became a means of circulation and payment. Many cities made gold coins. Before the tenth century, silver coins were widely circulated in Central Asia. After the eleventh century, due to the decline in the quality of silver coins, the scope of circulation narrowed. The undervalued silver coins could only circulate in the country that had issued the money.[12] Copper coins still occupied an important position in the field of currency circulation. Judging from the historical currency remains, which were unearthed in recent years, the coins of Karakhanid took up a large proportion of the circulating market of the Western Liao dynasty, in this period.

---

[12] Б. Г. Gafurov, *History of Tajikistan in Central Asia*, trans. Xiao Zhixing (Beijing: China Social Sciences Press, 1985), 216.

V. Arabization of Mongol Khanate Coins

In the Qin and Han dynasties, there were Eastern Hu people and Xiongnu people on the Mongolian grassland. Later, the Eastern Hu were defeated by the Xiongnu, and some of them fled to the Greater Khingan Range. The Mongolian people were the descendants of this branch of Eastern Hu people.

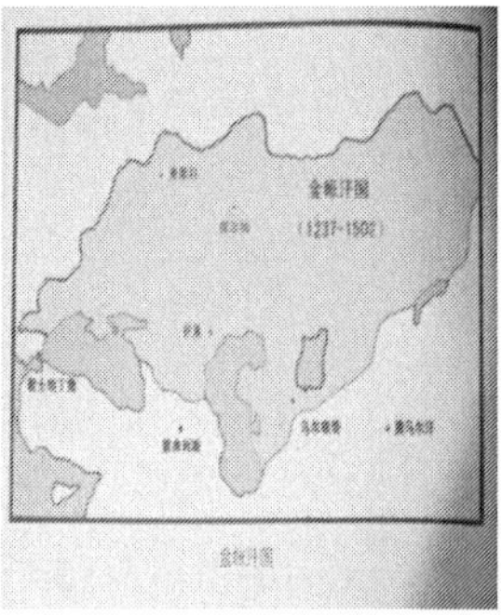

Fig. 6-2 Kipchak Khanate

At the end of Tang dynasty, the Mongolian ancestors returned to the Buerhan Mountains, on the upper reaches of the Onon Gol River. After several centuries of growth, Temujin, the leader of the Mongol people, annexed the Mongolian Plateau by force, and was called great Khan, with the honor title Genghis Khan. In AD 1206, when Genghis Khan unified all of the Mongolian tribes, he granted the land to his four sons. The four Khanates will now be described.

Kipchak Khanate was also called the Golden Horde. Genghis Khan's eldest son, Jochi, was granted the command of the region. Officially established in AD 1242, the Kipchak Khanate had the widest territory among the four Khanate states. As Jochi died earlier, the actual founder of this Khanate was his second son, Badu.

Ilkhanate was built by Hulagu, the son of Tolui, the fourth son of Genghis Khan. In 1256, IlKhanate was founded. When Kublai Khan called himself the Mongolian Khan, IlKhanate recognized him as the patriarch until his death.

Chagatai Khanate was the manor of Chagatai, the second son of Genghis Khan.

Fig. 6-3 Jochi branch after Genghis Khan

Gedei Khanate was the Fief of Ogodei, the third son of Genghis Khan. It had the smallest territory among the four.

The coins of the Four Great Khans (from Genghis Khan to Tai Zong Ogodei, Ding Zong Gui You and Xian Zong Meng Ge) have not been found in China. Their coins have been mainly unearthed in Central Asia, but their number is very small. There is a view in Western numismatics that, when Genghis Khan captured the Khwarazm, he then cast coins. At that time, Central Asia was already the world of Islam. On the obverse of these coins was Arabic inscription and on the reverse was: "Genghis Khan, the greatest Khan of justice." There are not many coins in the world with the name of Genghis Khan on them or thought to be related to Genghis Khan, so they are of high value. In England, a gold coin of Genghis Khan is worth one thousand to two thousand five hundred pounds. There have been only thirty-seven gold coins, four silver coins and three copper coins discovered so far. These coins of Genghis Khan should be studied carefully because, although China has a very rich collection of Mongolian historical materials, there is no record of Genghis Khan's coins.

Except for the several kinds of coins of Genghis Khan that were not regular in weight, the silver coins of the other three Khans weighed, on average, about 2.0 g-2.7 g each. Each Khanate had its own national emblem, which was put on the coins. Among the four Khanate States, only the coins of Kipchak Khanate and IlKhanate were specially struck and issued by the central government. In the other two khanates, the local rulers were responsible for the coinage. In Kipchak Khanate, on the money's surface was the place and year of its production, while the name of the Khan and compliments for him were on the back of the coin. The money design of Chagatai Khanate was slightly different. On the front, was the common Koran Scripture, while the back of the coin bore the praise of the Great Khan, the casting place, the year and the emblem of the clan.

Chagatai Khanate had a complete monetary system and coinage institution. There were three kinds of materials for coinage: gold, silver and copper. In the matter of the shape, each material had its own large, small or medium-sized coin. As to the text, there were no less than one hundred kinds. The characters, patterns and emblems on the coins were rich and colorful.

Chagatai coins have always been the concern of the coin circle. As early as a century ago, some Chinese and foreign archaeological explorers went to search for treasure, and successfully collected some Chagatai coins. In recent years, a large number of Chagatai coins have been unearthed in certain areas of Xinjiang. Even now, there are still sporadic or small batches of gold, silver and copper coins unearthed, and the specific quantity is difficult to estimate. At present, Chagatai silver coins have been found in Kuqa, Charkhlik, Turpan, Mori, Qitai, Changji, Bole, Huocheng, etc. In addition to the use of Kufi on the coins of Chagatai, Kublai Khan's Phag's-pa script, which had been created by Kublai Khan's national master, also appeared on the silver coins of this Khanate. Moreover, the Five Zhu coins had an impact on them too. Some Chagatai coins, unearthed in Xinjiang, had the simplified "Zhu" on the back.[13] In Beijing, there were also coins unearthed with Arabic inscriptions of Central Asia, from the fifteenth century. It has been confirmed that the silver coins were minted in the time of Shah Rukh (1377-1447) of the Timur Empire in Central Asia.

Fig. 6-4 "Ji Guo Hui Min" coin of Kipchak Khanate

Some Mongol Khanates also issued coins with Chinese characters, such as the Ji Guo Hui Min (means "aid the country and benefit the people") coins of the Kipchak Khanate. In the 1990s, two pieces of Chinese and Arabic coins were unearthed at the No.1 site of Hemelevka, near the city of Saratov, in the lower reaches of the Volga River, in Russia. On the coins, there were Chinese characters "Ji Guo Hui Min" and Arabic words, as well as the emblem of Mengu-Timur of The Golden Horde.

Fig. 6-5 Sargulid coin with Chinese character "Bao"

---

13 Qixiang Jiang, "On the Currency of the Western Regions in the Yuan Dynasty of Mongolia," *Xinjiang Coins*, no. 4 (1995).

In Sargulid, the vassal state of IlKhanate, coins with the Chinese character "Bao" were cast. Specifically, there were three types in existence. The first type was the silver coin weighing 2.7 g, 21.5 mm-22.3 mm in diameter. The obverse side was Arabic. Numismatists can only identify "minting," "year," "just Khan" and "Islamic calendar year 666 (AD 1267)." A Chinese character "Bao" was lying in the middle of the Arabic words. On the reverse side of the coin, were the Shahada and the name of the queen of Sargulid in Arabic. The second type was the copper coin. Besides the Arabic words above, there was the name of the casting place—"Shelazi." A Chinese character "Bao" was also in the middle. On the back, was the hexagonal Star of David. The name of the queen of Sargulid was in the center of the star in Arabic. The third was the silver coin that weighed 2.59 g and had a diameter of 21.5 mm. On the front side, the numismatists only recognize the Arabic "just" and "year 665 of the Islamic calendar (AD 1266)." There was a Chinese character "Bao" in the middle. On the back, were, also, Arabic Shahada and the name of the queen of Sargulid. In addition, some coins with similar shapes and inscriptions were made from different moulds. Each weighed 2.82 g and had a diameter of 28 mm. The year of casting was also 665 of Islamic calendar.

The issue of Bao coins by the vassal country Sargulid had something to do with the trade between the Persian Gulf and China, at that time. In 628 of the Islamic calendar, Sargulid controlled Kish Island, an important island in the Persian Gulf. Thus, Kish Island became an important transit point for trade between China and the West in the Persian Gulf, and business tax became an important source of tax revenue for Sargulid. In order to better trade with merchants from the Yuan dynasty, Sargulid issued Arabic-style currency with the

Chinese character Bao.[14]

The Chagatai Khanate issued coins with Chinese characters, in the Bukhara area. During the Mongolian Yuan dynasty, Chagatai Khanate issued two kinds of silver-plated copper coins in the Bukhara area, with the Chinese characters "Buhua" and "Ke," respectively. The Buhua silver-plated copper coin weighed 4.3 g. On the obverse side, there was a single coil in the bead pattern around the coin. Inside the coil, the Arabic "Bukhura coin" was in the center, surrounded by the Arabic "the coin was struck in 660 (AD 1262) in a glorious city." In the center of the back side of the coin were the Chinese characters "Bu Hua." The surrounding Arabic words and patterns were the same as those on the front.

The silver-plated copper coin of Ke weighed 6.6 g. On the obverse side, there was a single coil in the bead pattern around the coin. Inside the coil was Arabic, and in the center was the Arabic "Bukhara coin." There were six arched patterns around it. Between each pattern was an Arabic word, "King." On the back of the coin, there was a Chinese character "Ke," in the center, and the Arabic words around it were a little vague; they read, "The coin was cast in xx in 663 (AD 1265)."

From 1262 to 1272, Chagatai Khanate, Kipchak Khanate and IlKhanate all issued coins with both Chinese and Arabic words on them. This was not just a coincidence, or out of the trade demand of the Silk Road, but, instead, because of their recognition of Kublai Khan, the Mongolian Khan, who the Chinese tended to assimilate. Later, they stopped issuing coins with Chinese characters, partly because of the gradual disintegration of the Mongol Empire and partly because of the difference between their Islamic culture and the Chinese

---

[14] Tong Cheng, "A Study on the 'Bao' Coins in Fars Area of Ili Khanate," *Research on the Western Regions*, no. 4 (2008).

culture of the Yuan dynasty. Therefore, the Islamic Kipchak Khanate, the Chagatai Khanate and the IlKhanate stopped issuing coins with Chinese characters, one after another.[15]

VI. Coins in the Areas to the West of Qing Dynasty

1. Yarkand

Yarkand Khanate was founded in 1514, and its capital was Yarkand (now Shache). The territory included today's southern Xinjiang and the part to the west of Jiayuguan, in the Hexi Corridor. After the mid-sixteenth century, the Yarkand Khanate entered its heyday.

In 1646 (the third year of Shun Zhi), Turpan and Hami regions first paid tribute to the Qing dynasty, with the consent of Yarkand Khan Abdulla. In 1653 (the tenth year of Shun Zhi), Abdulla Khan sent envoys to the Qing dynasty and established its subordinate relationship. From then, the friendly relationship of tribute and trade was maintained for nearly a hundred years.

Located in the main part of the ancient Silk Road, in Xinjiang, the trade in Yarkand Khanate was prosperous and the commodity economy was developed. The coins of the Khanate have been mentioned many times in historical records, but, so far, no coin of Yarkand has been found.[16] Through field investigation, Xinjiang's coin researchers found that, before the Qing dynasty, there had been workshops for coin casting in Yarkand. Soon after destroying Yarkand, in 1678, the Junggar Khanate ordered the people of Yarkand region to make them a large number of coins. Obviously, they intended to use the original mint facilities and craftsmen in this area.

---

[15] Wei Yuan, "Research on the Issuance of Coins with Han and Arabic Words in Mongolian Khanates in 1262-1272," *Gansu Finance*, no.11 (2016).

[16] Liangtao Wei, *An Outline of the History of Yarkand Khanate* (Harbin: Heilongjiang Education Press, 1998), 201.

2. Junggar

At the end of Ming dynasty and the beginning of Qing dynasty, Wala rose in Northwest China, with the name of Oyirad. It was divided into four parts: Junggar, Heshuote, Dorbet and Torghut. At the beginning of the seventeenth century, the Junggar tribe gradually expanded under the leadership of Batur Hongtaiji, pushing the other three tribes aside. Before that, the Oyirads had paid tribute to the Ming and Qing dynasties.

At the time of Galdan, Junggar took control over the vast area to the south of Mt. Tianshan. Galdan sent envoys to Russia many times and, instigated by Tsarist Russia, invaded Kharka Mongolia in 1688 (the twenty-seventh year of Emperor Kang Xi). Galdan even proposed to divide the country equally with Emperor Kang Xi. In 1698 (the thirty-fifth year of Kang Xi), the Qing army annihilated Galdan's main force in Zhaomoduo. The following year, Galdan died.

After the death of Galdan, Tsewang Arabtan (1697-1727) and his son Galdan Tseren (1727-1745) became Junggar Khan, successively. The social situation in Junggar was relatively stable and its social economy made great progress. During their reign, Junggar strengthened its trade with the Central Plains. The social economy of Junggar had reached unprecedented prosperity.

After the destruction of Yarkand Khanate, the Junggar Khanate forged Junggar Poole coins, in the Yarkand area. Since there was no mint base in Junggar, they could only use the equipment and technology of Yarkand Khanate. The coins were dated from 1700 to 1745, that is to say, during the reign of Tsewang Arabtan and Galdan Tseren. Poole coins were made of pure copper, without lead or tin, so they were red. They were oval in shape and sharp at one end, like peach kernels. They was small and thick with no holes in the middle. The name of the casting place was inscribed on one side in the language of Chagatai. The name of Junggar Khan was cast on the other side in Oyirad scripts. The weight ranged from 6.3 g to 8.2 g. The casting method was striking and pressing. Every fifty pieces of Poole were worth one Liang of silver. The Poole was generally considered to be circulating in the vast area from the south of Mt. Tianshan and to the Yili area in the north.

3. The Coins of Yaqub Beg

After occupying the vast areas of Southern and Northern Xinjiang, Yaqub Beg forcibly abolished all the currencies issued by the Qing government, in Xinjiang, and minted coins himself. The gold coin of Yaqub Beg was called the Tilla, which was round and nonporous, with an outer diameter of 21 mm and a weight of 7.3 g. The outer ring of the front was of Arabic style pattern, and the inner ring was Chagatay scripts of "Sultan Abdul Aziz Han (Khan)." The scripts on the back were "Zarb Daris-Saltanati Kashgar 1291" (meaning "made in the capital Kashgar in 1291"). 1291 in the Islamic calendar is equivalent to AD 1874. A Tilla amounted to twenty pieces of Tanga coins, or one Liang of silver.

Tanga was the general name of silver coins in Central Asia, also the name of the traditional silver unit in southern Xinjiang. Each silver coin of Tanga, made by Yaqub Beg, was worth five cents of silver, and twenty pieces were one Liang. Each Tanga was about 12-13 mm in diameter, 0.5 mm or 0.75 mm in thickness, and 1.45 g-1.7 g in weight. Chagatay scripts were used on both sides. On the obverse were the words "Abdul Aziz Han (Khan)." "Zarb Kashgar Latif 1291" were on the reverse side. Of course, the year of casting may have been different. Having been struck coarsely, the patterns and characters on a Tanga coin were always biased to one side, so it was almost impossible to see the whole picture. The shape, size and thickness of each Tanga silver coin was extremely different, and some were even thick in one half and thin in the other half, so it was difficult to find two coins that were exactly the same as each other.

The copper coins of Yaqub Beg were minted from 1874 to 1876. They each weighed 3.3 g and were about 2 mm thick, with a diameter of about 14 mm. They were made of red copper. On both the front and the back sides were Chagatay scripts, “Abdul Aziz Hanan” and “Zatb Kashgar,” respectively.

Among the three kinds of coins—Tilla, Tanga and Poole—the gold and copper coins were very few, and the Tanga silver coins were the most widely used.[17] Yaqub Beg’s coins were purely the currency of foreign invaders. The inscription “Abdul Aziz Han (Khan)” on the front was the name of the Turkish Sultan because Yaqub Beg colluded with Turkey and regarded Turkey as its suzerain.

[17] Yuan Mu, *Currency History of Xinjiang in Qing Dynasty* (Urumqi: Xinjiang University Press, 1994), 120.

CHAPTER SEVEN

CURRENCY CULTURE EXCHANGE BETWEEN CHINA AND SOUTHERN ASIAN COUNTRIES

I. Trade and Currency Culture Exchange between China and India

China and India are close neighbors. Trade between China and India has been carried out since an early time. It is said that the history of trade between China and India is longer than that of the Silk Road. Before the world-famous Silk Road was opened, India had been, to a certain extent, a transit point for Chinese products to travel westward.

As early as the second century BC, a large number of Chinese products appeared in the market of Bactria. These Chinese products were transited from India, or the, so-called, Sindhu. At that time, the Han dynasty tried, many times, to open up a commercial route through India to Central Asia, but all the attempts failed because of the bad geographical conditions. In the Han dynasty, when Chinese and Indian merchants were trading along the coast, they found the narrow Kra Isthmus in Thailand. Chinese merchants landed in Patan (the city of Nepal), crossed Kedah (in Northern Malaysia) and the Chongli River, and then transported their goods to Southeast Asia.[1]

In the Han dnasty, the maritime trade between China and India had been opened up, and it was also the terminal of Chinese merchants' navigation, at that time. The Chinese merchant ships set out from Hepu

[1] Doreen Soas, "Local Currency of Singapore," trans. Sheng Guanxi, *Inner Mongolia Financial Research: Special Issue of Coins*, no. 3 (1993).

and Xuwen in Guangdong Province and, after more than ten months' voyage, reached Huang Zhi, or Conjevaram on the east coast of India. There was another commercial route to Huang Zhi, which first arrived at Myanmar (then called Fushoudulu) by land, and then sailed to the Indian peninsula. In the Han dynasty, Guangdong was the center of economic exchanges between China and India.

Since the time of Emperor Han Wu Di, Huang Zhi had sent envoys, or rather, businessmen, to China many times. They exchanged their local products with the Han dynasty. According to the records of the Han dynasty, people at that time knew that the climate of India was similar to that of Hainan Island, in China. In the Han dynasty, the purpose of trade between China and India, from the perspective of the Chinese side, was to seek rare things, such as night pearls, gems and so on. At that time, the Han imperial court sent its own translators, with the sailors, to trade with the countries in India. Gold, ironware and the miscellaneous silk fabrics were the most attractive goods of Han. Iron, then, was still very new to India; they called iron "the thing from China." China's iron production technology had a great impact on India. Even after the people of India were able to produce iron for themselves, theyt still called iron "the thing from China."

After the opening of the Silk Road, the economic communication between China and India became even closer. The merchants of the two generally reached each other by land. Moreover, the records about the envoys from India to China are common in Chinese history books. In the Jin dynasty, Indian merchants had already built their own ships and crossed the South China Sea to trade with China. In the early Tang dynasty, the Ilysha dynasty rose in India. Its feudal economy was rather developed at the time the Chinese monk Xuanzang went to India. The thriving commodity economy boosted the economic exchanges between China and India more and more. It was also in the Tang dynasty that India was officially called Tintu, or Sindhu in Chinese.

In the Tang dynasty, there were mainly two commercial routes between China and India, namely, the sea route and the land route. Some trades were direct between China and India, while some were done through entrepot of Arabs. Chinese businessmen could reach the Persian Gulf then. The land route was a branch from the Silk Road to India for trade. The types of commodities for trade between the countries also became more various in that period. China exported silk, ceramics, metal ware, paper, lacquerware and so on. India's exports to China mainly included ivory, pearls, glass, sugar, Ceiba pentandra cloth, spices, Buddhist scriptures and religious goods.

During the Song dynasty, the Indian subcontinent maintained trade with China. Due to the highly frequent trade between China and India, some Indian businessmen came to settle in China's commercial ports and built some Hindu temples there. During the reign of Emperor Tai Zong in the early Northern Song dynasty (984-987), an Indian monk came to Quanzhou, China. Some Indian businessmen came to him with high respect, and donated gold and silver to him in great amounts, with which he finally built a Hindu temple, in Quanzhou. The temple, known as Baolin temple, remained in the Southern Song dynasty. In the South Gate of Quanzhou, there is also a temple site of Brahmanism. A large number of stone columns, column heads, pillar bases and door frames of ancient Indian style were found in the buildings of Kai Yuan Temple and Tian Fei temple, together with some sculptures of half-man-half-beast, or half-bird-half-beast shapes, which reflected the myths and stories of ancient India and Ceylon. All of these are relics of Brahmanic temples. In addition to Quanzhou, China, Quilon of India's Zhunian dynasty was also a good port for Chinese and Indian ships. Starting from Quanzhou of China, the ships sailed to Lamburi (today's Sumatra), for the winter, and they arrived in Quilon of India after another month's navigation the succeeding year, with the help of the trade wind.

In the Yuan dynasty, the trade between China and India was more developed, and the means of trade were various. There were those who bartered, and those who exchanged with gold and silver. Moreover, some countries in the Indian subcontinent used paper money, issued by the Yuan Empire. For example, Uday (Ulpur in the western part of the Indian subcontinent) used silver coins, seashells and the paper money of the Yuan dynasty at the same time. Ten Liang of Zhong Tong *Chao* could be exchanged for one silver coin or more than 11,520 seashells (Chao means bank notes). Marco Polo wrote in his travel notes that the most foreign merchant ships he had seen in the ports of India were Chinese ships. Ibn Battuta, the famous Arab traveler also mentioned that Chinese ships were the largest ones he had seen on the maritime route from India to China, some of which had four floors, with a capacity of more than one thousand people. What's more, he mentioned the great volume of gifts he had seen from the Chinese Emperor to the Delhi Sudan of India.

During the Ming dynasty, the trade between China and India was still very developed, but the center of transfer between the two sides had shifted to Guri port. Zheng He arrived in Guri of India, during his voyages to the West. The trade between China and India had also concentrated in the coastal areas of the Southwest. Guri (Garikuli) and Kezhi (Keqin) were both prosperous places. At that time, China exported silk, celadon, camphor and medicinal materials, while India exported pepper, betel nut, colored fabrics, banksia rose, frankincense, pearl and coral.

In 1964, Guangzhou Cultural Relics Administration Office cleaned up the tomb of a Ming dynasty eunuch, in Dongshan. Three foreign silver coins were found in the tomb, two of which were Bengali silver coins, cast by King Rukn al-din Barbak (AD 1459-1474). The owner of the tomb was Wei Juan, a famous eunuch of the Ming dynasty, who had been in charge of Shi Bo Ti Ju Si (equivalent to the present-day department of foreign trade affairs), in Guangzhou city. The unearthed Bengali silver coins show the prosperity of Sino Indian trade at that time.

At the beginning of the ninth century, customs checkpoints were set up, in Quilon of South India, which imposed duties on Chinese ships. Each Chinese ship was charged one thousand dirhams, while the ships of other countries paid only ten to twenty dirhams. The Dirham is a silver coin, weighing about 2.91 g-2.95 g.[2]

Some scholars have pointed out that the southern Silk Road had not only a "Sea Route" to the South of India, but also a "Land Route," directly leading to the North of India, namely, the road from Annam to Tintu, and the Magadha kingdom was the end of this passage. The Square Hole coins in South Asia were mainly brought to these countries through ancient Sino foreign trade. Although there are not yet many reports of Chinese ancient coins being unearthed in India, according to the analysis of the existing data, the quantity should be relatively large. In the late 1930s, the University of Sagar, in India, and then the Department of Archaeology of the Indian central government excavated the Sirpur ruins at the junction of the northern Andhra Pradesh and Maharashtra states, and unearthed a rich collection of ancient artifacts. In one Buddhist temple site, a Kai Yuan Tong Bao coin, cast in the Tang dynasty, was found.[3] In October 1942, twenty Chinese coins were unearthed in Vikraman village, Tamil Nadu, India, among which, three were Kai Yuan Tong Bao coins, eleven were Northern Song coins and four were Southern Song coins. All were

---

[2] Yizhong Yu, "Research on the Influence of Chinese Currency Culture on Neighboring Countries from the Perspective of Their Coins," in *Proceedings of the Sixth Symposium on Southeast Asian Historical Currencies and Maritime Silk Road Currencies,* ed. Zhejiang Coin Society (Ningbo: Ningbo Numismatic Society, June 1995).

[3] Guanxi Sheng, "Overseas Circulation and Significance of Ancient Chinese Coins," *Asian Coins*, no. 1 (1999).

collected in the Madras Government Museum of India.

On February 18, 1944, 1,787 Chinese coins were unearthed from a depot in Thaliketai village, in India. Of this batch of ancient Chinese coins, the earliest dated back to the Five Zhu coins of the Han dynasty, and the latest to the Xian Chun Yuan Bao coins of the Southern Song dynasty. Besides the 114 Kai Yuan Tong Bao coins of the Tang dynasty, the coins of Northern Song dynasty accounted for the next great in number to be found. In the late 1960s, another ancient Chinese coin hoard was found in Olayakunam village, in Southern India. It is of great significance that a Three Zhu coin was identified from the 323 Song dynasty coins. The Three Zhu coins were made in the first year of Jianyuan (AD 140) of Emperor Han Wu Di, and were abolished after only four years. Due to the small amount of casting and the short time of circulation, few of these coins have been unearthed, even in China. In the first century AD, Emperor Wu Di of Western Han sent Zhang Qian to the Western Regions twice to develop a good neighborly relationship with the countries in Central Asia and South Asia. According to the research of scholars, there were Chinese merchant ships at this time by sea route to the Huang Zhi state on the east coast of South India. The ancient Chinese coins unearthed in India reflect the friendly exchanges between China and India in economy and culture.[4] There are seventy-seven pictures of round blank coins with square holes in *Quan Zhi*, most of which are from the Southeast Asian countries, such as India, Afghanistan, Pakistan, Nepal, etc., in ancient times.[5]

Indian coins have been found in Mulei County, Xinjiang, China. On the coins was a person holding a spear, with a snake under him. The figure was dressed in tight clothes and a robe that was not over the

---

[4] Sheng, "Overseas Circulation."

[5] Yanzhi Tu, "A Brief Account of Southeast Asian Money in *Quan Zhi* of Southern Song Dynasty," *Asian Coins*, no. 1 (1999).

knees. There were no inscription on the back.[6] After India became a British colony, in modern times, the British made a large number of British-Indian Rupees in India. The silver coins, produced by machine, soon flowed into Tibet and affected the local currency system. During the reign of Dao Guang, this kind of Rupee flooded in in large amounts. It even circulated in Yunnan, at the time of Guang Xu.[7] In 1902, the Chengdu Mint was ordered to cast Sichuan Rupees, by imitating the Indian ones, in order to resist the loss of interest caused by the use of Indian Rupees. In terms of the portrait of Guang Xu on them, the silver coins were obviously influenced by the Indian Rupees, which had the British king's portrait on them as well.

There were also India coins with Chinese characters, that is, the coins of Aham kingdom of the Assam state. With its capital located in Upper Assam, the kingdom was once considered the most powerful empire in the region, but it was not until 1648 that it first minted its own currency. The coinage of Jayadhvaja Simha was octagonal, exquisite and weighed about 11.3 g, which was different from that of other kingdoms. There was no name of the king on the first batch of the coins that were cast. From 1663, legends began to appear on the coins, in the traditional language of Aham, to commemorate the gods of the kingdom. This was not changed until the succession of Rudra Simha, in 1696. Brahman was very influential in the court of Rudra, so he issued coins to commemorate the gods of India and marked the date of the coinage on the coins.

---

[6] Elken Rozi, "On the Ancient Coins Found in Mulei County," *Xinjiang Finance*, supplement II (1988).

[7] Head Office of the People's Bank of China, *Materials of modern Chinese Monetary History* (Beijing: Zhong Hua Book Company, 1964), 840.

254

Fig. 7-1 Octagonal rupee of Jayadhvaja Simha (1648---1663), 11.34 g, Saka 1570.

With four lines of Assam scripts on each side and a circle of dots between the two lines on the edge, the rupee was extremely exquisite. The rulers of the Aham Kingdom used the octagon as the standard shape of the currency. This shape remained until the fall of the kingdom. The texts on the coins were the prayers for the protection of Hari Hara, a god of both Vishnu and Shiva.

The rough Chinese character "Bao" was cast in the square on the reverse side, surrounded by a circle of small dots, and the character "Zang" was cast on the front with the number 1570 at the bottom.

258

258 (x2)

Fig. 7-2 Octagonal rupee of Jayadhvaja Simha (1648---1663), 11.36 g, Saka 1570.

The Burmese invaded Assam in 1821. After expelling the Burmese from Assam, the British supported Purandara Simha, the former Prince of the Aham royal family, to the throne. But he was denied the right to have coins cast. Britain demanded that the new

Aham ruler pay tribute to it as a compensation for its help in the expulsion of the Burmese. Since he couldn't cast coins, the British demanded that he pay tribute with the old Aham coins because they knew the Aham coins were of better quality than their own coins, therefore, such tribute would be in their interest. Soon the whole Assam area came under British jurisdiction.

Fig. 7-3 Chinese coins with cinnabar characters

In addition, in the collection of ancient Chinese coins in the Calcutta Museum, India, there is a Kai Yuan Tong Bao coin with cinnabar characters on its back.

II. Currency in Nepal and Tibet

Before the Yuan dynasty, both gold and silver were equally used as Tibetan currency. However, there was a shift from gold to silver for the needs of trade after the Yuan dynasty. During the Yuan and Ming dynasties, Tibet did not cast coins, but used silver ingots supported by the Chinese government, which were inconvenient for use. In the sixteenth century, most of the silver coins used in Tibet were provided by the Ballarpur people in the Yangbu (Kathmandu) River Valley of Nepal. After the silver ingots, collected from Tibet, were made into silver coins, they were transported back to Tibet for use. This was the situation after the agreement between Mahendra Mara (1560-1574), the King of Kathmandu, and the local government of Tibet, according to which, Tibet should pay monthly silver for the silver coins made by Nepal. This kind of silver currency transaction lasted for more than two hundred years. The Nepalese silver coins were of different weights,[8] bluish in color because of a mixture of copper.

In the middle of the eighteenth century, the Gurkha conquered Nepal and monopolized the coin minting for Tibet. The Nepalese government gained 12 percent of the profits.[9] The Gurkha "exchanged the coins for silver, and then mixed the silver with copper to make coins, which were traded again in Tibet." Silver coins mixed with copper were called "alloy coins" in Nepal.[10] The silver in Tibet was gradually exchanged by the Gurkha, resulting in a large outflow of Tibetan silver. The pattern of Nepalese coins also strongly influenced Tibetan ones, which can be seen from the patterns on the two coins.

In 1788 and 1791, the Gurkha invaded Tibet twice. The Qing Empire decided to give the Gurkha a heavy counterattack. On one hand, it deployed armed forces to suppress the Gurkha invaders. On the other hand, Qing began to plan for the establishment of a local currency system in Tibet, in order to, fundamentally, solve the disputes between Tibet and the Gurkha. In September 1791, Emperor Qian Long gave an order: "The Qing Empire should unite both the interior and the exterior land with the same system. The officially made coins should circulate without any obstacles. Why should the small land of Tibet turn to a foreign currency? We should set up furnace seats and assign officials and craftsmen to cast coins in Tibet conforming to the example of the mainland. A minister would be stationed in Tibet as the supervisor who

---

[8] Huaiyuan Xiao, *History of Local Currency in Tibet* (Beijing: Nationalities Publishing House, 1987), 11.

[9] Lucette Boulnois, *Gold and Silver Coins in Tibet* (Beijing: China Tibetology Publishing House, 1999), 204.

[10] I. R. Ariyal, *Newly Organized History of Nepal* (Chengdu: Sichuan People's Publishing House, 1973), 160.

would manage the production."[11] In the following year, the Tibetan local government made Zhangga silver coins and Bao Zang copper coins. However, both were stopped the next year because too much copper was used in making the silver coins, which made the quality of the coins unmatched with their value. As to the copper, there was not enough for long-term use. At the end of the fifty-sixth year of Qian Long reign (1791), General Fu Kang'an, who came to Tibet to preside over the aftercare regulations, had discussions with the people from all the parties concerned. The proposal of making silver coins in Tibet was put forward. After examining the three silver coin samples proposed by Fu Kang'an, the Qing government decided that the characters "Qian Long Bao Zang" would be cast in Chinese on the obverse, with the words "fifty-eighth year" beside them, and the Tibetan words on the back.[12]

Fig. 7-4 Qian Long Bao Zang coins

[11] Zhong Hua Book Company, *Authentic Records of Qing Dynasty: Reign of Gaozong*, vol. 1387 (Beijing: Zhong Hua Book Company, 2008), 27.
[12] Ling Li and Ming Yi, "Research on Tibetan Local Coins in Chongqing Museum," *Special Issue of the Founding Meeting of Chongqing Numismatic Society* (1988).

Fig. 7-5 Jia Qing Bao Zang coin

At the beginning of the establishment of the local money system in Tibet, the Qing dynasty had considered the use of Tangut font to cast the Bao Zang coins. Tangut is the appellation of the Qinghai-Tibet region and local Tibetans in the documents of Qing dynasty. The realization of the intention was sped up by the consumption demand of the army there.

Fig. 7-6 Silver Bao Zang coins cast by the Qing dynasty in Tibet.

The Qing dynasty began to send troops to Tibet at the end of the fifty-sixth year of Qian Long's reign. The need for money exchange of the army stationed in Tibet became an urgent problem to be solved. Having planned to cast coins in Tibet, plus the military demand, the

Qing government inevitably issued the Bao Zang coins.[13] Later, it set up a Money Bureau in Sichuan Province to cast silver coins for circulation in Tibet, which remained through Qian Long, Jia Qing, Dao Guang and other emperors' reigns, until the Xuan Tong period. Since the Bao Zang coins were cast in a small number, a new type of Zhangga Dan Qi silver coin, known as White Dan Qi, was cast later. These coins had a high silver content and a unified form; therefore, they were well accepted by the Tibetan people. White Dan Qi was used until the twentieth century.

In 1855, the Gurkha army, under the support of Britain, invaded Tibet, which was strongly resisted by the Tibetan army and people. In the following year, conducted by the Qing minister to Tibet, the Tibetan local government and the Nepalese government signed a peace treaty, which stipulated that Gurkha merchants enjoy the privilege of being exempted from business tax and road tax in Tibet. As a result, a large number of British Indian commodities and rupees were transferred to Tibet by the Gurkhas. Made by machine, British Indian rupees had a good quality and were widely used in Tibet.

Due to the special geographical location and history of Tibet, its history of currency exchange with the neighboring countries is complex. In the Dao Guang period of the Qing dynasty, the French priest Guberta had visited Tibet, in China, and recorded, "the monetary system of Tibet is only composed of silver coins, which are slightly larger and thinner than our one Franc coins. One side of the coin is written in Tibetan, Persian or Hindi, and on the other side is a crown of eight small flowers. For the facility of trading, people split the money for use. Its value, then, is determined by the number of small flowers remaining on the split. The whole piece of silver is called 'Zhang Ka.'

[13] Ming Yang, "On 'Baozang' Copper Coins during the Reign of Qianlong," *Special Issue of the Founding Meeting of Chongqing Numismatic Society* (1988).

Half a coin is called 'cut money.' The fragment with five flowers is called 'Shuo Gan,' with three 'Kagan.' "[14] Moreover, he recorded that Kashmiris were the richest merchants in Lhasa, at that time. They were local silver coin changers, and gold and silver dealers.[15]

Besides, about one thousand five hundred Chinese coins have been unearthed in Yaphuwa, Central Sri Lanka. They were all coins of the Song dynasty, from Tai Ping Tong Bao to Jing Ding Yuan Bao. The casting time was from 976 to 1264. In addition, coins of the Song dynasty have also been unearthed in other places in Sri Lanka.

---

[14] Evariste Huc, *Travel in Tartar Tibet* (Beijing: China Tibetology Publishing House, 1991), 501.

[15] Huc, *Travel in Tartar Tibet*, 504.

CHAPTER EIGHT

CURRENCY CULTURE EXCHANGE BETWEEN CHINA AND AMERICAN COUNTRIES

I. Cradle of Modern Silver Dollars — Spanish Colonies

In the fourteenth and fifteenth centuries, the handicraft industry in Western Europe had a great development. Capitalism sprouted. Gold and silver money became necessary for the development of commodity economy. However, the source of metal ore in Europe was nearly exhausted and, in the process of trade with China and India, Europe exported a large amount of silver. Therefore, the trading media became the main problem of the European economy. Finding new gold and silver mines, by way of discovering new routes, became the dream of some European adventurers.

After Columbus discovered the new world, he immediately began to force the Native Americans to pay gold, and the Spanish colonialists turned their eyes to Latin America. After the silver mines were developed, near Mexico City, in 1530, the mining industry expanded in Tasco, Trabouyahua, New Galicia, Zacatecas, Guana Huato, Pachuca, Sambret, St. Louis, Potosi, etc. Among them, Zacatecas had the highest silver production.

At the beginning of the sixteenth century, the average annual production of silver in the world was about 1,511,000 ounces. In the middle of the sixteenth century, it had increased to 10,017,000 ounces. By the middle of the eighteenth century, that is, the Qian Long period of the Qing dynasty, the world's silver production was maintained at

9,000,000-17,000,000 ounces. Once silver was mined, it was initially controlled by merchants, who bought silver ingots from smelting plants or itinerant traders, then minted them into silver coins and lent money at an interest of 5 percent. Silver foreign trade was under the control of foreign trade merchants.

The Spanish used the encomienda, the levy system, the debt bondage system, black slaves and other ways to mine silver. The output of silver in Mexico increased in the eighteenth century. By the end of the eighteenth century, it had accounted for 67 percent of the total production in America. According to the order of the Spanish royal family, all silver produced had to be transported to the mints for silver coins casting.

Coinage in Mexico, 1690-1808[1]	
years	peso
1690-1699	43971340
1700-1709	51933145
1710-1719	65828482
1720-1729	84151727
1730-1739	93677484
1740-1749	108124854
1750-1759	130219836
1760-1769	119556109
1770-1779	174772560
1780-1789	193403561
1790-1799	231080280
1800-1808	200112734

Table 8-1 Coinage in Mexico (1690-1808)

[1] Hubert H. Bancroft, *History of Mexico* (San Francisco: Bancroft, 1883), 598.

The search for a new trade road, by the Spanish, symbolized the rise of colonialism. This new maritime trade road later replaced the land Silk Road and changed the course of the world history. Due to the difference in trading commodities, later generations called it the silk and silver road. The Southern Song dynasty could be said to have the most distinctive maritime characteristics of all the ages in Chinese history. At this time, China changed its past westward or northward direction of development, and turned to the blue sea instead. Of course, this was also the result of oppression from the northern ethnic groups. The Ming dynasty and Spain, almost simultaneously, chose to go to sea. Although, this, for China, was an expedition as great as Ban Chao's feat in the Western Regions, China only came into contact with the backward civilization this time, which, consequently, intensified China's belief in being the leader of a divine kingdom. As a result, China turned away from the sea. However, the Spanish and the Portuguese succeeded. They won the Americas and created an era of colonialism.

Ancient China has long been associated with the American continents. There is a historic site called Lilingtai in Canada. Xu Weijing, a Chinese man, bought it one hundred years ago. An urn of ancient Chinese money was unearthed there. When Kang Youwei studied and made rubbings from the inscriptions on the coins, all sorts of feelings welled up in his mind.[2] In the third year of Wan Li in the Ming dynasty (1575), Chinese silk and porcelain were sold to Mexico and other Latin American regions by merchants, and many Cantonese went to Akarp, Mexico, to engage in shipbuilding and other industries.[3]

---

[2] Yongwu Huang, "Native Americans," *Central Daily News of Taiwan* (February 10, 1999).

[3] Guoxin Huang, *Cantonese Merchants Engaged in Trade between China and Foreign Countries* (Hangzhou: Zhejiang People's Publishing House, 1997), 155.

America was the largest silver producing area in the world from the sixteenth to the eighteenth century. A large number of silver mines in the Western American colonies were exploited in the sixteenth century. For example, the silver in Northern Mexico was mined from 1546 to 1590, and the most famous Potosi silver mine in Peru reached its peak in the 1580s. During the three decades from 1581 to 1609, Potosi produced 254,000 kg of silver annually, accounting for more than 60 percent of the world's total silver production at that time. Spain, with its huge wealth of silver, occupied Manila in 1571. The Philippines colony developed into a famous trading place. The silver transported from Spain to the East flowed into China through the hands of Chinese and foreign maritime merchants.[4] In recent years, there have been many studies on this issue in foreign countries, such as that of Takeshi Hamashita of Japan, who starts his study from the tributary trade system of China,[5] and Gunder Frank of Germany, who looks at the world from the Eastern perspective in his *Reorient*.[6]

The Chinese did not expect that Columbus' discovery of America would have caused great changes in China's monetary system. During the one hundred fifty years from 1503 to 1660, the gold and silver mines in America transported 18,600 tons of silver and 200 tons of gold to Spain.[7] On April 27, 1565, the Spanish fleet arrived at Cebu Island, in the Philippines, thus establishing Spain's first colonial stronghold in the South Ocean. In 1571, the Spanish captured Manila. Three years later, they began their formal colonial rule in the area.

---

[4] Yuxun Wang, "On the Amount of Silver from Domestic Mining and Foreign Inflow in Ming Dynasty," *China Numismatics*, no. 3 (1998).

[5] Takeshi Hamashita, *The International Opportunity of Modern China—Tributary Trade System and Modern Asian Economic Circle* (Beijing: China Social Sciences Press, 1999).

[6] Gund Frank, *Reorient—Attach Importance to the East in Economic Globalization* (Beijing: Central Compilation and Translation Press, 2000).

[7] Song Zhu, "Geographical Discovery—Western Global Colonial Expansion," *Guangming Daily* (November 20, 1999).

From 1565 to 1815, there was a big sailing ship trade between the Philippines and Mexico. The medium of the transaction was Spanish silver. Due to the huge volume of trade, Spain once regulated that ships sailing from Mexico were not allowed to carry silver coins exceeding two hundred and fifty thousand pesos.[8] During the period from the middle and late Ming dynasty to the middle of the Qing dynasty, Spanish people exchanged silver coins for silk and porcelain, from China, through trade. As a result, China, which was not rich in silver, began to use silver money in circulation, a kind of boat-shaped silver ingot, obtained by melting and recasting the Spanish silver coins. According to some Spanish archives, at the beginning of 1800, more than 2.5 million pesos of silver were transported to Manila to pay for trade with the East, of which, about 1.5 million was paid to China. From the first sailing ship, in 1565, to the last one, in 1815, the silver paid to China amounted to the equivalent of about two hundred million US dollars, in today's money.[9]

The total amount of silver mined during the Ming dynasty was about 26,353,326 Liang. In the 152 years from Hong Wu to Zheng De, the total amount was 12,533,226 Liang, accounting for more than 47 percent of the total domestic silver mining in the Ming dynasty.[10] The middle of the Ming dynasty witnessed an unprecedented peak in the development of monetary economy in China's feudal society. The domestic exploitation of silver was far from enough to meet the demand for it. Only when a large amount of foreign silver flowed into China, in the years of Long Qing, was the contradiction between the two solved.

---

[8] Jianying Chen, "Some Issues on the Inflow of Spanish Silver Dollars into China," *Fujian Coins*, no. 3-4 (1994).

[9] Boji Liu, *The Unofficial History of Overseas Chinese in the United States* (Taipei: Taiwan Liming Culture Co., Ltd, 1976), 47.

[10] Yuxun Wang, "On the Amount of Silver from Domestic Mining and Foreign Inflow in Ming Dynasty," *China Numismatics*, no. 3 (1998).

As the Ming dynasty had officially banned the sea trade, from the fourth year of Hong Wu, it had always kept the policy of "forbidding the people near the sea from communicating with overseas countries." Before the Long Qing years, the trade between the East and the West was mostly conducted by envoys paying tribute and the imperial court giving rewards back to them, and no tax was levied on this. What's more, what the Ming dynasty paid was several times of the value of the tribute goods. After Hong Zhi, the merchant ships from various countries frequently came to China for the thick profits, even during the non-tribute period, and the number of merchant ships was also increasing; ships pretended to be tribute ships but, in fact, traded in China. As a result, the outflow of silver continued to rise, which became one of the factors that aggravated the problem of silver shortage. Not only had the ban on maritime trade failed to curb the growth of foreign trade in China, but it also failed to hold back the development trend of non-governmental maritime trade of the Chinese people.[11] In 1567, Mu Zong ascended the throne and officially replaced the "ban on maritime trade" with an open-up policy. With the absolute advantage of China in maritime trade, at that time, China always maintained the position of trade surplus, which led to the inflow of foreign silver in large amounts.

Macao was a center of the global maritime trade in the fifteenth and sixteenth centuries. In 1557, the Portuguese formally occupied Macao. After more than twenty years of operation, Macao entered a golden period of economic prosperity for eighty years, being an important international commercial port, connecting the East and the West, and a place where the East and the West cultures converged. It was in this golden era that the silk and silver road of the Ming dynasty

[11] Yuxun Wang, "On the Amount of Silver from Domestic Mining and Foreign Inflow in Ming Dynasty," *China Numismatics*, no. 3 (1998).

came into being, with the Chinese mainland as the hinterland and Macao as the transit port. Three routes were opened up, taking Macao as the center: Macao-Goa-Lisbon, Macao-Nagasaki, Macao-Manila-Mexico. These three routes radiated overseas, with Macao as the center, forming a great cycle of international trade. With the operation of these three major routes, a large amount of silk was transported away from the Chinese mainland via Macao, while a formidable volume of silver flowed into Macao and, then, was transferred to the Chinese mainland. Therefore, it was, literally, a silk and silver road. Thanks to the opening of these three routes, Macao had become the world's silver trading center.

Located on the silk and silver road, Macao, the world-wide silk trade center, gradually formed a world-scale silk market. Of the raw silk exported by China to Japan every year, almost 60 percent was exported by Portuguese merchants from Macao. According to the records, the amount of silver flowing into Macao from Japan was 2.35 million Liang, in 1636, while the total amount over the sixty years from 1578 to 1638 might have reached one hundred million Liang.[12] During the ten years from 1580 to 1590, the amount of raw silk transported from Macao to India-Goa was about three thousand Dan (a unit of weight) per year. During the two hundred years from 1574 to the end of the eighteenth century, Chinese silk and cotton fabrics quickly ranked first among the commodities from Macao to Mexico, via Manila. China's silk accounted for more than 60 percent of Mexico's total import value.

At first, the trade between China and Portugal was mostly the barter. After 1582, it turned from physical goods to silver, including the taxes Portuguese merchant ships paid to China, which were also

---

[12] "The Long Maritime Silk and Silver Road," *Macao Daily News* (August 2, 1999).

calculated in silver. According to statistics, in 1631, fourteen million Liang of silver was exported from the Philippines to Macao. This figure was 2.1 times the total output of China's official silver mines in the thirty years from Yong Le to Xuan De (1403-1434) of the Ming dynasty, or 3.8 times the revenue of the Ming state treasury during the Wan Li period.[13] In the reverse of these three routes, a large number of precious metals flowed to Macao to make it the world center for them. Much silver was used by Portuguese merchants to exchange for gold to realize their Oriental Dream—the pursuit of gold. Still, more silver had entered the Chinese mainland.

In addition to importing a large amount of Japanese silver into China, in the "triangle trade" of the East, the Portuguese also transported a certain amount of local silver from Lisbon to Macao every year to buy Chinese goods. There are records in Portugal which say that, in 1601, three Portuguese ships sailed for Macao, one of which sank in the coastal area of Guangdong Province and lost three hundred thousand Portuguese silver coins.[14] During this period, the total amount of silver flowing into China from Portuguese domestic trade was 5,008,250 Liang.[15]

Based on the analysis of historical materials at home and abroad, Wang Yuxun, a Chinese scholar, believed that China obtained more than three hundred million Liang of silver from foreign trade in the Ming dynasty. The specific figures are as follows: 87,750,000 Liang from Spain, 200,000,000 Liang from Japan, 42,762,750 Liang from Portugal, totaling 330,512,750 Liang, equivalent to 439,581,960 pesos.[16]According to Mr. Wang Shihe's estimation, in the early Qing

---

[13] "The Long Maritime Silk and Silver Road," (August 2, 1999).

[14] Yuxun Wang, "On the Amount of Silver from Domestic Mining and Foreign Inflow in Ming Dynasty," *China Numismatics*, no. 3 (1998).

[15] Wang, "On the Amount of Domestic Silver Mining."

[16] Wang, "On the Amount of Domestic Silver Mining."

dynasty, more than one million pesos of silver were imported into China from the Philippines, during the reigns of Shun Zhi, Kang Xi, Yong Zheng and Qian Long.[17] The Thirteen-Trade Monopoly existed from 1757 to 1842, during which the revenue of Guangdong Customs increased day by day. In the middle of the Qian Long period, the average annual revenue of Guangdong Customs was 500,000 Liang, which increased to 1,020,000 Liang, in the later Qian Long period, then 1.43 million Liang per year in the Jia Qing period and 1.52 million Liang in the Dao Guang years.[18] Wu Lianyan believed that the inflow of foreign silver was about 18,600,000 Yuan, in the period from 1551 to 1643, and 343,000,000 Yuan, from 1644 to 1839.[19] In his *History of Foreign Relations of the Chinese Empire*, Ma Shi said: "In the whole eighteenth century, silver dollars were the main things that were imported into Guangzhou, and the goods were nothing but auxiliary. In the 24th year of Kang Xi, only silver was used when foreign countries came to Fujian and Guangdong for trade. In the early years of Qian Long, foreign money began to be used. Forty years later, it expanded to Jiangsu and Hangzhou."[20] During the reign of Jia Qing, it was already the world of foreign silver dollars in Guangdong. In the reign of Dao Guang, foreign businessmen also used foreign silver dollars when they came to China. "Since 1825, all kinds of silver coins were found in China. Before that, there were only Spanish silver coins of Carola IV, commonly known as 'the old man,' which had the

---

[17] Shihe Wang, "The Development of Trade between China, Manila and Mexico in the Late Ming Dynasty," *Collected Papers on Geography*, no. 7 (1964).
[18] Guoxin Huang, *Cantonese Merchants Engaged in Trade between China and Foreign Countries* (Hangzhou: Zhejiang People's Publishing House, 1997), 155.
[19] Lianyan Wu, "History of the Influx of Foreign Silver Dollars into Guangdong in Great Amount," in *Free Thoughts on Silver Currency*, ed. Cultural and Historical Materials Research Committee of the CPPCC of Guangdong Province (Guangzhou: Guangdong People's Publishing House, 1992).
[20] Head Office of the People's Bank of China, *Materials of Modern Monetary History in China* (Beijing: Zhong Hua Book Company, 1964), 54.

highest value, and were thought most highly of by the Chinese people."[21]

After foreign silver dollars circulated in China, local money houses (old-style Chinese private banks) marked all the silver dollars they handled with their own business name as a credit sign for fixed exchange. As each firm would make a credit mark on the silver dollar it handled, after many times of repetition, a silver dollar quickly became riddled with holes, and was called a rotten board. This kind of rotten board could only be used in Guangdong. During the reign of Dao Guang, silver dollars were freely circulated in the following provinces: Guangdong, Guangxi, Fujian, Jiangxi, Zhejiang, Jiangsu, Anhui, and southern and eastern Hunan. In the thirteenth year of the reign of Emperor Guang Xu, the circulation scope of foreign silver dollars was further expanded to such trading ports as Yantai and Tianjin. In the thirteenth year of Dao Guang, there were many places in China that imitated the casting of foreign silver dollars. Those cast in Guangdong were called Guang Ban, in Fujian they were called Fu Ban, in Hangzhou they were called Hang Ban, in Suzhou they were called Su Ban, Wu Zhuang or Xi Ban. Whatever the name, they were all imitations.[22]

The Spanish silver coin was generally known as Ben Yang, in China. In its early stage, it had the names of double columns, double ropes or lace. The later ones, with figures such as Charles III, IV and Ferdinand VII, were called Big Ji, Small Ji, Old Man, Gong Tou, Ghost Head, New Head, Fan mian, Fo Fan, etc.

From the 1500s to 1732, Spanish silver coins made in America

---

[21] History Society of China, *Collections of Materials on Modern Chinese History (First Opium War)*, *Records of Guangzhou Foreigners* (Shanghai: Shanghai People's Publishing House, 1957), 263.

[22] Head Office of the People's Bank of China, *Materials of Modern Monetary History in China* (Beijing: Zhong Hua Book Company, 1964), 43.

were handmade struck ones with irregular shapes. They were called COB, with the Spanish national emblem or double pillars on the front, water ripple at the bottom, and a cross, in the middle, on the back, surrounded by a curve. There were marks for different casting places on these coins, with M for Mexico, L for Peru and P for Bolivia. A large number of Spanish COB coins were unearthed in China. On January 9, 1975, a batch of thirty-seven ancient foreign coins was unearthed in Manjianghong Hospital of Quanzhou City. They were all coarsely struck coins of irregular silver pieces, with uneven thickness. Besides the patterns, there was a cross on each of the coins.[23]The casting time was dated from 1634 to 1665. In 1971, ten COB coins, weighing 4.9 g-27.45 g each, were also unearthed in Anhai Township, Jinjiang, Fujian Province. On the obverse of each coin, there were the Spanish national emblem and the letters OMP. These coins were estimated to be cast between 1634 and 1665. Spanish silver coins were also unearthed in Guangzhou, many times. In 1988, ninety-nine pieces of Spanish silver coins were unearthed in Jianyang village, Chenghai County, Guangdong Province, dated from 1691 to 1699.[24]

The Spanish silver coins from 1732 to 1772, known as "the old double pillar," were a new type of silver coin, which were cast by machine. They were added with decorative patterns on the border that only modern coins have. There were famous patterns of the earth and double pillars, as well as crown and emblem, but there was no portrait of the king. In 1987, 134 pieces of Spanish silver coins were unearthed in Chikan, Hongjiang City, Guangdong Province. They were dated from 1736 to 1771, with the inscription "Ferdinand VI, King of Spain

---

[23] Relics Publishing House, "Ancient Foreign Currency Unearthed in Quanzhou," *Cultural Relics*, no. 8 (1975).

[24] Ping Wu and Lanying Chen, "On Currency of Maritime Silk Road," in *Proceedings of the Sixth Symposium on Southeast Asian Historical Currencies and Maritime Silk Road Currencies*, ed. Zhejiang Coin Society (Ningbo: Ningbo Numismatic Society, June 1995).

and India," or "Charles III, King of Spain and India." The silver coins had two lions on the front and two columns on the reverse. They also had the characters struck by the Chinese commercial firms.[25]

Fig. 8-1 Spanish silver dollars

From 1772 to 1825, the silver coins with the portrait of the Spanish King were minted, including that of Carlos III (1772-1788), Carlos IV (1789-1808) and Ferdinand VII (1809-1821 or 1825). They were known as "new double pillars" or the "double pillars with portrait." Chinese people usually called it "Fo Yang." The "portrait double pillars" coins were cast in the fifty-four years from 1772 to 1825. Not only did they have many different casting places and a large amount of casting, but they also circulated widely. They had exerted a profound impact on both the casting countries (regions) and the countries or regions into which they flowed. On April 1, 1996, a batch of Spanish silver coins was unearthed from Putuo Mountain, a scenic resort in Zhejiang Province. According to the estimation of the witnesses, the total number should have been about one thousand, but only about seven hundred pieces were collected. All were Spanish silver dollars. The date of coinage ranged from 1779 to 1895. They were machine-made coins with the portrait of the Spanish King on the

[25] Wu and Chen, "On Currency of Maritime Silk Road."

front and a crown on the back. In the middle of the back side, was a four-corner grid with two castles and two lions in the opposite corners. There was an upright column on each side of the grid surrounded by Spanish words. On the surface of the silver coins, there were concave marks with various symbols, including some stamps of Chinese characters, which confirmed that they had been in circulation in China.

Fig. 8-2 Silver plate with Spanish King's emblem

In addition, some ancient silver plates with the design of the Spanish King's emblem have been found in Guangzhou. The silver plates are irregular pentagonal, 22 mm in length, 38 mm in width, 3 mm in thickness, and weighing about 27 g. There are pictures on both sides of the silver plates, but no text. On one side, is the design of lions and castles, which can be identified as the Spanish King's emblem, while the picture on the other side looks like a Gothic windowsill. Thirty or forty pieces of such silver plates were also unearthed in Taiwan, at the end of the Qing dynasty. Although the production of these kind of silver pieces were primitive and simple, their design and weight were in accordance with the standard of Spanish silver dollars, which indicated that they must have served as Spanish silver dollars for a certain time.

After the withdrawal of the new double pillars, both China and Nanyang regions were suffering from the shortage of Ben Yang. Although Ben Yang was still the main currency, it became less and less, and the Ying Yang was not yet fully accepted by the market in China. It was a reasonable moment for the appearance of this kind of silver plate. Originally, there was a crown in the Royal emblem on Ben Yang, but, on the silver plate, the crown had been removed. Perhaps the Spanish had stopped the rule there, but the silver plate still retained some signs of Ben Yang in order to replace it. It is thought-provoking. It might be speculated that the silver plates were made by the former Spanish colonies, such as Peru or Bolivia, in 1821-1850, between the cease of new double pillars and the wide circulation of Mexican Ying Yang in China.[26]

II. Mexican Silver Dollars Spreading All Over the World

After the independence of Mexico, it stopped casting double pillars in 1823 and began to cast Mexican silver dollars. Their face value, diameter, weight and quality were the same as Spanish ones. Mexican silver dollars were cast until 1905, when the gold standard was carried out.

The Mexican silver dollars were originally called Bian Fu (which means bat, in English) in China. They flowed into Guangdong Province as early as 1829[27] and poured in tremendously, after the first Opium War. So far, they are the foreign silver dollars unearthed in the largest amounts in stock in China. Due to the good production and quality of

---

[26] Xuewen Dai, "Ancient Silver Plates with the Emblem of Spanish Kings," *Chinese Coins*, no.3 (1998).

[27] Lianyan Wu, "History of the Influx of Foreign Silver Dollars into Guangdong in Great Amount," in *Free Thoughts on Silver Currency*, ed. Cultural and Historical Materials Research Committee of the CPPCC of Guangdong Province (Guangzhou: Guangdong People's Publishing House, 1992).

the Mexican silver dollars, the double pillars were replaced around 1850. The circulation areas and the quantity of the Mexican silver dollars even exceeded those of double pillars. Later, Hong Kong, Japan, the United States (silver dollars for trading), Annam (French), China and the United Kingdom (silver dollars for trading) all successively made silver dollars, most of which, under the influence of the Mexican silver dollars, were similar to the Mexican ones in diameter, weight and quality.

Fig. 8-3 Mexican silver dollars

The Ying Yang, whose real name is the Mexican Dollar, had both an old version and a new version. The old version entered China in the eighteenth century. After a tremendous impact on the Spanish silver dollars, which had been the main currency in the market, it finally replaced them. The new version of Ying Yang was first made in 1823, after Mexico's independence. At first, Chinese people mistook it for British dollars, so they called it Ying Yang (Ying means British). On the front side, was an eagle standing on the cactus with a long snake struggling and twisting in its mouth, thus it got the name Ying Yang in China (here, Ying means eagle). It circulated, mainly, in Southern and Central China, especially in Shanghai. After the nineteenth century, it became the main currency and the standard for currency exchange.

In addition, Portuguese Cross money and Japanese Dragon money also circulated in China, in the Qing dynasty.

CHAPTER NINE

IMPACT OF WESTERN CURRENCY ON THE MODERN CHINESE CURRENCY SYSTEM

I. Circulation of Silver Dollars of Western Countries and the Casting of Silver and Copper Dollars in China

"In the coastal areas of Fujian and Guangdong, foreign money was often used. The money carried by every Dutch or Spanish merchant ship was usually calculated in tens of millions of dollars."[1] Horse money, also known as Horse Sword, was made in Holland from the seventeenth to the end of the eighteenth century. It had two kinds, big and small, and was widely popular in the early Qian Long period of the Qing dynasty. It was called Horse Sword because the pattern on the coin was a knight riding a horse with a sword in his hand. Horse Swords were made in different provinces of Holland, so their patterns and shapes were slightly different. The Dutch attacked Macao as far back as the Wan Li years of the Ming dynasty. Defeated by the Portuguese, they turned to attack Fujian but lost again. Then they went to Fujian for trade. During the reign of Qian Long, they set up commercial halls in Guangzhou. The amount of Dutch silver that flowed into China from the Wan Li period was less and less after the middle period of Dao Guang. In 1792, Holland was occupied by the French army, and the casting of Horse Sword was stopped.

---

[1] Tingyu Zhang et al., *A General Study of Imperial Documents: Study on Coins IV* (1787).

The Portuguese silver dollars got the name of Cross Money because of the pattern of a cross on the coins. During the Qian Long period of the Qing dynasty, Spanish Ben Yang competed with the Dutch Horse Sword money and the Cross Money of Portugal in circulation, in China. After 1821, Spanish coins were greatly reduced, due to the independence of American countries, and began to be replaced by Mexican silver dollars.[2] Britain once cast Hong Kong silver dollars. Although these silver dollars had the same style, size and weight as Mexican silver ones, the Hong Kong dollars failed because their silver content was only 90 percent. They were only issued for three years (1866-1868) before the Hong Kong Mint stopped casting. Even the mint machinery was sold to Japan.[3] About two hundred thousand dollars were cast. After that, Britain made a total of 153,360,000 silver dollars for trading in India; the so-called "standing man" coins.[4] They were mainly used for the trade with China, about one-third of which flowed there.

Since all countries used Mexican silver coins in trade, Japan forged trade silver dollars with the same size and weight as Mexican ones, and, further, made the trade silver dollars its standard currency, in 1878. Since Columbus discovered the new world, the colonists have exploited a large number of silver mines in South America. The vast majority of the silver in the world was produced in this area. When the old colonists did business with the Chinese, before the Opium War, they had no commodity that could open up the Chinese market.

---

[2] Saran Singh, *The Encyclopaedia of The Coins of Malaysia, Singapore and Brunei 1400-1967* (Kuala Lumpur: A Malaysia Numismatic Society Publication, 1996), 540.

[3] Singh, *The Encyclopaedia of The Coins of Malaysia, Singapore and Brunei 1400-1967*, 548.

[4] Lianyan Wu, "History of the Influx of Foreign Silver Dollars into Guangdong in Great Amount," in *Free Thoughts on Silver Currency*, ed. Cultural and Historical Materials Research Committee of the CPPCC of Guangdong Province (Guangzhou: Guangdong People's Publishing House, 1992).

However, China's ceramics, silk and tea became the hot goods for Western countries, so they had to trade the silver from South America for these products. As a consequence, China's monetary system underwent significant changes, from the Ming dynasty onwards. Year after year, the Chinese people had made a lot of money from overseas trade. They converted from their single currency standard of copper coins and paper money into a double standard of silver and copper, which had a great impact on China's society and economy, at that time.

First of all, some fundamental changes had taken place in China's traditional single monetary system, which was, a combination of copper coins and paper money. Although silver had been a member of the monetary family for a long time, its currency property was mostly limited to saving. The rich people in China regarded silver as the treasure of the house and buried it underground. It didn't play a role as a circulation medium in the traditional social and economic life. Since American silver dollars poured into China, in the mid and latter Ming dynasty, the status of silver in the Chinese monetary system had been immensely strengthened. The government's policy of levying silver for taxes had intensified the importance of silver in China's social economy. Silver played an irreplaceable role in large transactions and government finance.

Secondly, great changes had taken place in the form of silver in China. In the Song and Yuan dynasties, Chinese silver was generally cast into a narrow-waisted block. Since the Ming dynasty, Chinese silver had generally been cast into the boat shape, as commonly seen in movies. The vulgar name for it was Yuan Bao. There are not yet deep studies as to the reasons for this change in shape, but we can be sure that this change must have been related to the influx of silver into China.

It was the Chinese people who played an important role in the big sailing ship trade. Not only were these ships built by the Chinese, but also the overseas Chinese directly participated in the business in America, where the sailing ships set out. The earliest Chinese silver dollars were the imitation of foreign ones, such as the Spanish or Mexican silver dollars. The coinage mould for the imitations has been found now. Throughout the period of Dao Guang, there were many changes in the history of Chinese currency, one of which was the imitation of foreign money. In the thirteenth year of Dao Guang (1833), Huang Juezi said, "When foreign money flowed into China, the public liked its way of evaluation by pieces, thinking it easy to use. Because the price was equivalent to the fine silver, while the percentage of silver in a dollar could be slightly lower, some mean fellows just took advantage of this to make profits by melting the fine silver to forge foreign dollars. Those cast in Guangdong are called Guang Ban, in Fujian Fu Ban, in Hangzhou Hang Ban, in Jiangsu Su Ban, Wu Zhuang or Xi Ban. Whatever the names, they are all imitations from the mainland of China. The fraud did not start in one day, nor was it spread only in one province."[5] In the same year, Lin Zexu mentioned the problem in his memorial to the throne. In order to deal with this kind of forgery, and to return the right to the government, Lin Zexu also cast a number of foreign silver coins in his term of office. According to the historical records, this imitation was actually a kind of silver cake, which was only in circulation for a short time before it was abolished.

In April 1981, the villagers of Nanyang brigade of the Hongxing commune in Daxing County, Beijing, discovered a wooden box in a hoard, 0.7 m underground, during the construction of infrastructure. Nineteen silver cakes were unearthed from the hoard. The silver cakes were round, 2.6 cm-2.8 cm in diameter and 0.3 cm in thickness. The front was slightly convex with three lines of seals. In the middle, was

[5] History Society of China, *Collection of Materials on Modern Chinese History Vol. I, Opium War* (Shanghai: Shanghai People's Publishing House, 1957), 477.

the horizontal Ku Wen and the vertical seven Qian two Fen; on the right, was the county name of Zhejiang Province, such as Yongjia, Fenghua, Changle, Longquan, Haiyan, Qiantang, Huangyan, etc. On the left, was the name of the issuing Yin Hao (Chinese, old-style private bank), as Zhenchang on six pieces of the silver cakes, Xiefeng on two pieces, Xingcheng on four pieces, and Dunyu on three pieces. Still, there are four pieces on which the words were unclear. The weights of these silver cakes ranged from 18.6 g to 24.6 g, and the fineness was 95 percent. There may have been two kinds of silver cakes in Zhejiang Province: the officially made ones and the folk, Yin Hao, made ones. The former weighed one Liang, while the latter weighed seven Qian and two Fen.[6] They were believed to have been cast during the years of Dao Guang. The silver cakes made in Zhejiang Province were an important event in the modern monetary history of China.

During the Xian Feng period, some Yin Hao, in Shanghai, made silver cakes that were similar to silver dollars. For example, in the sixth year of Xian Feng, Yin Hao Wang Yong Sheng made silver cakes that were not much different in size from the silver dollars. Wang Yong Sheng, Yu Sen Sheng and Jing Zheng Ji were the three Yin Hao known to issue silver cakes in the Xian Feng years, in Shanghai. The silver cakes issued in Wang Yong Sheng had the weight of one Liang, while the other two issued two kinds of silver cakes, weighing one Liang or five Qian, respectively.

In Zhangzhou, Fujian, the Qing government used the local method to cast silver dollars in order to pay the local garrison. Now, people generally divide these kinds of silver dollars into three categories: the first with the words "Zhangzhou Military Pay" on the

---

[6] Editorial Board of Beijing Financial Records, *Financial Historical Materials of Beijing (Edition of Currency)* (Beijing: Beijing Financial Publishing House, 1994), 190.

surface, the second with many seals and stamps on, and the third with the characters, which were generally considered to be, Jin Shen (meaning prudent, in English) on.

In Taiwan, during the reign of Dao Guang and Xian Feng, the local government, in the face of peasant uprisings, cast silver dollars, with the hundreds of thousands of Liang silver in stock, to pay for the military expenditure. Three forms were used for casting: the god of longevity, the flower basket, and the sword scale. Each of the coins weighd seven Qian and two Fen, and had the words "Ku Fu" on it. These were the first silver dollars cast in Taiwan. Now, people tend to call the silver dollars with flower basket Ru Yi silver dollars.

Since the Spanish silver dollars began to circulate in China in the late Ming dynasty, the currency advantage of capitalism had manifested itself in the dollars. Conformed to the law of currency circulation, these dollars expanded their market day by day in the South, and the coastal cities, of China. After the Opium War, in 1840, China lost its control over the sea, and the Western powers invaded China eighty-four times from the sea, with more than 1,860 invading ships.[7] From then on, China entered a semi-colonial and semi-feudal society, and its currency culture was also tinged with this pathos. The Chinese currency culture, which had been in parallel with that of ancient Greece, gradually lost its radiance.

As early as the eighth year of Guang Xu (1882), general Xiyuan of Jilin Province began to make silver dollars, with machines, without reporting to the imperial court in advance. In order to solve the shortage of Zhi Qian (the officially cast coins according to the standard monetary system in the Ming and Qing dynasyies) in transactions, Xiyuan also ordered the establishment of a Bureau, called Bao Ji

[7] Hua Xu, "Historical Reflection on the Sea Power of China in Modern Times," *Guangming Daily* (November 19, 1999).

Money Bureau, to cast Zhi Qian on the abandoned official iron furnaces in the provincial capital. In the fifteenth year of Guang Xu (1889), Changshun, the general of Jilin Province, added furnaces and materials, and purchased machines from Shanghai to manufacture Zhi Qian in large quantities. On the back of the coins, were words Bao Ji in Manchu.

In Hubei Province, Zhang Zhidong, governor of Huguang, converted the gun making machines into coin casting ones. Then, through the Mao Sheng foreign bank, he ordered pressers, and shearing machines, as well as lettering money molds from Hanlicner, the US factory, and built a Copper Coin Casting Bureau on the old base of the Bao Wu Bureau.

In 1895, one hundred sixty thousand Liang of silver was collected and stored in Shanghai, and was used to buy the first-class Japanese copper and foreign lead, which, then, was transported to Guangdong and handed over to the Guangdong money bureau to make two hundred thousand strings of Zhi Qian. With a ratio of six-to-four, between copper and lead, each Wen of the Zhi Qian weighed eight Fen. This was the common Bao Su machine-made money, with Manchu characters on the back.

In the beginning of the twenty-second year of the reign of Guang Xu (1896), Liu Kunyi, governor of Liang Jiang, felt that the limited amount of money made by Guangdong could not meet the needs of the market, so he bought machines from Britain and Germany. In March, the Jiang Nan General Bureau of Silver Dollars and Zhi Qian Making was established. Each machine-made copper coin of Jiangnan Province weighed seven Fen. On the back of the coins, were "Bao," in Manchu, and "Jiang," in Chinese. On October 28 of the twenty-third year of Guang Xu's reign (1897), the factory was divided into East and West parts. The West Factory specialized in casting Zhi Qian and began its casting on December 15. The factory also made a kind of machine-made Zhi Qian, with the Manchu "Bao Ning" on the back.

Fig. 9-1 Guang Xu Tong Bao coin

Since the Westernization Movement copied the modern Western industrial technology, China's coinage industry changed from using the original local method to buying machines and building factories. In order to earn China's silver, many countries actively "helped" China to set up new factories. Generally speaking, the machine casting of Zhi Qian in most provinces was forced to stop in one or two years. Guangdong had the longest time of casting, but, in the twenty-sixth year of Guang Xu (1900), it also turned to casting copper dollars. The appearance of the copper dollars marked the complete failure of the machine-made Zhi Qian. The main reason for the failure lay in the fact that Zhi Qian was made at a loss. Finally, in many places, the task of making Zhi Qian was entrusted to the local method, while machines were used to cast profitable copper dollars.

Profits were made after the machines were used to cast copper dollars instead of Zhi Qian. The advantages of copper dollars greatly attracted the feudal rulers, which led to excessive casting. The malady immediately appeared. In 1906, Cen Chunxuan, governor of Liang Guang, for the convenience of circulation, began to cast holed one Wen Guang Xu Tong Bao, with reduced weight, which was quickly imitated by Fujian Province. In the first month of the thirty-fourth year of Guang Xu (1908), the Qing government ordered all provinces to copy and cast one Wen coins but rejected the holed pattern for the design of small coins without holes. This was far from the original intention of the Qing government, which was to restore the making of

Zhi Qian. After the newly cast one Wen coins were then incorporated into the copper dollar system, the monetary system of Zhi Qian, in the Qing dynasty, actually collapsed.

Fig. 9-2 Guang Xu Yuan Bao dollar

At the end of the Qing dynasty, the machine-made money was a great shock to the modern currency system. The Qing government was not interested in machine-made silver dollars, at the beginning, but regarded the, officially, machine-made Zhi Qian as the key to rescuing the currency system of the late Qing dynasty. The silver dollars were originally cast to make up for the insufficiency of the Zhi Qian. However, the rulers of Qing never thought that their subjective desire to restore the Zhi Qian, by machine, would cause great changes to the currency system of the late Qing dynasty. From then on, machine coinage began to replace the local casting method in China. The copper dollars defeated the Zhi Qian, and the silver dollars also posed a threat to silver taels. As a turning point in the Chinese modern currency system, the machine-made Zhi Qian had a far-reaching significance.

II. Circulation of Foreign Bank Notes and the Issuance of Bank Notes in China

The different monetary systems of local places in the Qing dynasty, namely, the different coin casting bureaus and the different purity of silver, laid the foundation for the rise of local, official "Yin Hao," in the future. Especially after the original centralized financial system was destroyed, the local currency became more and more important, and the local property of currency was strengthened day by day. Take Zhi Li, the province guarding the capital, as an example. The coin casting institutions in the province included Bao Zhi Bureau, Bao De Bureau, Bao Ji Bureau and Bao Jin Bureau. In addition to being different from other provinces, silver taels were also different within the province, represented by Hang Hua silver, in Tianjin; Yu Zhou Bao, in Zhangjiakou; Xiao Xi Bao, in Shijiazhuang; and Zhou Hang silver, in Xingtai. The Bei Yang Machinery Bureau and the Bei Yang Silver Dollar Bureau cast silver dollars. The Bei Yang Silver Dollar Bureau and the Zhi Li Mint branch of Hu Bu were in charge of the casting of copper dollars. Based on the circulation of these local coins, the emergence of local paper money became an inevitable trend.

The proliferation of foreign paper money and the limited circulation of central government paper money also contributed to the development of local paper money. The banknotes issued by the imperialist banks, such as HSBC, in China, were widely used in the capital city and big ports. In addition, some foreign banknotes also spread, unchecked, in the bordering provinces. For example, in the Northeast, Russian banknotes almost became the main currency; while, in Guangxi, the French paper money was powerful. Considering the various kinds of coins in different parts of China, paper money was more convenient for circulation. Besides, the regions also had their own financial needs. The wave of establishing official Yin Hao came, unavoidably, to each province, to issue paper money that was exclusive to the province only.

The official Yin Hao in the provinces experienced three peaks in terms of the time of establishment, except in Xinjiang and Ili, where the official Yin Hao were established earlier (in 1889). The first climax was around the outbreak of the Sino Japanese War, in 1894-1895, and especially after the war. The provinces included Shaanxi, Hubei, Shandong, Henan, Fengtian, Hunan (Fu Nan official money bureau), Sichuan (Shu Tong official money bureau), Tianjin and Jilin, of which Shaanxi set up its Yin Hao in 1894, while all the rest established their Yin Hao in 1896. The second climax was after the Incident of Gengzi, when Fujian, Zhili, Jiangxi, Shanxi, Jiangsu, Guangxi and Hunan (Hu Nan official money bureau, 1903) established their official Yin Hao, of which Jiangsu set up two—Yu Su and Yu Ning. The third climax happened after the implementation of the new deal, in the late Qing dynasty. The provinces that set up official Yin Hao were Guangdong, Sichuan (Jun Chuan Yuan bank 1905), Anhui, Gansu, Guizhou, Rehe, Zhejiang, Heilongjiang and Guangxi. These three climaxes corresponded to the three periods of financial dilemma of the Qing government.

The banknotes issued by the official Yin Hao were basically for cashing, and they were mostly linked with local coins. Therefore, the types and denominations of banknotes were very complicated. The notes of silver taels were usually marked with the purity of the silver of different places. Similarly, the notes of silver dollars varied from place to place because of the different types of dollars in circulation.

At that time, the following local financial institutions issued banknotes in Zhili.

Bei Yang Tian Jin Yin Hao, also known as Tian Jin official Yin Hao, began to issue the notes of silver taels and silver dollars, in 1893. In 1906, silver tael notes were issued in Baoding and Tianjin, respectively. Due to the different purity of silver taels, they were divided into four kinds, with the denominations of one Liang, five Liang, ten Liang, fifty Liang and one hundred Liang. The silver dollar notes also had five kinds: one Yuan, five Yuan, ten Yuan, fifty Yuan and one hundred Yuan. The notes of Zhi Qian had seven kinds: one string, two strings, five strings, ten strings, twenty strings, fifty strings and one hundred strings. The Yin Hao, altogether, issued 384,500 Liang of silver tael notes, 732,000 Yuan of silver dollar notes and 64,794,000 Wen of notes of Zhi Qian.

The Bei Yang Silver Dollar Bureau was originally a mint for silver dollars, but it also issued notes of copper dollars in the last years of Guang Xu. Some had the denomination of one hundred Wen or five hundred Wen.

The Chahar Official Money Bureau issued banknotes in the late Qing dynasty.

The Rehe Official Yin Hao was founded in 1906, and issued silver tael notes and notes of Zhi Qian. But only notes of Zhi Qian were found now.

In Fengtian, the Hua Feng Official Paper Money Bureau was set up, in the 20th year of Guang Xu (1894), to issue the banknotes of Zhi Qian. In November, of the thirty-first year of Guang Xu (1905), the Fengtian Official Yin Hao was set up to issue notes of Zhi Qian, in the denominations of one Diao, two Diao, three Diao, four Diao, five Diao, six Diao, seven Diao, eight Diao, ten Diao, fifteen Diao, twenty Diao, twenty-five Diao, thirty Diao, forty Diao, fifty Diao, sixty Diao, seventy Diao, one hundred Diao (Diao was the unit of coins in ancient China, one Diao was one thousand Zhi Qian), etc. All were withdrawn and destroyed in two years. It then issued silver dollar notes of one Jiao, two Jiao, five Jiao, one Yuan, five Yuan and ten Yuan (Jiao was the unit of money, ten Jiao is one Yuan). In the first year of Xuan Tong (1909), it was renamed as the Official Yin Hao of Eastern Three Provinces.

The Guang Xin Company was the local financial institution of Heilongjiang, in the late Qing dynasty. It was founded in Qiqihar, in October of the thirtieth year of Guang Xu (1904), and issued notes of Zhi Qian amounting to 39,736,673 strings, until the second year of Xuan Tong (1910). The notes of silver taels issued totaled to 6,918,101 Liang, and the company started to issue silver dollar notes in the Xuan

Tong years. The company still existed after the formation of the Republic of China. In Jilin, the local financial institution was the Yong Heng Official Money Bureau, which was founded in June of the twenty-fourth year of Guang Xu (1898). It also existed after the Republic of China was formed. In Shanxi, it was the Jin Tai Official Money Bureau.

In the Qing dynasty, Jiang Nan Province was set up in Jiang Nan regions, which was administered by the governor of Liang Jiang. In the twenty-ninth year of Guang Xu (1903), the Jiang Su Official Money Bureau was established, and, soon after, the Yu Ning Official Money Bureau of Jiang Nan was established too.

The Shandong Tong Ji Official Money Bureau was the first local financial institution in Shandong Province. It was established in August of the twenty-seventh year of Guang Xu (1901), headquartered in Jinan, and was renamed the Shandong Official Yin Hao, in May of the next year. At the beginning of its establishment, the Bureau issued banknotes of Zhi Qian in large denominations, including one thousand Wen, two thousand Wen, three thousand Wen, five thousand Wen and ten thousand Wen. It also issued the banknotes of silver taels, from the twenty-eighth year of Guang Xu (1902) until it was closed in 1911.

In the spring of the twenty-first year of Guang Xu (1895), the governor of Sichuan ordered the establishment of an official money shop in Sichuan, which was the Shu Tong Official Money Bureau. The government allocated capital for it to issue notes of Zhi Qian. The headquarters was in Chengdu. It ended in November of the twenty-third year of Guang Xu (1897). The Jun Chuan Yuan Bank was established in 1905, which was, at first, jointly run by government and businessmen and, then, by government singly. The bank issued a great volume of banknotes, and the issuing fund was forcibly withdrawn by the military many times. In 1920, Sichuan Finance Department ordered the closure of the bank.

At the end of Qing dynasty, many official money bureaus were set up, in Xinjiang, to issue banknotes. Ili and Kashgar Official Money Bureaus were established, respectively, in 1881. In December of the fifteenth year of Guang Xu (1889), the Xinjiang Official Money Bureau issued oil cloth notes, at the beginning of its establishment. The denomination of each note was four hundred Wen of Xinjiang red money, which was worth one Liang of silver. Later, it placed an order for printing a new type of paper money, in Shanghai, with a denomination of four hundred Wen, which was still issued after the Republic of China had been formed. Also, in 1889, money bureaus were set up in Suiding and Ningyuan to issue oil cloth notes. In 1894, the Suiding Money Bureau merged into the newly founded Huiyuan Official Money Bureau. In 1902, Aksu official money bureaus were set up, in Wensu and Yanqi counties, which issued the paper money, with the denomination of four hundred Wen of red money.

Under the influence of foreign banknotes, China's feudal rulers began to reflect on the differences between Chinese traditional paper money and foreign banknotes. Furthermore, they established China's first bank, the Chinese Commercial Bank, and issued banknotes. After learning from the West, they established the first central bank of China, Hubu Bank, to issue banknotes. These banknotes were issued in a mode different from the paper money of the traditional official Yin Hao. Everything developed in the direction of a separation from the financial issuance.

Due to the influx of foreign banks, in modern times, Shanghai became one of the financial centers in Asia. The capitalist economy led to economic globalization, influenced by which, China's economy gradually integrated into the world economic system. The traditional financial and currency issuing system was shaken. This was never a superficial shake. In effect, the issuance ruled by traditional government has turned to the issuing of credit currency, by banks, and modern financial thoughts have gradually entered the minds of Chinese people.

The replacement of silver taels with silver dollars, copper coins with copper dollars, and Guan Tie (Chinese traditional paper money) with banknotes, indicated the decline of China's traditional monetary culture. The ancient financial theory has retreated in front of the reality of foreign financial activities. Due to the exchange of monetary culture, changes have occurred to China, in its process of opening up to the world economy and integrating into it. The pace of modernization first made itself known in the field of finance and currency. The exquisite stamping of machines defeated the traditional casting. The evaluation of silver dollars by piece exempted Chinese people from the burden of weighing money. Banknotes magnified the shortcoming of the traditional paper money, in the matter of cash preparation. Since the soul of the financial and monetary system has changed, there is nothing surprising about the disappearance of the traditional Square Hole money and the clumsy silver taels. Hellenistic figures, plants and patterns finally appear on the Chinese currency. With the progress of history, all of these are the inevitable requirements for the cultural fusion, as a result of the world economic integration.

A Centennial Review of the Research Achievements of Currency Cultural Exchange between China and Foreign Countries

Jianbing Dai and Xiaorong Chen

Numismatics is known as a unique study of the lost knowledge in academic circles, which has two meanings: on the one hand, it takes coins as the research object and involves many fields such as history, archaeology, economy, culture, printing, casting, language, religion and so on; on the other hand, in the early 1980s, the study of this subject in China was close to extinction, so it got the name. Numismatics has a very high status in the West, just like the study of inscriptions, because the regeneration of many ancient monarchies depends on it. In China, numismatics also has a long historical tradition. It originated in the Song dynasty, developed into the School of Qian Jia (the school of coins during Qian Long and Jia Qing times) in the Qing dynasty, then merged Chinese and Western studies in the Republic of China, until the subject flourishes today. The currency cultural exchange between China and foreign countries, in one important aspect, is actually the cultural exchange of the currency research between the two.

I. Chinese Scholars' Research on Foreign Coins

1. Textual research and achievements from the early twentieth century to the 1970s

The Chinese study on currency has a long history, but the research on the currency cultural exchange between China and foreign countries only took shape in the last one hundred years. It is inseparable from China's political, economic and cultural exchanges with the outside world. Chinese numismatics, since its birth, has attached great importance to the study of foreign coins. Hong Zun of the Song dynasty had some special chapters for foreign coins in his *Records of Money*. When textual research had a distinct development, in the middle of Qing dynasty, scholars still paid close attention to foreign coins. Weng Shupei's *Gu Quan Hui Kao*, from the Qian Long period, and other works conducted a preliminary study on foreign coins.

During the period of the Republic of China, especially in the 1930s, Ding Fubao, a famous scholar, devoted himself to the study of ancient money. He had successively founded the Ancient Quan Society and the Quan Coins Society. After 1938, he compiled and published *The Dictionary of Ancient Money*, *The Illustration of Ancient Money in History* and *The Outline of Ancient Quan Studies*. His *Dictionary of Ancient Money* was a great work, of twelve volumes, which contained hundreds of foreign coins. The first six volumes mainly introduced the Chinese and foreign coins from ancient times to the Qing dynasty. Each picture of a coin was also marked with the average market price, at that time. The latter six volumes contained the descriptions of the coins collected in the former six. The book, with its rich cites of materials about the coins, and the bibliography and index that were more abundant than books of the same kind, provided a valuable reference for Oriental numismatics, at that time. During this period, there were also a group of researchers of foreign coins, such as Yuan Kewen, who specialized in the study of ancient foreign gold coins and wrote the work *Quan Jian*. Due to its unique geographical and economic status, Shanghai became the gathering place of many Chinese and foreign numismatists. In addition to the Chinese scholars' numismatic research, organized by Ding Fubao, some Westerners living in Shanghai also had their own coin gatherings and published a number of works in English.

Zhang Xinglang, a well-known contemporary scholar, edited *Collection of Historical Materials on Transportation between China and the West*, which preserved many data about foreign coins. The historian Xiang Da translated Stein's archaeological achievements in Central Asia and published the book *The Archaeological Records of Stein in Central Asia*, which made an introduction to the ancient coins Stein had unearthed there. Peng Xinwei's *History of China's Currency* (Shanghai People's publishing house, 1958) can be rated as the pioneer work of Chinese currency history and monetary studies. The book pays special attention to the foreign coins passed to China through the Silk Road. It points out that the moon patterns on the back of Tang's Kai Yuan Tong Bao maybe closely relate to those on the coins of the Western Regions states. This book also introduces the foreign silver dollars circulating in China in modern times, analyzes their influence on the prices of goods in China, and makes a price comparison of the gold and silver coins, between China and foreign countries.

From the 1950s to the 1970s, Chinese archaeologists attached great importance to the foreign coins unearthed in China, mainly represented by the famous archaeologists Xia Nai and Huang Wenbi. As early as the 1930s, Huang Wenbi discovered many ancient Central Asian coins along the Silk Road, during his archaeological survey in Xinjiang, based on which he has accomplished archaeological writings: *Archaeological Records in Tarim Basin*, *Report on the Archaeological*

Excavation in Xinjiang and *Archaeological Records of Turpan*. In the 1940s, Mr. Xia Nai investigated from Shaanxi to Gansu to Xinjiang, along the Silk Road. In his decades of field investigation, he collected a large number of objects or relative materials of Parthian coins, Eastern Roman gold coins, Persian Sassanian silver coins, Arabian gold and silver coins, and other Central Asian coins. He engaged in further collection and research, which led to the publication of dozens of research papers, including "Persian Sassanian Silver Coins Unearthed in Xining, Qinghai Province" and "A Summary of Sassanian Silver Coins Unearthed in China," published in the first issue of *Journal of Archaeology*, in 1958 and 1974, respectively; "Arabic Gold Coins Unearthed from Tang Tombs in Xi'an," published in the eighth issue of *Archeology*, in 1965; and "Byzantine Gold Coins Unearthed from the Tomb of Emperor Li Xi Zong," published in the sixth issue of *Archeology*, in 1977.

2. More systematic research of foreign currency by China, since the 1980s

2.1 A special study on the currencies along the Silk Road

Since the 1980s, under the promotion of the Chinese Numismatic Society, the Silk Road Monetary Research Group has been established, which was composed of eleven provincial and regional numismatic societies from Gansu, Inner Mongolia, Xinjiang, Tibet, Qinghai, Ningxia, Shaanxi, Henan, Shanxi, Sichuan and Yunnan. It promoted the development of currency research on the Silk Road in China, and a number of high-level research results emerged, facilitating the academic communications on Chinese coins with foreign countries. Until now, ten monographs have been published by Lanzhou University Press, including *Silk Road Currencies*.

Xinjiang is the most authoritative place, in recent years, to study the currencies of the Silk Road and the related countries, in China. Mr. Jiang Qixiang has made outstanding contributions. In the late 1980s,

Jiang Qixiang published many papers on the currency of the ancient Western Regions, for example, the papers "A Textual Research on Xinjiang Silver Coins Unearthed in Beijing," "Re-exploration of the Taugust Khan Coins in Suleiman Kader" and "A Brief Report on the Cleaning up of Karakhanid Coins Hoard Unearthed in Artushi County, Xinjiang," published in Supplement II of *Xinjiang Finance*, in 1988. In 1990, he wrote *Xinjiang Black Khan Dynasty Coins*, which was published by Xinjiang People's Publishing House. After that, he devoted himself to the study of the coins of the Mongol Khanates in the Western Regions. Papers on that study include "A Preliminary Study on the Jagatai Gold Coins Discovered in Bole, Xinjiang," in *Collection of Papers on Chinese Coins II*, in 1992; "On the Currency of the Western Regions in the Mongolian Yuan Dynasty," in *Xinjiang Coins*, in the fourth issue of 1995; and "Shah Rukh Silver Coins Found in Beijing," in *Chinese Coins*, in the third issue of 1999.

Coin researchers from some provinces in Northwest China have also conducted in-depth studies on the Silk Road currency, such as Kang Liushuo and Liu Dayou, in Gansu Province. Mr. Lin Meicun's research on ancient Silk Road currency has always been in a leading position in China, with many influential articles, such as "The Western Spread of Han Culture in Tang Dynasty from the Perspective of Tujishi Coins," in *Cultural Relics*, in the fifth issue of 1993. Kang Liushuo mainly wrote "A Summary of the Foreign and Western Region Coins along the Silk Road Unearthed in Gansu Province," in *Inner Mongolia Financial Research: Special Issue of Coins*, in the fourth issue of 1993; and "The Present Situation and Prospect of Currency Research on the Silk Road," in supplement II of *Lanzhou Finance*, in 1995. The works of Liu Dayou are *A Record of Cycling along the Silk Road to Look for Ancient Coins*, published by the Editorial Board of Quanyou Series of Books in China in 1991; "Persian Sassanian Silver Coins Found in Tianshui;" and "Discovery of Tujishi Coins in Tianshui," in *Inner Mongolia Finance*, in 1987. Mr. Wang Guizhen studied the Persian silver coins unearthed in Guangdong as well.

The issues concerning the maritime Silk Road and the influence of American silver dollars on China have gradually become the focus of research, in recent years. Dai Xuewen, from Taiwan, has made excellent research on Spanish silver coins, such as his article "An Ancient Silver Piece with the Emblem of the Spanish King," in *Chinese Coins*, in the third issue of 1998. Other representative works include Wang Yuxun's "On the Amount of Silver from Domestic Mining and Foreign Inflow in Ming Dynasty," in *Chinese Coins*, in the third issue of 1998 and Sheng Guanxi's "Spanish Silver Coins Unearthed from Putuo Mountain, Zhejiang Province," in *Chinese Coins*, in the fourth issue of 1996.

2.2 Deep research on the currency of East Asia and Southeast Asia

Since the 1980s, Chinese numismatic scholars have made studies on the currencies of East Asia and Southeast Asia, which were greatly influenced by Chinese currency. The above two regions belong to the category of the Chinese monetary culture circle because they have been deeply influenced by Chinese monetary culture for hundreds of years before the Qing dynasty. Therefore, the research on the coins of East Asian and Southeast Asian countries is based upon the study of Chinese currency as a deepening and extension of the study of ancient Chinese monetary culture. The papers "Overseas Circulation and the Significance of Ancient Chinese Coins," by Sheng Guanxi, and "The Relationship between Chinese Ancient Coins and Coins in East and Southeast Asia," by Dai Zhiqiang, summarize the influence of Chinese coins on the neighboring countries in Asia. Both were published in *Asian Coins*, the first issue of 1999.

Chinese scholars pay much attention to the currency exchange between China and Japan. *Chinese Coins* is one of the main research journals, which has published many influential papers, such as "A Detailed Study on Japanese Gold and Silver Coins," by Tu He, and "The Twelve Kinds of Imperial Coins in Japan," by Geng Zongren, in the third issue of 1985. Zhou Aiping's "The Flow of Chinese Currency to Japan and Its Influence," in the fourth issue of 1995, and "A Brief Talk about the Vassal Currency in the Edo Period of Japan," in the fourth issue of 1999, extended the study of Japanese currency from coins to paper money.

The study of Annam coins is, at present, a new hot spot in the field of Chinese numismatics. In the past, due to various reasons, Annam money was rarely seen in the domestic currency market. However, with the increasingly frequent communication between the two countries, especially the large-scale construction in Vietnam since the 1990s, more and more Annam coins have come to light, which provides an opportunity for the study of the money. The papers about Annam coins are as follows "The Money of Ming Dynasty Cast in Annam," by Wong Yixiang, in *Shaanxi Finance*: *Special Issue for Coins 18*, in 1992; "A Brief Talk about the Three Kinds of Dang Mo Money 'Ming Ming,' 'Shao Zhi' and 'Si De' in Annam," by Guo Ruoyu, in *Chinese Coins*, in the fourth issue of 1996; and "Vietnam Bar Silver in Circulation in China," by Dai Xuewen, also in *Chinese Coins*, in the fourth issue of 1996. "Vietnam Currency in History," co-edited by Yunnan Numismatic Research Association and Guangxi Numismatic Society, was published by China Financial Publishing House in 1993.

In addition, Chinese scholars have also studied the coins of Korea, Malaysia, Thailand, Indonesia and other countries, and written the following articles "Chinese Copper Money in Indonesia," by Zhou Jingnan, in *Chinese Coins*, in the second issue of 1986; "Siam (Thailand) Porcelain Money Tong Bao," by Wei Yuewang, and "Thailand's 'Porcelain Money' Is Used for Gambling Tally," by Yao

Shuomin, which were published in the first and the third issue of *Inner Mongolia Financial Research: Special Issue of Coins*, respectively, in 1995.

In the last ten years, due to the establishment of the Asian Numismatic Society in Singapore and the joint efforts of Chinese scholars, the study of Southeast Asian coins has become hot in the field of numismatics. A large number of articles have been published in *Asian Currencies*, the Journal of the Asian Numismatic Society, and high-level papers are emerging constantly.

2.3 Systematic arrangement and research of foreign currency materials in recent years

Since the 1980s, especially from the 1990s up to now, Chinese scholars have systematically researched the world coins, by sorting out the related materials, and published a large number of documents. Their achievements have emerged with an accelerating tendency. Here are the main publications: the English version of *Chinese Currencies in History* (China International Book Trading Corporation, 1983); *Coins Collected in Shanghai Museum • Foreign Coins*, edited by Bronzeware Research Department of Shanghai Museum (Shanghai Shu Zhou Publishing House, 1995); *Currency in the Bund of Shanghai*, by Ma Chuande, Xu Yuan and Hu Youwen (Shanghai Education Press, 2000); *Old Shanghai Currency*, edited by Ma Chuande, Tang Weikang, et al. (Shanghai People's Fine Arts Publishing House, 1998); *On Foreign Coins*, by Zhu Jianqing (Shanghai Classics Publishing House, 1998); and *Shi Jiagan's Old Collection of Chinese and Foreign Coins*, by Shanghai Museum (Shanghai People's Fine Arts Publishing House, 2000).

After the establishment of the Foreign Currency Professional Committee in the Chinese Numismatic Society, domestic foreign currency research has entered a new stage. Li Tiesheng, as a representative, has successively published such works as *Appreciation of Ancient Greek and Roman Coins*, *World Coins* 1-3, and *Appreciation of Eastern Roman Coins*. Besides, *Research on the Currency Culture Exchange between China and Foreign Countries*, published by China Agriculture Press, in 2003, written by the author of this book, also gives a thorough reflection on the relevant research achievements of this period.

II. Western Scholars' Research on Eastern Coins

1. Research achievements of foreign scholars on Silk Road currency

Numismatics has a very prominent position in the Western academic circles. There are a group of profound scholars and experts in Britain, France, the United States, Japan, Germany, Sweden, the Netherlands, Russia, India and other countries. The works of the study on coins in ancient Greece, Rome and India are countless, in Western countries. In terms of Silk Road currency, from the late nineteenth century to the early twentieth century, Stein (UK), Pelliot (France), Le Coq (Germany), Kozlov (Russia), Ju Ruichao (Japan), Sven Hedin (Sweden), etc. all excavated and took away, from Xinjiang, Inner Mongolia, Gansu and other places, many precious cultural relics and coins, during their archaeological investigation in Central Asia and Western China. They were preserved in the British Museum, the French National Museum, the Russian Petersburg Museum, the German National Museum, and the Nagashi Temple in Japan. The numbers of these coins are very large.

In recent decades, Western scholars have made great achievements in the study of Silk Road currency. Western countries published a number of monographs on Persian Sassanian coins, in the 1950s, including Morgan's *Handbook of Ancient Oriental Coins*, Wolke's *Catalogue of Arabic Sassanian Coins* and Puppo's *A Summary of Persian Art*. Valentine's *Sassanian Coins* was the first monograph on the coins of this dynasty. He also wrote *Indian Coins* and a book on Arab coins, *Modern Copper Coins of Muhammad States*. Goebel's *Sassanian Numismatics*, Baruch's *Sassanian Coins* and Sellwood's *Introduction to Sassanian Coins* came out in 1968, 1976 and 1985, respectively. Before that, Sellwood had published *Parthian Coins*. Mr. Du Weishan of Canada collected a large number of Silk Road coins and donated them to the Shanghai Coin Museum. In 1992, he compiled *the Coins of Ancient Countries along the Silk Road*, which was edited and published by the Shanghai Museum. The former Soviet Union published a number of research results on ancient coins in Central Asia, among which was Smirnova's *Sogdian Copper Coins*.

Since the 1970s, there have been more papers and works on Silk Road currency in foreign countries, and the research scope is also more extensive, such as India's research on the coins of the Kushan Empire, the British Museum's research on the coins with both Chinese and Kharosthi by Kleib, the Dutch scholar Dr. T. D. Yih's research on the Karahan coins, the Russian Petersburg museum's research on Central Asian coins by Temar, the French scholar Thierry's research on Byzantine Gold coins, the Polish scholar Bopelavic's research on Bactria coins, the Japanese scholar Ikuo Hirayama's collection of the coins in Central Asia, etc.

2. Research on Islamic coins in European countries

Hennequin of France edited *Catalogue of Islamic Coins—The Seljuk Dynasty and Subsequent Dynasties until the Mongolians' Invasion into Asia,* which was published, in 1985, by National Library of Paris. Of the 932 pages, fifty were illustrations. The book collected information of more than two thousand coins. Among the fifty pages of illustrations, sixty-two pictures were of the original size. The coins collected in this catalogue were from the Seljuk dynasty to the time of Mongol invasion. There were no Turkish coins. Geographically, it included what is now Syria, Iraq, Iran and the Asian part of Turkey. In terms of time, it was dated from 433 to 869 on Islamic Calendar (AD 1041-1464). The British Museum has long since compiled a relatively complete catalogue of the Islamic coins in its collection, the last volume of which was published nearly a century ago. This ten-volume catalogue has great value for reference. Even now, the British Museum is still an important base for the study of Oriental coins in the world. Cribb, Wang Hailan and others have made great achievements in the study of Chinese coins and the exchange between Chinese and foreign coins. Moreover, its Oriental Numismatic Society (ONS) is very influential in the world.

III. Foreign Scholars' Research on Chinese Currency

1. Japanese scholars' fruitful study on Chinese coins

The depth and breadth of Japanese scholars' research on ancient Chinese coins makes it worthy of serious study by Chinese numismatics scholars. In the 1930s, Japan's Hirao Juquan compiled *Quan Pu*, a series of books about Japanese, Chinese and Korean coins, which were published by Lidezhuang, in Tokyo. He has made outstanding achievements in the following aspects. First, in the matter of Japanese currency, he compiled monographs for each of the Twelve Coins of Imperial Dynasty. Second, he compiled monographs for the Chinese coins of different dynasties. Third, on the subject of Korean currency, he published *Quan Pu of Koryo Money* (1935) and *Quan Pu of Korean Tong Bao* (1936). Fourth, he also did further comprehensive compilation work; *Newly Set Zhao He Quan Pu* (1931) was focused on Far East currency. Having been constantly supplemented, by 1939, the book had included all types of Japanese and Chinese coins, except gold coins, silver coins, and ancient Chinese Bu coins and Knife coins. Another of his books, *Lidezhuang Quan Pu* (1934), was a collection of the phased research results.

Other influential books on the coins in China and the neighboring countries in Japan include Honida Tadomo's *History of Chinese and Foreign Money,* which was first published in 1831 and reprinted in 1916; Mikaya Kaya's *Currency,*—a book about history of Chinese currency, with a large number of Chinese coins rubbings of various periods—which was published by Tokyo Yusankaku in 1936; Yoshida Toruo's *China Currency Research*, published by Tokyo Osaka Star House Bookstore in 1933, which introduces Chinese coins, paper money and China's currency system at that time; and Opyeong Changhong's *Records of East Asia Money*, a total of eighteen volumes, 3,034 pages, published in 1938 by the Tokyo Iwanami Bookstore. This was Japan's most influential work on the Far East coins in the 1930s, in which the author made a scientific collation of the Far East coins, and made a study ranging from the Eastern coinage materials, the academic language of Numismatics, to the coin moulds, the coin calligraphy, etc. Its summary of Japanese, Chinese and Annam coins, as well as the textual research on the calligraphy of Oriental coins, was especially original and unique.

Since the beginning of the twentieth century, many Japanese periodicals have become the platform of Oriental coins research, such as the journals of coins, *Fang Quan Chu* and *Journal of Ancient Numismatics*; the archeology journals, *Journal of Archaeological Science* and *Archaeology*; the journals of history and culture research, *History and Geography*, *Public Opinion on History*, *Journal of History*, *China* and *Sinology*. Japan's research on Chinese currency, in recent years, is represented by Akiu Yuaki. Mr. Akiu Yuaki is a scholar who is keen on Chinese coins. Self-titled "dragon craze," he was born in 1921, in Hokkaido, and now lives in Osaka. In the 1970s, he founded the "China Copper Coins Research Association," which set off a wave of research on Chinese copper coins overseas, with members all over Japan, Taiwan and North America. From 1974 to 1976, Akiu Yuaki published *Guang Xu Yuan Bao*, *Qing Dynasty Copper Coins* and *Republic of China Copper Dollars*, successively. They were the only monographs on the study of Chinese copper coins to be published in the forty years after Tracy Woodwards, a French native, wrote *Chinese Ten Wen Copper Coins*, in 1936. Akiu Yuaki once founded the monthly *Copper Coins Bulletin*, and, also, published *The Dragon Craze's Collection of Rubbings*.

2. Western scholars' research on Chinese coins

In the first half of the twentieth century, some Western numismatists began to collect and study ancient Chinese coins. The representative figures were Arthur B Coole, Eduard Kann, Woodward, etc.

Arthur B Coole was born in Kansas, in 1900. When he was very young, he moved to Fujian with his father. Later, he worked in a church school and began to collect ancient Chinese money. His collection is divided into two parts: ancient Chinese coins and coin books and periodicals. There are more than six thousand pieces of Chinese coins, including fifty-six moulds of money, hundreds of Knife and Bu coins, and fourteen pieces of Da Ming Bao Chao (the paper money of the Ming dynasty). Most of the collection is still in the United States. His collection of Chinese coin books is also called "the richest in the world," among which, more than two thousand Chinese coin books and periodicals are precious relics. The books were donated to the American Numismatic Association (ANA) after his death, in 1978. The association has set up an oriental library, named after Arthur B Coole, in Colorado, where its headquarters are located. His early works are *Currency in Chinese History* (1936) and *Hardware Currency of Chinese Dynasties* (1937). Later, he compiled *Encyclopaedia of Chinese Coins* (1973), which was left unfinished in the seventh volume of Sui and Tang Dynasties because of the death of the author.

Another world-class coin collector was the Austrian Eduard Kann (1886-1962). He was sent to work in North China, in the early twentieth century, and began to trade gold and silver in Shanghai, in the 1920s. In 1948-1949, many foreigners sold rare Chinese coins, while Eduard Kann took the opportunity to put them into his collection, especially gold and silver coins. Later, Kann moved to California and took most of the collection with him. What he collected is extremely precious and in large numbers, including more than two hundred pieces of silver Yuan Bao and over five hundred Xinjiang coins, mostly gold and silver coins. In 1954, he wrote *A Collection of Illustrated Chinese Coins*, in which all the illustrations came from his collection. As he had been engaged in the gold and silver industry for a long time and had considerable attainments in the research of China's silver dollars, it is still an important reference book for the study of Chinese silver dollars. He was also the author of *On Chinese Currency*, a Chinese version of which was published by the Commercial Press. As an early scholar of China's economy and finance, his statistics on China's financial and monetary data were well founded and frequently cited by later generations.

M Tracey Woodward (1876-1938) was unique in his collection of Chinese coins. At the age of twelve, he took over his father's stamp collection and developed his lifelong habit of collection. After 1916, he immigrated to China, until 1930. His *Chinese Dang Shi Wen Copper Dollars* was originally serialized in a Chinese economic journal, from 1926 to 1936, and then compiled into a book and published.

The works of Stewart Lockhart were also influential, such as *Currency of the Far East* (Hong Kong: Hong Kong Noronha and Co., 1907). He was born in Scotland, in 1858, and, later, worked in Hong Kong. He became the Commissioner of Weihaiwei Customs, in 1902, and stayed in the position for fifteen years. *The Collection of Chinese Copper Coins by Stewart Lockhart* was published in 1915 by Shanghai

Geely Huashi Company. Of the 174 pages, there are 2,070 pictures of Chinese bronze and copper coins, which provide a lot of monetary data and materials for later research.

The above-mentioned foreign numismatists had different emphases in collecting Chinese currency. Not only did they have a rich collection, but they also had their own monographs published. They made certain contributions to China's coin research. Their works were all in English, which has played a positive role in the spread of Chinese culture of coins in the world. However, it can't be denied that the large amounts of Chinese coins they took away was a great loss to Chinese culture, which we must face squarely.

3. Foreign scholars' attention to the currency culture exchange between China and foreign countries

When studying the Silk Road coins, foreign numismatists were very interested in the Chinese coins unearthed from Central Asia, India, Japan and Southeast Asia, and published many research papers. For example, Professor Smirnova, of the former Soviet Union, has studied the Chinese Kai Yuan Tong Bao coins unearthed in Tajikistan, in Central Asia; Indian scholars have studied the coins of Chinese Song dynasty unearthed in India's Tamil DuPont; Russian scholars have studied Chinese Five Zhu coins unearthed in the Fergana area of Uzbekistan; and Japanese scholars have studied Chinese coins of the past dynasties unearthed in Japan.

As early as 1930s, Japanese scholars paid attention to the exchange of currency culture between China and North Korea. For example, Kuroda Koichi's "On the Ming-Character Knife Unearthed from North Korea Again," in *Hai Dong*, No. 8 of 1938, and "On the Gold and Silver of Silla Era," in *Hai Dong*, No. 10 of 1937; Opyeong Changhong's "Korean Tong Bao Coins," in Hamada Gengzuo's *Research on Antiquities*, published by Business Press, in 1936; etc. In recent years, Li Jianmao, of South Korea, also discussed the currency exchange between China and South Korea in the "Ming Knife Money" part of his *Encyclopaedia Dictionary of National Culture* (1992).

Singapore's numismatic scholars, such as Huang Hansen, have organized the Asian Numismatic Society. The exchange of monetary culture between China and Southeast Asia is an important topic of their research. They founded the *Asian coins* journal and have accomplished a series of achievements. Thierry, of France, and Dr. Tjong Ding Yih, of the Netherlands, are especially fond of the research of the currency culture exchange between China and foreign countries. They have published a series of relative articles, in various media.

In recent years, the study of currency history, as a deeper part of coin studies, has also accomplished a lot in foreign countries, the representative works of which have aroused great repercussions in the academic circle, such as *the Gold and Silver Coins of Tibet—History, Legend and Evolution* ([France] Boulnois, China Tibetology Publishing House, 1999); *The International Opportunity for Modern China—Tributary Trade System and Modern Asian Economic Circle* ([Japan] Takeshi Hamashita, China Social Sciences Press, 1999); and *Reorient* ([Germany] Gund Frank, Central Compilation and Translation Press, 2000). In his recently published papers, such as "Silver Monetization in the Ming Dynasty—a New Perspective of China's Connection with the World" (*Hebei Academic Journal*, no. 5, 2004) and "the Preliminary Investigation of Silver Monetization in the Ming Dynasty" (*Research on China's Economic History*, no. 2, 2003), Wan Ming claimed that it was the domestic economic development that led to the change in the function of silver, as opposed to the theory of external motivation, held by Western scholars on the monetization of silver as a currency in China.

BIBLIOGRAPHY

Ariyal, I. R. *Newly Organized History of Nepal*. Chengdu: Sichuan People's Publishing House, 1973.

Bancroft, Hubert H. *History of Mexico*. San Francisco: Bancroft, 1883.

Bank Financial Research Institute of Japan. "The History of Japanese Currency: In Relation to China." *Chinese Coins*, no. 1 (2000).

Bao, Hui. "An Application for the Provincial Decree of Copper Coins Banning." *My Manuscripts*, vol. I. http://www.guoxuedashi.com/SiKuQuanShu/2265x/.

Bauslaugh, Robert A. "The Numismatic Legacy of Alexander the Great." *Archaeology*, no.7 (1984).

Bernstein, A. "On Turkic coins." In *Collected Papers of Oriental Museum*, edited by Winter Palace Museum. St. Petersburg: Winter Palace Museum, 1940.

Boulnois, Lucette. *Gold and Silver Coins in Tibet*. Beijing: China Tibetology Publishing House, 1999.

Chen, Caijing. "On the Exchange of Currency Culture between China and the West from the perspective of the Ancient Local Currency Unearthed in Xinjiang." *Miscellaneous Cultures*, no. 1 (1991).

Chen, Gaohua and Wu, Tai. *Overseas Trade in Song and Yuan Dynasties*. Tianjin: Tianjin People's Publishing House, 1981.

Chen, Jianying. "Some Issues on the Inflow of Spanish Silver Dollars into China." *Fujian Coins*, no. 3-4 (1994).

Chen, Taimin. *Sino Philippine relations and Overseas Chinese in the Philippines*. Hong Kong: Hong Kong Chaoyang Press, 1985.

Cheng, Tong. "A Study on the 'Bao' Coins in Far Area of Ili Khanate." *Research on the Western Regions*, no. 4, (2008).

Dai, Xuewen. "Vietnam Bar Silver Circulating in China." *Chinese Coins*, no. 4 (1996).

Dai, Zhiqiang. "The Relationship between Chinese Ancient Coins and Coins in East and Southeast Asia." *Asian Coins*, no. 1 (1999).

D'ohsson. *History of Mongolia*. Translated by Feng Chengjun. Beijing: Zhong Hua Book Company, 1962.

Dong, Chao. "Bianchen and Gaya's Iron." *Ancient culture of East Asia*, no. 68 (1991).

Du, Jianyi and Du, Doudou. "The Management and Influence of the Central Dynasty on the Western Regions from the Perspective of the Coinage History of Xinjiang." *Xinjiang Coins*, no. 4 (2010).

Duan, Lisheng. "A Thai Coin with Chinese Characters." *Chinese Coins*, no. 3 (1985).

Editorial Board of Beijing Financial Records. *Financial Historical Materials of Beijing (Edition of Currency)*. Beijing: Beijing Financial Publishing House, 1994.

Frank, Gund. *Reorient—Attach Importance to the East in Economic Globalization*. Beijing: Central Compilation and Translation Press, 2000.

Gafurov, Б. Г. *History of Tajikistan in Central Asia*. Translated by Xiao Zhixing. Beijing: China Social Sciences Press, 1985.

Guo, Ai. "Sino Japanese Economic Trade and the Outflow of Copper Money in Yuan Dynasty." *Zhoushan Coins*, no. 2 (1994).

Guo, Zhengzhong. *A Study on the Commodity Currency Economy of Urban and Rural Areas in the Song Dynasty*. Beijing: Economic Management Press, 1997.

Head Office of the People's Bank of China. *Materials of modern Chinese Monetary History*. Beijing: Zhong Hua Book Company, 1964.

History Society of China. *Collections of Materials on Modern Chinese History (First Opium War), Records of Guangzhou Foreigners*. Shanghai: Shanghai People's Publishing House, 1957.

Huang, Guoxin. *Cantonese Merchants Engaged in Trade between China and Foreign Countries*. Hangzhou: Zhejiang People's Publishing House, 1997.

Huang, Jun. *A Brief Record of Gold and Stone in Hengzhai*. Beiping: Zunguzhai, 1935.

Huang, Yongwu. "Native Americans." *Central Daily News of Taiwan*. (February 10, 1999).

Huc, Evariste. *Travel in Tartar Tibet*. Beijing: China Tibetology Publishing House, 1991.

Issat al Nuss. *Outline of Syrian Geography and History*. Shanghai: Sanlian Publishing House, 1974.

Ji, Liqun ed. *On Chinese Culture*. Beijing: Beijing Yanshan Publishing House, 1998.

Jiang, Qixiang. "A Brief Report on the Cleaning Up of the Kiln of Karahan Dynasty Coins Unearthed in Artux County, Xinjiang." *Xinjiang Finance*, Supplement II (1988).

Jiang, Qixiang. *Karakhanid Coins of Xinjiang*. Urumqi: Volksverlag Xinjiang, 1990.

Jiang, Qixiang. "On the Currency of the Western Regions in the Yuan Dynasty of Mongolia." *Xinjiang Coins*, no. 4 (1995).

Kang, Liushuo. "An Overview of the Silk Road Foreign and Western Regions Currency Unearthed in Gansu Province." *Inner Mongolia Finance Research: Special Issue of Coins*, no.4 (1993).

Kang, Liushuo. "Silk Road Currencies Study: Present and Forecast." *Lanzhou Finance*, no. 2 (1995).

Kang, Liushuo. "Some Problems in the Circulation of Persian Sassanian Silver Coins in Northwest China." In *Anthology of Chinese Currency*, vol. 5, edited by Chinese Numismatic Society, 464-474. Beijing: China Financial Publishing House, 2010.

Kang, Liushuo. "A Summary of the Silk Road Foreign and Western Region Coins Unearthed in Gansu Province." *Financial research in Inner Mongolia: Special Issue on Coins*, no. 4 (1993).

Konig, G. "Byzantine and Sassanian Coins Unearthed in China." In *Collection of Papers at the First Annual Meeting of Shanghai Numismatic Society*, edited by Shanghai Numismatic Society. Shanghai: Shanghai Numismatic Society, 1986.

Li, Guoqing. *The Formation and Development of Overseas Chinese Capital*. Fuzhou: Fujian People's Publishing House, 1985.

Li, Han. "Foreign Copper Coins in Chinese Market in Late Qing Dynasty." *Chinese Currency*, no. 1 (1985).

Li, Jinxiu. "A study of Yin Ting of Persian Ishaq unearthed in Xi'an." In *Silk Road: A Study of the History of Relations between China and Foreign Countries in Ancient Times*, Vol.II, edited by Yu Taishan and Li Jinxiu, 250-273. Beijing: Commercial Press, 2012.

Li, Jingde, ed. *Zhuzi Yu Lei Vol. VIII*. Beijing: Zhong Hua Book Company, 1986.

Li, Ling and Yi, Ming. "Research on Tibetan Local Coins in Chongqing Museum." *Special Issue of the Founding Meeting of Chongqing Numismatic Society* (1988).

Li, Mingwei, ed. *History of Trade on the Silk Road*. Lanzhou: Gansu People's Publishing House, 1997.

Li, Tao. *Continuation to Zi Zhi Tong Jian Vol. 317, Item of Oct. 1081*. Beijing: Zhong Hua Book Company, 2004.

Li, Tiesheng. "Examples of Multi-currency Culture on the Silk Road." In *Collection of Papers on Ancient Coins and Silk Summit Forum and the Fourth International Symposium on Turpan Studies*, edited by Academy of Turpan Studies and Turpan Museum, 8. Shanghai: Shanghai Classics Publishing House, 2015.

Li, Tiesheng. "Four English Monographs about Sassanian Coins." *Special Issue of Inner Mongolia Financial Currency*, no. 3 (1994).

Liu, Boji. *The Unofficial History of Overseas Chinese in the United States*. Taipei: Taiwan Liming Culture Co., Ltd., 1976.

Liu, Dezhen. "Discovery of Lead Cakes with Foreign Inscriptions in Lingtai, Gansu Province." *Archeology*, no. 6 (1977).

Liu, Sen. "On the Three Platinum Products of Emperor Wu of the Han Dynasty." *Anhui Coins*, no. 1 (1995).

Liu, Xu. *Book of Tang Vol. 48: Food Records I*. Beijing: Zhong Hua Book Company, 1975.

Liu, Yingsheng. *Silk Road Culture: Maritime*. Hangzhou: Zhejiang People's Publishing House, 1995.

Lopez, R.S. "The Dollar of the Middle Ages." *The Journal of Economic History Vol.II*, no.3 (1951).

Ma, Huan. *Wonders Overseas*. Beijing: Commercial Press, 1935.

MacDonnell, Arthur Anthony. *History of Culture in India*. Translated by Long Zhang. Beijing: Zhong Hua Book Company, 1948.

Mu, Yuan. *Currency History of Xinjiang in Qing Dynasty*. Urumqi: Xinjiang University Press, 1994.

Na, Zhong. *Inheritance and Blending: Arab Culture*. Hangzhou: Zhejiang People's Publishing House, 1993.

Netcher, E. and Van der Ghigs, J. A. *Dutch East Indian Currency*. Batauia: DeMunten Van Nederlandsch Indie, 1863.

Niu, Ruji. "A Study of Tujishi Coins." *Chinese Coins*, no. 3 (1988).

Peng, Xinwei. *The Currency History of China*. Shanghai: Shanghai People's Publishing House, 1965.

Pilazoli, Mi. "Shell and Copper Coins in Culture of Yunnan." *Academic Journal of Yunnan Nationalities Institute*, no. 1 (1994).

Rashid. *Collections of Historical Documents*. Vol. III. Beijing: Commercial Press, 1997.

Relics Publishing House. "Ancient Foreign Currency Unearthed in Quanzhou." *Cultural Relics*, no. 8 (1975).

Rozi, Elken. "On the Ancient Coins Found in Mulei County." *Xinjiang Finance*, supplement II, (1988).

Rui, Chuanming. *Research on Ancient Turkic Inscriptions*. Shanghai: Shanghai Classics Publishing House, 1998.

Sheng, Guanxi. "The Overseas Circulation and Significance of Ancient Chinese Coins." *Asian Coins*, no. 1 (1999).

Singh, Saran. *The Encyclopaedia of the Coins of Malaysia, Singapore and Brunei 1400-1967*. Kuala Lumpur: A Malaysia Numismatic Society Publication, 1996.

Soas, Doreen. "Local Currency of Singapore." Translated by Sheng Guanxi. *Inner Mongolia Financial Research: Special Issue of Coins*, no. 3 (1993).

Song, Qingling. "Report on Visiting Indonesia." *The People's Daily* (September 27, 1956).

http://data.people.com.cn/rmrb/s?type=2&qs=%7B%22cds%22%3A%5B%7B%22fld%22%3A%22dataTime.

Song, Xian and Zhou, Suzhen. "The Circulation of Ancient Arabic Coins in China." *Research on Western Regions*, no. 3 (1993).

Takeshi, Hamashita. *The international opportunity of modern China—Tributary Trade System and Modern Asian Economic Circle*. Beijing: China Social Sciences Press, 1999.

Tu, He. "On Japanese Gold and Silver Coins." *Chinese Coins*, no. 3 (1985).

Tu, Yanzhi. "A Brief Account of Southeast Asian Money in *Quan Zhi* of Southern Song Dynasty." *Asian Coins*, no. 1 (1999).

Tuo, Tuo and Arutu. *History of Song Dynasty Vol. 490: Foreign Countries VI Khotan*. Beijing: Zhong Hua Book Company, 1985.

Wang, Dadao. "On the Coins Unearthed in Yunnan." *Yunnan Cultural Relics*, no. 5 (1988).

Wang, Dayuan. *A Brief Account of Foreign Islands.* Beijing: Zhong Hua Book Company, 1981.

Wang, Shihe. "The Development of Trade between China, Manila and Mexico in the Late Ming Dynasty." *Collected Papers on Geography,* no. 7 (1964).

Wang, Yongsheng. "The Imitation of the Currency System of the Yuan Dynasty by the Persian Ilikhanate." *Chinese Coins*, no. 4 (1994).

Wang, Yuquan. *The Origin and Development of Chinese Ancient Currency*. Beijing: Science Press, 1957.

Wang, Yuxun. "On the Amount of Silver from Domestic Mining and Foreign Inflow in Ming Dynasty." *China Numismatics*, no. 3 (1998).

Wei, Liangtao. *An Outline of the History of Yarkand Khanate*. Harbin: Heilongjiang Education Press, 1998.

Weng, Yixiang. "Coins of Ming Dynasty Cast in Annam." *Shaanxi Finance: Special Issue of Coins* (1992).

Wu, Lianyan. "History of the Influx of Foreign Silver Dollars into Guangdong in Great Amount." In *Free Thoughts on Silver Currency*, edited by Cultural and Historical Materials Research Committee of the CPPCC of Guangdong Province. Guangzhou: Guangdong People's Publishing House, 1992.

Wu, Ping. "Exploration of Maritime Silk Road Currencies." *Fujian Currency*, no. 3-4 (1994).

Wu, Ping and Chen, Lanying. "On Currency of Maritime Silk Road." In *Proceedings of the Sixth Symposium on Southeast Asian Historical Currencies and Maritime Silk Road Currencies*, edited by Zhejiang Coin Society. Ningbo: Ningbo Numismatic Society, June 1995.

Xi, Yanzhao. "Rare porcelain money." In *Research on Coins*, edited by Henan Numismatic Society. Beijing: Science Press, 1996.

Xia, Nai. "Arab Gold Coins Unearthed from the Tombs of Tang Dynasty in Xi'an." *Archeology*, no. 8 (1965).

Xia, Nai. "Byzantine Gold Coins Unearthed in the Tomb of Li Zongxi in Zanhuang." *Archeology*, no. 6 (1977).

Xiao, Huaiyuan. *History of Local Currency in Tibet*. Beijing: Nationalities Publishing House, 1987.

Xiao, Zhihua. "East-West Communications and Byzantine Gold Coins." *Newspaper of China Cultural Relics* (February 7, 1999).

Xu, Hua. "Historical Reflection on the Sea Power of China in Modern Times." *Guangming Daily* (November 19, 1999).

Xu, Song. *The Important Manuscripts of Song Dynasty • Foreign Land*, book 4. Shanghai: Shanghai Classics Publishing House, 2009.

Yang, Ming. "On 'Baozang' Copper Coins during the Reign of Qianlong." *Special Issue of the Founding Meeting of Chongqing Numismatic Society* (1988).

Yang, Shouchuan. *Study on Currency of Shells*. Kunming: Yunnan University Press, 1997.

Yao, Shuomin. "Thailand's 'Porcelain Money' Is Used for Gambling Tally." *Inner Mongolia Financial Research: Special Issue of Coins*, no. 3 (1995).

Yih, Dr. Tjong Ding. "Cash Coins of the Gongsi on Borneo and Banka." Accessed https:// www.Charm.ru

Yu, Yizhong. "Research on the Influence of Chinese Currency Culture on Neighboring Countries from the Perspective of Their Coins." In *Proceedings of the Sixth Symposium on Southeast Asian Historical Currencies and Maritime Silk Road Currencies*, edited by Zhejiang Coin Society. Ningbo: Ningbo Numismatic Society, June 1995.

Yuan, Wei. "Research on the Issuance of Coins with Han and Arabic Words in Mongolian Khanates in 1262-1272." *Gansu Finance*, no. 11 (2016).

Zhang, Tingyu. *A General Study of Imperial Documents: Study on Coins IV*. (1787).

Zhong Hua Book Company. *Authentic Records of Qing Dynasty: Reign of Gaozong*. Vol. 1387. Beijing: Zhong Hua Book Company, 2008.

Zhou, Aiping. "The Flow of Chinese Currency to Japan and Its Influence." *Chinese Coins*, no. 4 (1995).

Zhou, Jingnan. "Chinese Copper Money in Indonesia." *Chinese Coins*, no. 2 (1986).

Zhou, Shirong. "A Study on the Coins of the Western Han Dynasty Unearthed in Hengyang, Changsha." In *Anthology of Chinese Coins*, edited by Chinese Numismatic Society. Beijing: China Financial Publishing House, 1985.

Zhu, Huo. *New Classic of Ancient Money*. Xi'an: Sanqin Publishing House, 1994.

Zhu, Jieqin. *History of Relations between China and Iran*. Xinjiang: Xinjiang Publishing House, 1988.

Zhu, Song. "Geographical Discovery—Western Global Colonial Expansion." *Guangming Daily* (November 20, 1999).